ALSO BY ALLEN C. GUELZO

Robert E. Lee: A Life

Reconstruction: A Very Short Introduction

Redeeming the Great Emancipator

Lincoln: An Intimate Portrait

Gettysburg: The Last Invasion

Fateful Lightning: A New History of the Civil War and Reconstruction

Lincoln Speeches (editor)

Lincoln: A Very Short Introduction

Abraham Lincoln as a Man of Ideas

*The New England Theology: From Jonathan Edwards to
Edwards Amasa Park* (editor, with Douglas Sweeney)

Lincoln and Douglas: The Debates That Defined America

Lincoln's Emancipation Proclamation: The End of Slavery in America

Abraham Lincoln: Redeemer President

*Edwards in Our Time: Jonathan Edwards and the Shaping
of American Religion* (editor, with Sang Hyun Lee)

Josiah Gilbert Holland's Life of Abraham Lincoln (editor)

*For the Union of Evangelical Christendom: The Irony
of the Reformed Episcopalians, 1873–1930*

*Edwards on the Will: A Century of American
Philosophical Debate, 1850–1856*

Our Ancient Faith

Our Ancient Faith

LINCOLN, DEMOCRACY, AND THE
AMERICAN EXPERIMENT

Allen C. Guelzo

Alfred A. Knopf
New York
2024

Library of Congress Cataloging-in-Publication Data
Names: Guelzo, Allen C., author.
Title: Our ancient faith : Lincoln, democracy, and the
American experiment / Allen C. Guelzo.
Description: First edition. | New York : Alfred A. Knopf, 2024. |
"This is a Borzoi Book published by Alfred A. Knopf." |
Includes bibliographical references and index.
Identifiers: LCCN 2023026851 | ISBN 9780593534441 (hardcover) |
ISBN 9780593534458 (ebook)
Subjects: LCSH: Lincoln, Abraham, 1809–1865—Political and social
views. | Lincoln, Abraham, 1809–1865—Influence. | Democracy—United
States—History. | United States—Politics and government—1861–1865.
Classification: LCC E457.2 .G8855 2024 | DDC 320.473—dc23/eng/20231023
LC record available at https://lccn.loc.gov/2023026851

Jacket image: *Portrait of Lincoln* by Otto Henry Schneider. Private
Collection. Photo © Christie's Images / Bridgeman Images
Jacket design by Ariel Harari

*For my beloved grandchildren, to whom I offer
Abraham Lincoln as an invitation to democracy:*

*Abigail, Sophia, Caleb, Cora, Isobel,
Violet, Sonny, and Patrick*

I believe in democracy. I accept it. I will faithfully serve and defend it. I believe in it because it appears to me the inevitable consequence of what has gone before it. Democracy asserts the fact that the masses are now raised to a higher intelligence than formerly. All our civilisation aims at this mark. We want to do what we can to help it. I myself want to see the result. I grant it is an experiment, but it is the only direction society can take that is worth its taking; the only conception of its duty large enough to satisfy its instincts; the only result that is worth an effort or a risk. Every other possible step is backward. . . .

—HENRY ADAMS, *Democracy: An American Novel* (1880)

I understand a ship to be made for the carrying and preservation of the cargo, and so long as the ship can be saved, with the cargo, it should never be abandoned. This Union should likewise never be abandoned unless it fails and the probability of its preservation shall cease to exist. . . . *So long, then, as it is possible that the prosperity and the liberties of the people can be preserved in the Union, it shall be my purpose at all times to preserve it.*

—ABRAHAM LINCOLN, *New York Daily Herald*
(morning edition), February 21, 1861

Quarry the granite rock with razors, or moor the vessel with a thread of silk; then you may hope with such keen and delicate instruments as human knowledge and human reason to contend against those giants, the passion and the pride of man.

—JOHN HENRY NEWMAN, "Knowledge Its Own End," in *The Idea of a University*

Abraham Lincoln: It seems to me that when he walks the streets of the New Jerusalem that angel wings are bowed in reverence as he passes, and angel fingers are pointing, while angel lips are whispering, "There goes the great emancipator."

—ROBERT P. KENNEDY, "Address" (October 13, 1903), in *Antietam: Report of the Ohio Antietam Battlefield Commission* (1904)

This coronet of freedom, brighter than ever decked monarch's brow, all radiant with freedom's stars, a grateful, loving, trusting people . . . placed on the head of Abraham Lincoln; and the head was worthy to wear it. . . . Freedom made and freedom crowned him; and that crown shall ever be ours,—for never—no, never, no, never— shall our glorious national diadem be circled by a star or a gem that is not the willing offering of freedom and freemen.

—EDWARD F. CUTTER, *Eulogy on Abraham Lincoln, Delivered at Rockland, Maine, April 19, 1865*

It is doubtful if there ever was a death which seems to have produced so deep an effect on so many people, of all classes. It is almost incredible. The papers are full. The expression of feeling is not external merely as is often the case with great men, but Lincoln had a hold on the hearts of this great nation, such as no man but Washington ever had before. He had too a more difficult task to accomplish than Washington.

—JOHN LANGDON SIBLEY, diary entry for April 23, 1865 (Harvard University Archives)

Contents

Author's Note

This is a brief essay, in a time of shadows. My long life has been a hurdle race of public agonies, from the Vietnam War, through repeated and destabilizing economic convulsions and a "clash of civilizations," to a crazed and inhumane technological environment in which no reality seems stable, bullhorns trample debate, and the smiling threat of power is all too ominously real. I have taken delight in the life of a scholar, only to watch the scholarly life, and its withdrawn tranquility, besieged by economic shrinkage and invaded by political soap opera. I have been a lover of democracy, as only the descendant of immigrants can love it, and seen it shouted down in arrogance, and—all the more horribly—by those who have positioned themselves to reap its richest benefits. I have taken consolation, however, in the figure of one American who lived a very different life, in a time of follies, and who gave democracy a new lease on life and a fresh sense of its purpose. To all those who have despaired of the future or whose lives have been ruined by the failures of the present, I offer this man's example. And just as we, as a nation, were once rescued at the last gasp by an intervention so unlooked-for as to defy hope, I take up his principles with the yearning that once again, this last, best hope of earth may yet have a new birth of freedom.

This has been a work with a surprisingly long gestation, and there is a sense in which I have been working toward it for far longer than I even realized. So it should not be surprising that some pieces of it have appeared in preliminary and speculative shapes in a variety of places. I note here "Lincoln's Statesmanship in Navigating a Divided Nation," in *Orbis* 62 (Spring 2018); "Little Note, Long Remember: Lincoln and the Murk of Myth at Gettysburg," in *The Gettysburg Address: Perspectives on Lincoln's Greatest Speech*, edited by Sean Conant in 2015; "A. Lincoln, Philosopher: Lincoln's Place in 19th-Century Intellectual History," which appeared in *Lincoln's America, 1809–1865*, edited by Joseph Fornieri and Sara V. Gabbard, in 2008; "Lincolnomics: The Economic Mind and Policies of Abraham Lincoln" and "Government by Reason—or by Passion? On Lincoln and Democracy," published in *City Journal* (April 2021 and Autumn 2023); "Lincoln and Democracy," in *National Affairs* (Spring 2023); and especially "Was Lincoln a Racist?" in Brian R. Dirck's *Lincoln Emancipated: The President and the Politics of Race* (DeKalb: Northern Illinois University Press, 2007). I have also touched on some of these themes in some shorter pieces: "Mr. Lincoln's Economics Primer," in *National Review* (December 20, 2010); "What the Civil War Can Teach Us About Political Restraint," in *The Christian Science Monitor* (January 10, 2011); and "What If Abraham Lincoln Had Lived?" in *The Washington Post* (April 13, 2015). I also drew on this material for the three lectures I delivered in 2022 and 2023 on Lincoln and democracy at the New-York Historical Society as the Louise Lehrman Distinguished Fellow.

To the editors and agents who have opened the possibilities of appearing in print (that ultimate academic vanity)—and particularly to Andrew Miller at Knopf and to John Rudolph of Dystal, Goderich & Bourret—to my colleagues, friends, supporters, students, and alumni in the James Madison Program and the Department of Politics at Princeton University (and especially Robert P. George and Bradford P. Wilson), to the Thomas W. Smith Foundation, and to the family which has wrapped me in a love I cannot even pretend to have deserved, I lay down a lush carpet of thanks, gratitude, and tears.

Our Ancient Faith

The Disposition of Democracy

W e have all heard the dreary complaints at one time or another, and now perhaps more than ever. Democracy is the worst form of government, except for all the others (according to Winston Churchill). Democracy is the rule of hooligans (according to Jason Brennan).[1] Democracies are "historical accidents" that are "closing before our eyes" (according to Jean-François Revel), or worse, they slouch toward becoming "flabby, prosperous, self-satisfied, inward-looking, weak-willed states" (according to Francis Fukuyama).[2] Conventional democratic ideas are fairy tales (according to Christopher H. Achen and Larry M. Bartels).[3] Democracies have no use for beauty or community (according to Ryszard Legutko).[4] Democracies die at the hands of the governments they elect (according to Steven Levitsky and Daniel Ziblatt).[5] Two cheers—and only two cheers—for democracy (according to E. M. Forster).

Perhaps none of this should strike us with any surprising force. We have lived through a century in which democracies have been repeatedly tried, and repeatedly failed, or worse, been easily subverted or overthrown. And the most recent failures were cruelest in their impact for having arrived, after

1991, at a moment when democracy seemed to have emerged unchallengeable from a generation-long struggle with its most serious totalitarian rival. *Solidarność* triumphed in eastern Europe; the Berlin Wall crumbled and the Soviet overlords disappeared; the Goddess of Freedom reared her torch on Tiananmen Square.

And then, almost as quickly, democracy sagged and, in many places, collapsed. Tiananmen Square was brutally emptied; a former Soviet intelligence operative shrewdly twisted post-Soviet elections into a nationalist authoritarianism; the fastest-growing and most aggressive economy in the world belonged to a repressive dictatorship which had been fathered by one of the most genocidal minds of modern times. According to the annual surveys published by Freedom House, the number of people living in genuinely democratic states has fallen by more than half since 2003.[6] Even in places where the cardboard façade of democracy is maintained, the countervailing forces of state control of media, curbs on political assembly, judicial corruption, and bureaucratic metastasis make a mockery of the word.

Yet, at the same moment, real democracies too often allow themselves to be judged by the pitiless standards of their rivals. They drown themselves in guilt for any absence of perfection, ignore real imperfections with indignation, and imagine every difficulty to be a crisis. They are as vulnerable to their own self-criticism as they are to external aggression. The biographer of democracy's earliest champion has spoken of democracy as "one of the rarest, most delicate and fragile flowers in the jungle of human existence." After all, he reasoned, democracy was the rule of the day for only two hundred years in its birthplace, Athens, and disappeared thereafter for two millennia. If durability and persistence were the measure of political success, the intervening centuries of monarchy, oligarchy, and despotism would send democracy to the bottom of the most-desired list of political theories.[7]

The United States of America is the longest, still-functioning large-scale democracy in the world. Created as a republic on the model of republican Rome in the late eighteenth century, it had a strong democratic torque from the beginning which only became more pronounced in its first four decades of life. Its founding documents—its Declaration of Independence from Great Britain, and its federal Constitution of 1787—articulate many of what have become accepted as fundamental principles of a democracy: the natural equality of all humanity (as opposed to traditional or organic hierarchy), a national government of explicitly limited powers, and a separation of even those powers within the national government.

But the United States was—and is—by no means a pure democracy. Even in 1787, the sheer size of the American republic seemed to make the model of democracy everyone knew best—the face-to-face democracy of ancient Athens—impractical, if not downright dangerous, and that impracticality has only grown more mountainous as the average size of congressional districts spills over the line of 700,000 people. Even more troubling to the American founders were the reminders that Athens' democracy had not always behaved well or wisely. The Athenian assembly made heroes of scoundrels like Alcibiades, and martyrs of freethinkers like Socrates. "There is," warned James Madison, "a degree of depravity in mankind, which requires a certain degree of circumspection and distrust," and nowhere was that distrust more justified than in democracies. "Had every Athenian citizen been a Socrates," Madison warned, "every Athenian assembly would still have been a mob."[8]

With that caution in view, the American Constitution of 1787 laid major restraints on the way in which the American republic could be said to be democratic. The republic was to be a *federal* republic, a union, an association of quasi-sovereign states; and the chief officer of the republic, the president, would be elected by the states, through an ingenious mechanism that came to be called the Electoral College. The national legislature would be elected, partly by direct vote every two years (as the House of Representatives), but also partly by the state legislatures every six years (this body, in homage to republican Rome, would be called the Senate). The federal judiciary was elected by no one; its members were appointed by the president and confirmed by the Senate. Rome, not Athens, was the aspiration of the new republic, and its first president was hailed as a Cincinnatus, not a Pericles.

Still, the forces let loose by American independence and the Revolutionary War fought against Great Britain for that independence all marched in democratic directions. Many of the pre-revolutionary North American colonies were founded as private franchises, and frequently by Protestant religious dissenters who were devoted to face-to-face control of public affairs. For almost a century, successive British governments happily left them to their own devices, and to their own ad hoc legislatures and finances. That, as the Revolution's historian, David Ramsay, wrote in 1789, "generated ideas, in the minds of the colonists, favourable to liberty... They had in effect the sole direction of their internal government." So, when, in the 1760s, imperial planners in London tried to substitute forms of direct control from the imperial metropolis, the colonies balked. The colonial assemblies were small, met infrequently, and imposed little in the way of legislation; nevertheless they were based on a surprisingly broad spread of qualified electors—or at least broader than anything seen anywhere else in the world.[9] By the time the colonies revolted, Americans (wrote François-René de Chateaubriand, after his tour of America in 1791) "were already accustomed to the public discussion of the interests of the people...by virtue of which they governed themselves, and managed their own affairs."[10]

The American Revolution's aftermath did nothing to change that attitude. The American upper classes—the Washingtons, Jeffersons, and Madisons—had been *upper* only by contrast with the "lower sort" beneath them. Set beside the English landed gentry from whom they had disengaged themselves, the American elite were small potatoes, and the bumptious commercial classes of mechanics, artisans, shopkeepers, and speculators made them feel it, too.

By 1792, property restrictions on voting eligibility had disappeared in half of the states. By 1808, voter turnout for popular elections in Pennsylvania and Massachusetts had reached 70 percent of those eligible under the laws—in some Maryland counties, it actually exceeded 80 percent—and observers were shedding any reluctance to describe the American government as a *democracy*.[11]

If anything, Americans now boasted that their system was "not as some affirm, *democracy rejected,* but *democracy made easy,*" and constituted the "most splendid discovery of modern times."[12]

The fundamental notion of any democracy is that political sovereignty ultimately resides in the people of a nation (and *nation* can include everything from a classical city-state to a multi-ethnic federation). Especially in the American democracy, insisted Brown University president Francis Wayland in 1825, "the people are not only the real but also the acknowledged fountain of all authority."[13] That idea was itself the child of a larger cluster of ideas which had their origin in the eighteenth-century Enlightenment, and which came to be known as *liberalism*.

The Enlightenment began as a scientific revolt against the hierarchical notions of the physical universe as taught by Aristotelian scholastics. Rather than seeing all objects imbedded in a "great chain" of occult relationships that stretched from the base earth to the spotless heavens, all those relationships now appeared in the testimony of Galileo and Newton as individual entities, in no necessary order or relationship to each other, and moved only by measurable and predictable natural forces.

This "new philosophy" generated a parallel political universe, as European political theorists challenged political hierarchy as well, and replaced it with the notion that politics was the decision of people to quit the state of nature and create a government for themselves, rather than entering a place in a fixed hierarchical order, presided over by divinely chosen kings. In traditional societies, people arrived in an already-existing environment with a specific *status;* in liberal societies, they created new societies which were designed to allow them to exercise *rights.* In this new social and political culture of liberalism, the basic political unit became the free *individual* (unlinked to an organic or hierarchical identity), the basic political order became *equality* (since individuals possessed the same natural rights), while equality became *universal* (because these rights were hardwired into *every* individual, irrespective of race or origin) and *optimistic* (sure, as Enlightenment liberals were, that the logic of natural rights would prove everywhere as irresistible as the logic of scientific law).[14]

Liberalism did not necessarily require that government take the specific form of democracy.[15] But in the American environment, democracy swiftly emerged as liberalism's dominant shape, and with three basic tenets. The first was *consent*. Consent can be deployed in various ways—either directly through participatory assemblies, office-holding, and juries, or through the people's freely selected representatives. But even in the latter case, consent is still the rule; the people themselves set the limits of what those representatives may do. In tyrannies, governments *rule;* in liberal democracies, governments *represent.* Under the canopy of liberalism, the people are judged competent to direct their own lives, public and private, without needing or wanting the paternal tyranny of aristocrats and monarchs, and the state exists to do no more than secure individual rights.[16]

But consent is rarely, if ever, the same as unanimity. The people are too numerous, even in the Athenian assembly, to be of a single mind, and so there will invariably be divisions of opinion. In that case, the second rule of liberal democracy is *majority rule.* A minority, simply by having not convinced a sufficiently large number of the people, carries with it the stigma of very likely being wrong; and anyway, government by minorities is what aristocracies take for granted. On the other hand, no majority is perfect or infallible simply for being a majority. Self-interest, passion, and arrogance can turn righteous majorities into intolerable frauds, while persuasion, reason, and civility may be the means by which a minority convinces others that *they* are right, and can thus become the new majority.[17]

This is a pleasant balance in theory, but in practice, the temptation is always alive for both over-mighty majorities and desperate minorities to grab for the levers of state authority and use them to swallow up a political order completely. It is the abiding weakness of democracies to assume that a majority must, simply by the weight of being a majority, be right and good, and therefore have a license to *rule;* and second to that is the resentment of minorities who believe that the majority is neither right nor good and is therefore illegitimate.

Even if majorities do not actually hunt down minorities, they can still make life unpleasant for them in tremendously dreary ways; and minorities can find cheap ways to derail the rule of majorities when they talk themselves into believing that such subversion somehow works for the greater good. A frustrated or reckless minority could, by sheer truculence, undermine the will of a majority and short-circuit the majority's consent and, in Fisher Ames's worried analysis in 1805, "effectually defeat the authority of the national will" and "make it subservient to the worst designs of the worst men."[18] So, in addition to the rule of the majority and the toleration of the minority, liberal democracies must also submit to *law*, independent of both. This not only keeps violence at bay but gives equality a hard, substantial reality.

In effect, the lines of the democratic state are drawn vertically, with the ups-and-downs of majorities and minorities on the one side and the administrative apparatus of the state on the other, owned by neither the majority nor the minority, and a middle band between the two created by law. Without law, every choice could be made to harmonize with the will of whoever had achieved control of the government apparatus—and that *whoever* could as easily be a well-organized and ruthless minority as a vast but disorganized majority.

The tools by which democracies protect these balances are also threefold. The first is an agreement to understand all the legal participants in a state as *citizens,* possessing equal standing and access to political life—the right to vote, to hold office, to hold leaders accountable, to form political associations that shape policies, to be represented. This does not necessarily mean that these citizens will enjoy equal standing in other aspects of their lives. Periclean Athens was the most nearly perfect realization of a *polis* of equal citizens, but it also had no concern about economic inequality between those citizens or for the slaves who stood outside citizenship, and it ensured citizen equality by sharply limiting the extent of citizenship to the six thousand or so Athenians who turned out for the meetings of the assembly. What it did mean, though, was that every office was open to every citizen, and every citizen had an equal right to speak freely. Juries were chosen by lottery, and the participation of the poor was guaranteed by stipends.[19]

The second tool which protects democracies is elections— which is to say, events in which the citizens, authorized by themselves, cast votes for offices (and to hold officers accountable) and determine policies and laws which will govern all. And not merely elections as a fact, but elections as a regular, predictable, and inexorable sequence, so that every officer—whether elected or appointed—and every representative knows that a moment of accountability is inevitable. In the case of elected officials and representatives, the accountability is direct to the voters at election time; in the case of appointed officers—administrators, soldiers, and judges who are commissioned by the state with a charge to execute either the conclusions of the representative legislature or the laws the legislature adopts—the accountability is indirect, through the elected leadership. But it is still accountability, and the accountability leads back ineluctably to elections.

The third of democracy's protective tools are its forums for discussion and association, whether the Athenian *agora*, the London coffeehouse, or particularly in America, the newspaper and the political party. In America, claimed one Philadelphia publisher, newspapers are

*The gen'ral source throughout the nation
Of every modern conversation.*[20]

Newspapers, in turn, were the mouthpieces of the political party. At first, the American revolutionaries with one consent denounced political parties for weaponizing disagreement. But if parties were "an evil," then the great French observer of nineteenth-century American democracy, Alexis de Tocqueville, understood that they were "an evil inherent in free governments" because they resulted from the free association of citizens with each other. The reputation of political parties has never been high in the American experience, tolerated at best as a necessary excrescence and deplored at worst as the source of violence, corruption, and skulduggery. But Tocqueville found that parties in a liberal democracy could actually be surprisingly "peaceful in their objects and legal in their means." Even in their sharpest clashes, the Ohio jurist Frederick Grimke marveled at how political parties created "an arena on which all men may be active and useful" and inspired "a desire and a motive for understanding and taking part in political affairs."[21]

Democracies that use their tools well accomplish many great things. They allow their citizens the fullest expression of natural rights, and they permit mobility and self-transformation to a degree unprecedented in human history.[22]

But the adroit handling of these tools depends on something less visible, a set of shared assumptions that the ancients called *virtue* and which Tocqueville called *mores* (from the Latin for *character* or *morals*). These were the habits, conventions, assumptions, instincts, customs, codes that keep the free individual or a domineering majority from running—

freely—off the rails or degenerating—freely—into chaos. "It is not enough to constitute a democracy that the whole crowd of citizens should have the right to do whatever they wish or propose," warned the classical historian Polybius. It was only where "reverence to the gods, succour of parents, respect to elders, obedience to laws, are traditional and habitual" that "we may speak of the form of government as a democracy."

Likewise for Tocqueville two thousand years later: it was the "laws and *mores* of the Anglo-Americans" that "form the special reason for their greatness," because it was those *mores* that made Americans "capable of supporting the empire of democracy." The problem Tocqueville could not resolve was that while democracy was dependent on those *mores,* it could also prove destructive of them. In an atmosphere of citizen equality, the *mores* beloved of one citizen did not necessarily have any purchase on another. Unless those *mores* had some grounding in natural law or some other higher authority, they could be dismissed in a democracy as just another artificial anti-liberal restraint. Without some sense that there are truths which not even majorities can defy, democracy becomes rudderless, hollow, morally relative, and difficult to sacrifice for.[23]

Tocqueville was already worried in the 1830s that the vital underlayment of *mores* might not be able to contain a turn in democracies toward selfishness and crudity. He was particularly concerned that democracy's passion for equality would discourage Americans from developing anything noteworthy in the way of culture, since Americans would refuse to recognize the talents of anyone superior in natural gifts to themselves, and would invite increasing meddlesomeness from a central government which citizens would call upon to enforce equality. Still worse, a democracy unrestrained by *mores* might subside into anarchy. They would then prove the rule laid down by Thomas Hobbes, the Enlightenment's darkest light, that the natural law was merely a fancy term that described "any man's appetite or desire."

Tocqueville's doubts about American democracy would not have been assuaged if he had extended his great tour of the United States in 1831 to include the states lying below the lines of the Potomac and Ohio Rivers, where race-based slavery was the single most important political, social, and economic fact on the ground. European aristocrats who got to see American democracy first-hand—like Johann Georg Hülsemann, the Austrian empire's chargé d'affaires to the United States—berated "the tendency of things in America" as "directly opposed to the entire basis of our civilization." And not just aristocrats. Karl Marx derided "the old democratic litany . . . universal suffrage, direct legislation, popular rights, a people's militia, etc." as mere phantasms erected by liberals as a distraction from the economic class struggle, which Marx saw as the real driver of modern history, while the nihilist philosopher Friedrich Nietzsche sneered at liberalism's decline into "the most contemptible" end, that of "the *last man*," impoverished, tame, blinking.[24]

Criticize and doomsay as they liked, it was the aristocrats and philosophers who lost ground in the decades following the American Civil War. The attempt of a slave-based Southern Confederacy to disrupt the American democracy was defeated; a French attempt to establish in Mexico a New World outpost for Napoleon III's Second Empire failed miserably; and for all their bristle and tinsel, the monarchs were slowly eviscerated of real power and parliaments, dumas, assemblies, and reichstags increasingly laid hands on real political power. By the second decade of the twentieth century, it had almost seemed (as John Maynard Keynes remembered) that liberalism was fast overtaking "the projects and politics of militarism and imperialism, of racial and cultural rivalries, of monopolies, restrictions, and exclusion," and Max Weber could announce that the only real political choices in a world disenchanted by scientific and economic rationalism were between "a democracy with a leader... or a leaderless democracy."[25]

The First World War brought democratic optimism to a smash, partly because the extent to which liberal democracy had insinuated itself into the politics of the European powers had apparently done nothing to prevent Europe's headlong rush into the war's catastrophe, and partly because the promise of an American president that the war would "make the world safe for democracy" failed so dismally. Instead, new brands of anti-Enlightenment dictatorship, fueled by corrosive philosophies which glorified national identities based on cult-like worship of race and soil, claimed the stage of the future. Even the American democracy, suffering a disgusted isolationism in the 1920s and its greatest economic crisis in the 1930s, looked like it might settle into a compromise with centralized authoritarianism.

That the dictators were eventually defeated could not disguise how close they came to triumph, helped along unintentionally, and at times unwisely, by the democracies themselves. The United States and Great Britain joined hands, almost too late, to defeat the totalitarian tyrannies of Germany, Italy, and Japan, while turning another hand to an even bloodier totalitarian in the form of Joseph Stalin in order to solicit his aid. And the post-1945 democracies that emerged from Europe's Second World War ruins to replace the dictatorships appeared sickly and uncertain. For every Konrad Adenauer in Germany, there was a justifier of authoritarianism in Carl Schmitt; for every Pope John Paul II, there was an Ayatollah Khomeini. When the last of the dictatorships birthed by the First World War finally imploded in 1991, political theorists finally believed they could celebrate democracy as "the end of history." But the resurgence of a violent and aggressive Islamism and a near collapse of the global economy in 2008 once again brought democracy's doubters to the fore. The most pressing question became not whether, but *how* authoritarian regimes might replace democracies—by slow decay or by sudden overthrow, by the hyper-dominance of one political party and its leader, or by military interventions in the name of stability.[26]

Even in the United States, economic inequality, cultural polarization, and the surrender of representative legislation to bureaucratic process fed increasing amounts of anxiety and doubt among Americans that their democracy was prey to a depressing variety of intestinal cancers. Presidents like Lyndon Johnson, who were otherwise praised as champions of civil rights, were, in private, cynics who believed that "what the man on the streets wants is not a big debate on fundamental issues; he wants a little medical care, a rug on the floor, a picture on the wall." The glue of American democracy was dissolving in a welter of gender and racial identity demands, while the bureaucratic rationalism which Weber had predicted would paralyze American vitality had now become a demoralizing and arbitrary fact of American life, leaving vast swaths of the American heartland impoverished, directionless, and hopeless.[27]

But it is the collapse of shared *mores* which has emerged in American minds as the single biggest danger to liberal democracy, for without any underlying set of agreed assumptions, no majority can rule safely and no minority can sleep quietly. Absent those *mores,* the question which emerges is whether a democracy can remain a democracy (or even a nation) if all that holds them together is a set of political rules.

One answer has come from those progressives who are impatient to the point of contempt with liberal individualism for not granting them *enough* autonomy, and who decry the persistent inequalities in liberal democracies as evidence that democracy is nothing but a window-dressing for the powerful. Especially for "woke" progressives, the promises of American democracy are falsehoods, maintained by the powerful in order to oppress the marginalized and make them into partners in their own immiseration. For them, government must rule, and be ruled through their hands, to suppress the noxious exercise of privilege.

Another answer has been provided by religious "integralists" and "national conservatives," who have concluded that democracy in America has granted *too much* autonomy to the individual over the community, including the liberty to emancipate the individual "from morality, tradition, and even biology." Family dissolves; subsidiary social organizations shrink and fade; culture survives only in the most debased and corrupt forms of entertainment. Their solution has been to look to nationalist authoritarians who would defy liberalism's nerveless indifference to perversion and dissolution. In an ironic mirror-image of progressives, they too yearn to *rule*, and some even welcome the bureaucratic state as the most dependable provider of security, health, and safety.[28]

There now stand two definitions of the problems of American democracy and two sharp dismissals of its future, one which complains that liberal democracy is entirely too weak to survive against the onslaught of political authoritarianism, and one which concludes that it is entirely too strong, and has become the ally of political authoritarianism. And yet, against American democracy's cultured despisers, there has always been one figure to confound the doubters, then and now. His name is Abraham Lincoln. It will be worth our while to examine what he says about democracy.

Chapter One

The Cause of Human Liberty

The word *democracy* occurs only 137 times in the collected writings of Abraham Lincoln. But no other word described what he saw as the most natural, the most just, and the most enlightened form of human government. Nothing, he said, could be "as clearly true as the truth of democracy." And nothing demonstrated that truth more clearly in Lincoln's mind than the American democracy, which embodied "the great living principle of all Democratic representative government."[1]

Lincoln's confidence in democracy was based on three evidences, beginning in the plainest terms with what it had done for him. His own experience illustrated how the absence of a permanent hierarchy in American life permitted anyone to transform themselves. "The principle of 'Liberty to all'" was "the principle that clears the path for all—gives hope to all—and, by consequence, enterprize, and industry to all." As soon as he had entered into adulthood, he was intent on taking that path and "cutting entirely adrift from the old life" he had known on his father's farm. He was "not ashamed to confess" in 1860 "that twenty-five years ago I was a hired laborer, mauling rails, at work on a flat boat—just what might happen to any poor man's son."

Not ashamed, because in America, there were no artificial restraints of class, birth, or hierarchy: "every man can make himself." Lincoln had been "a strange, friendless, uneducated, penniless boy," but in the democratic air of America, "the prudent, penniless beginner in the world, labors for wages awhile, saves a surplus with which to buy tools or land, for himself; then labors on his own account another while, and at length hires another new beginner to help him." He can even aspire to the highest office of that democracy. "I happen temporarily to occupy this big White House," he told an Ohio regiment that he reviewed outside the Executive Mansion in August 1864.

> *I am a living witness that any one of your children may look to come here as my father's child has. It is in order that each of you may have through this free government which we have enjoyed, an open field and a fair chance for your industry, enterprise and intelligence; that you may all have equal privileges in the race of life, with all its desirable human aspirations.*

In a world still teeming with aristocracies and dictatorships, "such a race of prosperity has been run nowhere else."[2]

No one seemed to illustrate the power of democracy to transform "any poor man's son" more than the man he admired most in American politics: Henry Clay, his "beau ideal of a statesman, the man for whom I fought all my humble life." Like Lincoln, Clay was a "self-made man"—someone "who had risen by their own efforts and industry to professional and political distinction"—which was exactly what a democracy made possible.[3] Not only was Clay shaped by democracy, but he devoted himself to promoting it. The "primary and all controlling passion" of Clay's life was "the cause of human liberty" for "the oppressed every where." If Clay loved his country above all others, it was not a vainglorious or parochial nationalism, but "because it was a free country," and its "advancement, prosperity and glory" were the means to "the advancement, prosperity and glory, of human liberty, human right and human nature."

Still, Clay was not a perfect model: "Mr. Clay was the owner of slaves." But this was only incidental, Lincoln argued (not entirely convincingly). Clay had been "cast into life where slavery was already widely spread and deeply seated." To Clay's credit, Lincoln insisted that Clay "ever was, on principle and in feeling, opposed to slavery." What restrained Clay's good instinct was his uncertainty about "how it could be at once eradicated, without producing a greater evil, even to the cause of human liberty" by disrupting the American government. But that still placed Clay at a far distance from "an increasing number of men, who, for the sake of perpetuating slavery, are beginning to assail and to ridicule...the declaration that 'all men are created free and equal.'"[4]

Self-transformation, especially on the order of a Henry Clay, might serve for Lincoln as a justification for democracy, but for others, democracy needed a more transcendent rationale, and that was what Lincoln found in natural law. Modern jurisprudence has relegated much of natural law to the historical attic, but in Lincoln's day, it remained a potent intellectual resource and has undergone a significant revival among political theorists in our own. Natural law proceeded easily from the assumption, fostered mutually by the Enlightenment, Christian scholasticism, and classical philosophy, that if the physical universe functioned by natural physical laws, then the moral world should reveal similar evidence of law-likeness. "Every law"—meaning *physical* law—"is found to be in harmony with every other law," by analogy, in the *moral* realm, reasoned Francis Wayland (whose works Lincoln "ate up, digested, and assimilated"). Moral codes, and then positive law, form themselves around natural moral law as readily as physics forms itself around natural physical law.[5]

From natural law, it would be possible by "the light of reason" to discern a number of natural *rights,* or goods, and the Declaration of Independence taught Lincoln that "among these are Life, Liberty and the Pursuit of Happiness." The "love of liberty," for instance, is an instinct "which God has planted in our bosoms," and it is a love which is "the heritage of all men, in all lands, every where." It was so much a matter of nature that even "the ant, who has toiled and dragged a crumb to his nest, will furiously defend the fruit of his labor, against whatever robber assails him." In the same way, "the most dumb and stupid slave that ever toiled for a master, does constantly know that he is wronged." Each of these natural goods is a "right within itself," and moral uprightness requires that they receive "the protection of all law and all good citizens" for human flourishing. But the enjoyment of these rights could only exist fully within a democratic framework of self-government. Natural rights were "a standard maxim for a free society, which could be familiar to all, and revered by all; constantly looked to, constantly labored for." In turn, they rendered "the doctrine of self-government... right—absolutely and eternally right."

It was not always clear whether these rights were an imperative or simply a natural regularity. Either way, there could be "no just rule other than that of moral and abstract Right," and that "rule" began with "the right of a people to 'life, liberty and the pursuit of Happiness.'" Those "maxims" also rendered slavery morally wrong—not merely inconvenient and certainly not a "positive good," but *wrong*—since "there can be no moral right in connection with one man's making a slave of another." Was not the Declaration's assertion of the "equality of natural rights among all nations... correct"? And "have not all civilized nations, our own among them, made the Slave trade capital, and classed it with piracy and murder? Is it not held to be the great wrong of the world?" It was a loathing so fundamental that Lincoln could not "remember when I did not so think, and feel."[6]

Finally, democracy shone for Lincoln because it had the sanction of both the American past and the American future. It almost rings naïve, in our weary ears, to hear the abolitionist Wendell Phillips announce in 1864 that "the future and inevitable form of all governments is to be democratic; and that all progress tends toward that final and happy goal." And yet Lincoln was similarly confident democracy would not only triumph in his time but provide a "vast future" for generations to follow. "The popular principle applied to government," he told Congress in December 1861, has produced everything "which men deem desirable," and will continue to do so "if firmly maintained ... for the future." Americans must "diligently apply the means," he wrote in 1863, "never doubting that a just God, in his own good time, will give us the rightful result." But that result, if achieved, would "we hope and believe ... liberate the world."[7]

But just as powerful was the vindication given to democracy by the American past. Lincoln inherited from eighteenth-century politics the sense that political orders tend downward, toward decay and degeneration, rather than evolving upwards into something different and improved. The solution was to "recur to first principles," and especially the principles of the American Revolution (a "resuscitation" which had also been urged by Henry Clay). He "knew the tendency of prosperity to breed tyrants," and so "when in the distant future some man, some faction, some interest, should set up the doctrine that none but rich men, or none but white men, were entitled to life, liberty and the pursuit of happiness, their posterity might look up again to the Declaration of Independence and take courage to renew the battle which their fathers began."

In Lincoln's imagination, the Revolution had been more than merely a domestic rebellion against British taxing authority. He could remember from his boyhood reading of the Revolution's history that "there must have been something more than common that those men struggled for." Why else would the revolutionaries have fought so tenaciously? What Americans must do in this new age, he reasoned, is to "re-adopt the Declaration of Independence, and with it, the practices, and policy, which harmonize with it." If "you have been inclined to believe that all men are not created equal in those inalienable rights enumerated by our charter of liberty, let me entreat you to ... return to the fountain whose waters spring close by the blood of the Revolution." The Founders "could not have consented that these institutions shall perish; much less could he, in betrayal of so vast, and so sacred a trust, as these free people had confided to him." He might be living in a different century, but he would be the exponent of "those noble fathers—Washington, Jefferson and Madison."[8]

Democracy was "my ancient faith," and Lincoln's certainty of its triumph rose to the level of serenity. By the same token, those who have been the most distrustful of Abraham Lincoln have displayed more than a little distrust of democracy, too.

Lincoln did not merely espouse democracy; he *looked* like democracy. He was as common-looking and homely as a democratic people were themselves common and homely. Henry Clay Whitney, hearing Lincoln speak at Urbana, Illinois, in 1854, thought "he had the appearance of a rough, intelligent farmer." He was "Stoop Shouldered," long-armed, with "large and bony" hands, and an attender of the Lincoln-

Douglas debates in 1858 found "his general appearance any-thing but prepossessing" (and "his phiz is truly awful"). Above all, he was "not stiff" or formal. Jane Martin Johns described him in 1849 as "unaffected, unostentatious," and Whitney was impressed by how "he entered into conversation in a frank, genial, unconstrained manner as if the stranger was on terms of familiarity and mutual accord, and had been for years." Even after his election as president in 1860, Ada Bailhache could spend "an evening at Mr. Lincolns" before his depar-ture from his home in Illinois, scarcely realizing "that I was sitting in the august presence of a *real live President.*" William Howard Russell, *The Times* of London's reporter in America in 1861, was startled to find that at Lincoln's White House receptions "any one could walk in who chose." Even the hat he wore en route to Washington and his inauguration sent a democratic message: it was a "soft wool hat" with a wide brim and tall crown, known as a "Kossuth hat," from the style worn by the Hungarian revolutionary, Lajos Kossuth.[9]

Lincoln did not, however, offer a specific, or even lengthy, definition of *democracy,* or "representative" democracy, or "a representative Republic," or a "constitutional republic, or "a democracy—a government of the people, by the same people." A republic was clearly a democratic space, since its opposite was the suppression of "meetings," and through that, "to shut men's mouths," and he had no hesitation in jumbling together *republic* and *democracy* as though they were synonyms.[10] But Lincoln's only attempt at actually defining *democracy* occurred, almost in passing, in a note he jotted on the eve of the Lincoln-Douglas debates, and at that moment, it was more of an effort to set democracy apart from slavery:

> *As I would not be a slave, so I would not be a master. This expresses my idea of democracy. Whatever differs from this, to the extent of the difference, is no democracy.*[11]

This is a peculiar definition, since Lincoln makes no formal attempt in it at specifying the components of democracy (like the location of sovereignty), and makes no allusion to elections, or even to majority rule. What Lincoln did instead was to draw a contrast between slavery and democracy, so as to illustrate what democracy was *not,* and that contrast hinged on the point of *consent.* A slave is someone who has no autonomy, no say in their status, whose consent is unsolicited and undesired, and with no prospect of being delivered from that status.[12]

Consent was a key concept for Lincoln in considering both democracy and slavery. Consent was how sovereignty was exercised: his objection, in 1848, to war with Mexico over the disputed region between the Nueces River and the Rio Grande was based on whether the people in that region had ever "submitted themselves to the government or laws of Texas, or of the United States, by consent." And consent was what drew a line of separation between freedom and enslavement. "This is a world of compensations," Lincoln concluded, "and he who would *be* no slave, must consent to *have* no slave."[13]

"According to our ancient faith," Lincoln said in 1854, "the just powers of governments are derived from the consent of the governed." It was one of the Declaration's foundational arguments *that Governments are instituted among Men, deriving their just powers from the consent of the governed,* and Lincoln translated that "axiom" to mean "that no man is good enough to govern another man, without that other's consent. I say this is the leading principle—the sheet anchor of American republicanism." Slavery might have some justification if the slave is not a human being, and is incapable of consent. "If he is not a man, why in that case, he who is a man may, as a matter of self-government, do just as he pleases with him." But a slave, plainly, is "a man." So, Lincoln reasoned, "is it not to that extent, a total destruction of self-government, to say that he too shall not govern himself?" When one man "governs himself that is self-government; but when he governs himself, and also governs another man" without that vital element of consent, "that is more than self-government that is despotism."[14]

Consent could come in several forms. It could mean active agreement, either vocal or participatory. Democracy encourages "the people to judge and act for themselves," and in a functioning democracy, "all the governed" exercise "an equal voice in the government." In some contexts, consent could come with certain reservations. Lincoln himself would "consent to the extension" of slavery into the republic's western territories "rather than see the Union dissolved, just as I would consent to any great evil, to avoid a greater one"—although he suspected that yielding such a consent would, in fact, disregard any consent by the people living in those territories, forcing "Governors, and Secretaries, and Judges on the people of the territories, without their choice or consent," to tolerate the intrusion of slavery. And to the free laborer consent was what began and ended his labor for another. Consent was exactly what was absent from the slave's labor, either at its beginning or ending. In slavery, "the master not only governs the slave without his consent; but he governs him by a set of rules altogether different from those which he prescribes for himself." It appropriates the slave's labor, the slave's personality, even the slave's sexuality, since it allows the master to exploit the slave's physical being in "forced concubinage."

Or, consent could mean simple passive acquiescence. The Missouri Compromise of 1820 "was settled by the Northern members consenting to the admission of Missouri, with the understanding that in consideration thereof the South consented that slavery should forever be prohibited from entering any territory north of 36 degrees 30 minutes." This, however, was a low form of consent, in a grudging spirit, and only out of necessity to preserve the Union (and American democracy with it) from heading off disaster's cliffs. It was better, at least, than the conniving sort of consent Lincoln had known, in which shady lawyers "in advance, consent to be a knave."[15] But not by much.

Lincoln believed that slavery persisted in the American republic only by this low form of consent, a fact which was suggestive of how inconsistent slavery and democracy really were. Mere acquiescence fostered a political environment in which active consent is unsolicited, and sooner or later, disregarded. The crime of the "famous" Kansas-Nebraska Act, which erased even the Missouri Compromise and opened all the western territories to the possibility of legalized slavery, was that "it was done without the consent of the people" in those territories, "and against their wishes, for if the matter had been put to vote before the people directly, whether that should be made a slave territory, they would have indignantly voted it down." From that point in 1854, the record of James Buchanan's failed presidency was little more than a series of "fraudulent attempts of the administration and the slave power to force institutions upon a free people against their consent."[16]

On those terms, slavery is a condition Lincoln would not wish for himself or his country, and all the more so because he had tasted something of slavery in his own crude, backwoods upbringing. As an adolescent, Lincoln's father, Thomas, had, quite literally, rented him out to neighboring farmers and flatboaters, with all the proceeds going back into his father's hands. The memory of that "domination" still rankled Lincoln four decades later, leading him to claim that "I used to be a slave," but "now I am so free that they let me practice law." It rankled still further when protectors of slavery argued that slavery was, in fact, a "positive good" for the slave, because American slavery was confined to a race of natural inferiors—as though slavery was a benefit bestowed on those incapable of appreciating democracy. In its worst form, slavery was nothing but Thomas Hobbes's war-of-all-against-all, and slavery's most shameless defender, John C. Calhoun, did not hesitate to say that "property in man has existed in all ages, and results from the *natural* state of man, *which is war*." This was *nature* seen, not as a manifestation of orderliness, but of a violent contest of the strong and the weak, the intelligent and the imbecile. As such, Lincoln added, the slavery argument was indistinguishable from the excuses of monarchs, because kings "always bestrode the necks of the people … because the people were better off for being ridden."

Slavery was the antithesis of consent, because consent implied order, and the capacity of all human beings to perceive and embrace order; slavery was about power, not order. It prescribed what one must or must not do, irrespective of any thought or gesture on the part of the enslaved, and rendered the slave incapable of registering either. Arguments defending slavery excited as much contempt in Lincoln as arguments for kings. "As a *good* thing, slavery is strikingly peculiar, in this, that it is the only good thing which no man ever seeks the good of, *for himself*." Lincoln had "never known a man who wished to be himself a slave"; if that man would not consent to be a slave, he had no business overriding the consent of others and making them slaves. "If any should be slaves," he told the soldiers of an Indiana regiment during the Civil War, "it should be first those who desire it for *themselves*."[17]

Democracy implied a political Golden Rule: what you do not want done to yourself, do not try to impose on others; what you *do* impose on others, submit to yourself. Those who wish not to have consent trampled upon must not be party to such trampling themselves. If not a slave, then not a master; that is democracy, or at least, one key aspect of it.[18] There is no separation of people into the categories of those born naturally to freedom and those born, as in Aristotle's *Politics*, with slave-like traits and who are unable to live on any higher plane than subservience and unintelligence.

Democracy and slavery are so unalike that those who want to live in a democracy cannot, ultimately, reconcile that desire with the buying, owning, and keeping of slaves. That some people do manage this artful dodging is an evasion of logic and reason, growing out of pure self-interest and the irrational lust for power. It survives as it does only because some people cannot see the inconsistency of democracy and slavery "through 2,000,000,000 of dollars." It did not matter that, technically, democracy is a political system and slavery an economic one, for in Lincoln's mind, the boundary between economics and politics was thin to the point of evaporation.[19]

Lincoln's "idea of democracy" only establishes what democracy is *not*, or at least cannot include. He never offered a more thoroughgoing definition of what democracy *is*. But it is not difficult to piece together a larger "idea" from the vast outpouring of letters, speeches, briefs, notes, and state papers which he composed over the course of a public life that lasted thirty-three years, from the day he first announced himself as a candidate for the Illinois state legislature.

Even more than consent, Lincoln understood that democracy is characterized by its location of sovereignty in the body of the people. "This country, with its institutions, belongs to the people who inhabit it," he announced in his first inaugural address, and the great challenge of the Civil War—first, even before dealing with slavery—was proving that this is "not an absurdity." A sovereign people can amend their democracy's rules or replace their rulers, but it cannot suffer one portion of that democracy simply to walk away and call it "peaceful secession." If a minority balks at the policy endorsed by the majority, and then proceeds to break things up by armed force, then democracy would appear in the eyes of a not-very-sympathetic world to be a practical farce.[20] "We must settle this question now, whether in a free government the minority have the right to break up the government whenever they choose," Lincoln explained to his secretary, John Hay, less than a month after the war began. "If we fail it will go far to prove the incapability of the people to govern themselves."[21]

The way that they would govern themselves, however, would be by law. Universal "reverence for the laws" was the spirit of order; it restrained the state from becoming tyrannical and the people from becoming a mob, and had application as much to the high as to the low. Yield an inch on the law, and next the yard will be taken. "Allow the President to invade a neighboring nation, whenever he shall deem it necessary," he complained to William Herndon in 1848, "and you allow him to make war at pleasure."

Law, however, only ensured stability; it could not inspire participation, and in a democracy, the participation of the citizens was indispensable. Lincoln closed a speech in 1859 with "an appeal to all—opponents as well as friends—to think soberly and maturely, and never fail to cast their vote, insisting that it was not a privilege only, but a duty to do so." Even "with its incidental, and undesirable strife," an election is the only way of "demonstrating popular sentiment." It was the genius of the American democracy that its Constitution gave "public servants but little power for mischief." And what "mischief" they might inaugurate with that "little power" would be of no great duration, since the people,

through the Constitution, "have, with equal wisdom, provided for the return of that little to their own hands at very
short intervals."[22]

But a democracy practiced in this way would only function "while the people remain patient, and true to themselves." Patience—and the law it served—would turn out to
be in fearfully short supply in Lincoln's America, for there
were too many who were only too happy to be masters, and
to have others as slaves.

Chapter Two

Law, Reason, and Passion

I know the American People are much attached to their Government," Abraham Lincoln said in January 1838, when he was still a rising almost-twenty-nine-year-old state politician in Illinois. Curiously, that government was itself just shy of sixty-two years old, which is not a long political time for attachments to develop. The United States had no long descent to trace from toga-draped elders; it had no official language, no state church, no national university. It was built around a Declaration and a Constitution whose creators were guided by what they had read in a dozen or so treatises on political theory. "It will not be an easy matter to bring the American States to act as a nation," predicted the Earl of Sheffield in 1784. "We might as reasonably dread the effects of combinations among the German as among the American States." Even the Americans' allies agreed: "In all the American provinces," wrote France's chargé d'affaires in America in 1787, there will be "little stability."[1]

Sure enough, the republic fractured within three decades into rival political parties, suffered through two serious outbreaks of conspiracy and rebellion (the Whiskey Rebellion of 1795 and Aaron Burr's plot to set up his own private fiefdom in the Mississippi River valley), blundered into a near-fatal war with Great Britain in 1812, and then sagged into economic collapse in 1819. Political life seemed to grow more rowdy with every decade. Members of Congress brawled on the floor of the House of Representatives. Elections were riotous affairs where voters were "open to the promptings of every rascally agitator," where threats and intimidation turned away "numbers of native-born citizens" who "would say they had wives and children, and would not like to risk their lives in a useless attempt," and where the indifferent jack-a-nape who "cares not a farthing for the general good ... will sell his vote for a dollar."[2]

But far from any of this proving to Americans the folly of their government, Americans believed in it with an energy which approached religious reverence. They did not merely create a republic; they created a highly democratic one, and absorbed the democratic principle into their pores. "There is no such thing as class distinction here," wrote a Swedish immigrant in 1846, "no counts, barons, lords or lordly estates ... neither is my cap worn out from lifting it in the presence of gentlemen." The democratic citizen, wrote the democratic novelist James Fenimore Cooper, "insists on his independence and an entire freedom of opinion." For Henry Clay in 1819, the American government was the "only one bright spot" in the "political hemisphere of the west" which could "enlighten, and animate, and gladden the human heart."[3]

No one understood the Americans' devotion to their democracy, or shared it more thoroughly, than Abraham Lincoln. For the safekeeping of their democracy, Americans "would suffer much for its sake. I know they would endure evils long and patiently, before they would ever think of exchanging it for another." Certainly *he* would. "We have the best Government the world ever knew," Lincoln told a newly recruited regiment of New Yorkers twenty-six years later, a government in which "the people" had the "right to decide the question," whatever the question might be. And it was one which he was happy to share as broadly as possible. When "I see a people borne down by the weight of their shackles—the oppression of tyranny...rather would I do all in my power to raise the yoke, than to add anything that would tend to crush them."[4]

This was not because Lincoln had no eye for Americans' political excesses. But what mitigated the baleful tendency of passion in democracy was law. In one American law treatise and discourse after another in the fifty years after independence, the law was held up as "a moral science of great sublimity," wrote the Baltimore jurist David Hoffman in 1817. It was nothing less than "the public reason, uttered by the public voice." So long as Americans allowed themselves to be ruled by reason, they would choose to be ruled by law, and all would eventually be well with their democracy. But if Americans should surrender to "the dictates of passion and venality, rather than of reason and of right," warned Francis Wayland, at "that moment...will the world's last hope be extinguished, and darkness brood for ages over the whole human race."[5] Even democratic government's most reckless champion, Andrew Jackson, was—at least at first—a lawyer. The man who proposed to save it from Jacksonian passion—Abraham Lincoln—was a lawyer, too.

In 1828, Andrew Jackson won his second bid for the presidency, and rode to power the following March as the champion of the Democratic Party and "the direct representative of the American people." Once Jackson had that mandate in hand, his two terms as president wrought calculated havoc on the nation's bankers and banking system, expelled Indian tribes from their homelands, and turned presidential appointments into a "spoils system," all the while positioning himself as the people's tribune, "a democratic autocrat." He was the first singular example of what James Madison most feared from democracy—a weakness for demagogues who would play to fear, anger, and contempt, and persuade Americans to put more faith in power than in liberty.[6]

Jackson left office in 1837, just in time for the nation's economy to subside into financial panic. "At no period in its history has there been as great a degree of general distress as there is at this day," wailed a short-lived New York Democratic newspaper. "Of its mechanics and other working men, at least 10,000 are without employment, and their wives and families...are suffering...heart-rending want." In New York, "a mob of several hundred" ransacked merchants' warehouses for flour. Want kindled fury, and not just over the economy. Over 140 riots erupted, and mob violence in Boston, Philadelphia, and New York overran businesses, struck out at landlords, "monopolists and extortioners," and targeted white abolitionists and free blacks who looked like a source of labor competition. William Ellery Channing, addressing a convention of the American Anti-Slavery Society, was attacked with "repeated showers of stones and rotten eggs." What had been "a government of laws," declared the *Philadelphia Public Ledger*, now looked like a descent into "the reign of mobocracy and terror."[7]

Lincoln had already complained, in January of 1837, as a member of the Illinois state legislature, about Jackson's "lawless and mobocratic spirit...which is already abroad in the land; and is spreading with rapid and fearful impetuosity, to the ultimate overthrow of every institution, or even moral principle, in which persons and property have hitherto found security." The rising tide of "mobocracy" brought Lincoln, a year later, in January 1838, to the Baptist church in his hometown of Springfield to address the monthly session of the city's Young Men's Lyceum. The Lyceum had already been casting a worried eye on the upsurge in mobs, taking as its December 1837 topic of discussion "Do the signs of the present times indicate the downfall of this Government?"[8] Lincoln's speech a month later was his answer to that question.

Americans, he began, had inherited "the fairest portion of the earth" as their bounty, as well as a "government...conducing more essentially to the ends of civil and religious liberty, than any of which the history of former times tells us." Creating that government had been an immense task, but having accomplished it, it remained now for the newest generation to preserve and hand on—"undecayed by the lapse of time and untorn by usurpation"—the "political edifice of liberty and equal rights." Simple enough. But the evidence of the preceding year was that a successful handing-on was by no means certain. And the force which would fuel the mobs and dash that handing-on to the ground came not from war or invasion, but from Americans themselves and a "growing disposition to substitute the wild and furious passions, in lieu of the sober judgment of Courts; and the worse than savage mobs, for the executive ministers of justice." Was democracy inevitably the victim of the passions?

Lincoln's suspicion of passion had long roots, stretching back into the eighteenth-century Enlightenment, for law was simply the public embodiment of the Enlightenment's reverence for reason. After all, Lincoln was born in 1809, at the end of what is sometimes called the "long eighteenth century," and his intellectual growth was steeped in the classics of the Enlightenment: Tom Paine, Constantin Volney, Adam Smith. Central to the Enlightenment was its preference for reason over authority and hierarchy—which is to say, the justification of our beliefs and actions by material or logical evidence, not by testimony or personal emotion.[9]

The Enlightenment did not discover reason (as though no one had ever been reasonable before the Enlightenment's progenitors appeared in the seventeenth century), since the religion of the Old Testament urged minds to *come now, and let us reason together,* and the theologians of the Middle Ages devised scholastic inquiries which were monuments to rational inquiry. But the premises on which they erected those rational structures were inherited from authority, and especially the authority of the Bible or Aristotle, or both in tandem. What distinguished the Enlightenment's *reason* was the breaking up of the authority of those premises, and the employment of reason as an authority itself, to persuade rather than to threaten.

The first of the ancient premises to crack and founder under the inspection of reason were scientific ones—that the physical universe was a hierarchy, from the Earth at the base, through the realms of the planets and stars, to the high heavens—and the cracking was begun by Galileo and Newton. It was only a matter of time before *reason* deconstructed the political hierarchies of Europe as well. "We live in a century in which the philosophical spirit has rid us of a great number of prejudices," claimed Denis Diderot in his *Encyclopédie* in 1749, a century his countryman, the economist Anne-Robert Turgot, described as "the century of reason." And under the reign of reason, politics was no more exempt from scrutiny than physics. Once Americans decided that "no truly natural or religious reason can be assigned" to the rule of dim-brained or tyrannical monarchs, then (as Tom Paine declared) the "distinction of men into kings and subjects" vanished.[10]

But the reign of reason was itself threatened, partly by the bad example of what happened in Jacobin France in the 1790s, where another revolt against hierarchy turned into an incestuous bloodbath, and partly because of suspicions that reason could not penetrate every secret, or worse, that if it did, it would render them pale, bloodless, and boring.[11] Reason had no greater admirer than Immanuel Kant, and yet even Kant warned that reason made mistakes that experience did little to correct. The reasoning mind could deal only with the appearances of things, not the things-in-themselves, which required an entirely different way of knowing, apart from reason. "If we view the objects of the senses as mere appearances, as is fitting," Kant wrote, "then we thereby admit at the very same time that a thing in itself underlies them, although we are not acquainted with this thing as it may be constituted in itself, but only with its appearance...."[12]

However, Kant believed, tools did exist with which to penetrate and apprehend those underlying realities: one was criticism, another was intuition. And it was from this skepticism of reason that the Romantic antidote emerged, looking to find the real springs of human identity in the non-rational—in personal experience or tribal identity, in the bonds of tradition, in the sublime, in the occult power of class, nations, soil, race, religion—in *passion.*

The Enlightenment eyed passion warily, uncertain whether to banish it or co-opt it. Anthony Ashley Cooper worried that passion, undeniable as it might be as a human instinct, could nevertheless inspire demoniacal furies, "especially where religion has had to do." Passion can put people "beyond themselves... and in this state... the fury flies from face to face, and the disease is no sooner seen than caught." Especially in politics, "the prudent, the equitable, the active, resolute and sober character" will (according to Adam Smith) generate "prosperity and satisfaction," but "the rash, the insolent... and voluptuous... forbodes ruin to the individual, and misfortune to all who have anything to do with him." A century and a half later, those fears were all too well confirmed, as the "political passions" of the Romantics—"the thirst for immediate results, the exclusive preoccupation with the desired end, the scorn for argument, the excess, the hatred, the fixed ideas"—came within an ace of destroying civilization itself.[13]

It is unlikely that Lincoln ever laid eyes on Kant, but his school textbook, the *Columbian Orator,* taught him that "guided by reason," nations have "established society and government" and can even "remedy the imperfections, of nature herself." Reason, for Lincoln, was the guidance of human affairs by "observation, reflection and experiment," and there was hardly a more instructive lesson in that guidance than the American Revolution. "Fatally enamoured of their selfish systems of policy," the British "were deaf to the suggestions of reason and the demands of justice," and it cost them an empire.[14] Americans must profit from the reminder of that contrast, because it could only be a "Happy day"

> *when, all appetites controlled, all passions subdued, all matters subjected, mind, all conquering mind, shall live and move the monarch of the world. Glorious consummation! Hail fall of Fury! Reign of Reason, all hail!*[15]

No wonder, then, that in the ears of the Springfield Lyceum, Lincoln identified the mobs of the previous year as an unlovely manifestation of passions which had usurped reason and thrown aside truth, and a sign of political doom for democracy. The American republic, precisely because it was founded on "the capability of man to govern himself," was most in danger from Americans who had surrendered that "capacity" to passion through "the increasing disregard for law which pervades the country." In Lincoln's concept of democracy, reason stood on one side, passion and "outrages committed by mobs" stood on the other.

He had no difficulty summoning up examples: first, lynching gamblers in Vicksburg, and then hanging suspected slave rebels and their white allies (in the so-called Madison County slave insurrection of 1835), until "dead men were seen literally dangling from the boughs of trees upon every road side"; next, in St. Louis, a "mulatto man, by the name of [Francis] McIntosh" who was "chained to a tree, and actually burned to death" in 1836; and finally the "hundreds and thousands" who "ravage and rob provision-stores, throw printing presses into rivers, shoot editors, and hang and burn obnoxious persons at pleasure, and with impunity." (The editor he had particularly in mind was Elijah Lovejoy of the Alton *Observer*, who was shot to death in a gunfight by a mob who attacked his abolitionist newspaper two months before Lincoln spoke to the Lyceum.)

A government which rests itself on the people, and which does not require an aristocrat or a class of nobles or an oppressive imperial army to establish order, will rapidly lose its self-respect if this is how the people conduct themselves. "Good men, men who love tranquility, who desire to abide by the laws, and enjoy their benefits," but who now see "their property destroyed; their families insulted, and their lives endangered" will become "disgusted with, a Government that offers them no protection," and will soon enough welcome a monarch or a dictator—anyone on a white horse who will bring order out of chaos. This, after all, had been the pattern followed by one republican experiment after another, in France with Napoleon, in the South American republics with Bolívar and San Martín, in Mexico by Agustín de Iturbide and Santa Anna.[16]

But worse, if self-government went down in the United

States, it would drag down with it all hope for liberal democracy everywhere else. Despite democratic America's excesses over the years, nowhere had a democratic republic been more prosperous; nowhere had successive changes of administrations been more peaceful. If in spite of that, democracy yielded to the destructive uproar of passion—if Americans had forgotten the principles of the Revolution so quickly— "it will be left without friends, or with too few, and those few too weak, to make their friendship effectual" and spell the end of "that fair fabric, which for the last half century, has been the fondest hope, of the lovers of freedom, throughout the world." Self-government—a principle he would later cast in terms of "government of the people, by the people, for the people"—cannot survive by passion. Such government lives only by reason—and the instrument of reason in political life was law.[17]

So, the solution to the problem of passion was, for Lincoln, "simple": treat the laws as absolutes, almost as mathematical axioms. "Let every American, every lover of liberty, every well wisher to his posterity, swear...never to violate in the least particular, the laws of the country; and never to tolerate their violation by others." That oath would serve as a surrogate for passion, a "political religion of the nation," in which "all sexes and tongues, and colors and conditions" should "sacrifice unceasingly upon its altars." Even when laws proved "unwise," let them "be religiously observed" until a proper process of repeal could be effected. He had no sense of how a *civil* disobedience to laws could work; it was either strict adherence or "mob law."

Obedience to the laws would become the American democracy's fountain of youth, constantly replenishing its stability and prosperity. That did not mean that law was the solution to every situation. In the broadest sense, "the theory of our government is Universal Freedom" for the exercise of the "equal rights of men" and thus "secure the blessings of freedom."[18] Laws should be effective, fair, reverenced—but few. (It was, after all, "the great secret of government," according to Elnathan Winchester's 1796 school primer, "not to govern too much," since "the milder, simpler and more equitable the laws are, the more likely they are to be obeyed.") Lincoln had no notion that democratic government was responsible for securing a vague "common good." "Government is not charged with the duty of redressing, or preventing, all the wrongs in the world," he wrote in 1859 in notes for speeches he would give in Ohio; its power to promote a "general welfare" was preventative rather than regulative, to "redress and prevent, all wrongs, which are wrongs to the nation itself," and thus "avoid planting and cultivating too many thorns in the bosom of society." Its scope should be deliberately modest: "The legitimate object of government, is to do for a community of people, whatever they need to have done, but can not do, at all, or can not, so well do, for themselves in their separate, and individual capacities."[19]

For that reason, the laws Lincoln hoped Americans would religiously obey could be sorted into two simple and general categories, "those which have relation to wrongs, and those which have not." The first category largely involved criminal law, "all crimes, misdemeanors, and non-performance of contracts." The other was related to civil law: "All which, in its nature, and without wrong, requires combined action, as public roads and highways, public schools, charities, pauperism, orphanage, estates of the deceased, and the machinery of government itself."

Lincoln was certainly no libertarian. There had to be at least some common rules for "making and maintaining roads, bridges, and the like; providing for the helpless young and afflicted; common schools; and disposing of deceased men's property." And as a disciple of Henry Clay, he called from the beginning to the ending of his career for government sponsorship of economic empowerment. His earliest election speeches for the Illinois legislature are full of pledges to promote road and bridge construction, the creation of a state bank (on the model of the Second Bank of the United States so hated by Andrew Jackson), "setting a limit to the rates of usury," lobbying Congress for the sale of public land in Illinois, and even claims for "an estray horse, mare or colt." He mocked those who greeted any proposal "to remove a snag, a rock, or a sandbar from a lake or river" with the incessant cry of "no." Yet, this abiding rule remained: "In all that the people can individually do as well for themselves, government ought not to interfere." The "best sort of principle" is "the principle of allowing the people to do as they please with their own business."[20]

But this legal self-restraint was never entirely safe from the passions; nor could law banish passion from American life by its own strength. The slaveocracy of the South, wrote a Republican publicist, was "a reign of terror, which has muzzled the press and silenced free speech. In most of the slave States, nobody is permitted to speak unless he speaks in a particular way." Nothing seemed to underscore the threat posed by passion to law, and beyond it to the kind of government Lincoln spoke for, more than the attempt in 1861 of eleven Southern slaveholding states to secede from the Union. Secession thrived on passion, and all the more so because it set aside law and thrust the rule of power into the smallest crevices of society. "Madness rules the hour," Nathan Appleton (the pioneer merchant of American industry) wrote to a Charlestonian, and "loyal men ... live under a reign of terror which dismays, silences and paralyzes them." Across the South, denunciation, shaming, shunning, and silencing became the preferred responses. And worse: "at the South," enraged secessionists re-enacted the "case for lynching" that Lincoln had attacked in the Lyceum two decades before. "It is sufficient that a man is from the North," complained an Ohio newspaper in February 1861, "or if that is not enough, every Northern man is put to the inquisition, and if he is a Republican, or if he voted for Lincoln," that was more than enough justification for an atrocity to take place. No nation "ever submitted to such abuse of its subjects by foreign people." Yet secession-minded politicians drove wildly toward disunion "as if they were afraid that the blood of the people will cool down."

Across the South, "a system of espionage prevails which would disgrace the despotism and darkness of the middle ages," complained Michigan congressman Henry Waldron. "The personal safety of the traveler depends, not on his deeds, but upon his opinions." Frederick Law Olmsted found that "in Richmond, and Charleston, and New Orleans" free society seemed to have disappeared into the grasp of a system of "citadels, sentries, passports, grape-shotted cannon, and daily public whippings," while the South Carolina legislature was preparing "bills in relation to free negroes, itinerant salesmen, and traveling agents"—as though Lovejoy and McIntosh were examples of proper response.[21] The Confederacy had become, on a national scale, a mob.

In 1861 as much as in 1838, Lincoln fingered passion as the culprit at the root of this ideological bullying, and he even scolded his own party in 1860 for trying to fight Southern passion with Northern passion. "Let us do nothing through passion and ill temper," he said, and told the New York state legislature that we must "restrain ourselves" and "allow ourselves not to run off in a passion."[22] But Southern passion was the element he feared the most. "We must not be enemies," he pleaded in his inaugural address. "Though passion may have strained, it must not break our bonds of affection." In the cool light of reason, Southerners would find that they "can have no conflict without being yourselves the aggressors."

Passion—whether in the form of Jacksonian mobs or paranoid slave owners—threatened to send democracy off its legal rails; and ready to remind him of that threat were the mouthpieces of reactionary aristocracy. "With a democracy... passion is not the exception but the rule," jeered the *London Quarterly Review* in the summer of 1861.

> *Passion is fostered equally by the two main characteristics of the democratic sovereign—ignorance and numbers....A triumph gained by a majority under such feelings will preclude the possibility of moderation... but such discipline is impossible where the rude masses that form a nation are dashing forward at the bidding, not of their leaders, but of their own excited partisanship.*

Lincoln's task would be to show that reason, not passion, would triumph, that democracies were not doomed—and the United States would not be doomed—to self-destruction by passion. "This country, Sir, maintains, and means to maintain, the rights of human nature and the capacity of man for self-government," he told a newly arrived European envoy in November 1861. And he reminded Congress that the war "presents to the whole family of man, the question, whether a constitutional republic, or a democracy—a government of the people, by the same people" can be broken up and "organic law" shouldered aside.[23]

Lincoln promised to employ "all indispensable means" in suppressing the Confederate rebellion. But as much as he would reach for whatever tools he thought might save democracy, they would still be the reasonable tools of law. No "spirit of revenge should actuate his measures," he told

a Maryland legislative delegation, and writing to a Louisiana Unionist in 1862, he promised that "I shall do all I can
to save the government." But "I shall do nothing in malice.
What I deal with is too vast for malicious dealing." He was
the first to admit that "I frequently make mistakes myself,
in the many things I am compelled to do hastily," and there
were moments in dealing with scheming cabinet members
or unenthusiastic generals when Lincoln's temper darkened
into something close to malice. But he struggled to be guided
by "the dictates of prudence, as well as the obligations of law,"
and labored to convince himself that reason would eventually prevail, even among the Southern public. "At the beginning," the fire-eaters and war-mongers in the Confederacy
"knew they could never raise their treason to any respectable
magnitude, by any name which implies violation of law." But
the mob-stokers could only burn through so much political
fuel before Southerners came to their senses. "If that were
crushed," Lincoln assured John Hay, "the people would be
ready to swing back to their old bearings." Lincoln was more
anxious that too many Northerners at the end of the war
were as governed by "hate and vindictiveness" as the secessionists had been at the beginning and were fully as eager to
bring down unconstitutional vengeance on Southern heads.
Is there, after all, "in all republics, this inherent, and fatal
weakness?" he asked.[24] Is it passion which will make some of
us slaves, and others of us masters? It is a question which, to
Lincoln's dismay, was not precisely answered, except by an
assassin's bullet.

Chapter Three

An American System

G iven how much Lincoln is celebrated as the champion of democratic politics, it will be easy to miss the ways Lincoln's prescriptions for government are wound around economic issues. Laws he thought government could, and *should,* enact ought to involve "crimes" and "misdemeanors," but ought to concentrate equally on the "non-performance of contracts," as though refusing to repay a loan was on an equal standing with murder or drunkenness. Perhaps this was simply a reflection of the contours of his own law practice before the Civil War. Lincoln was involved in over five thousand cases over a quarter century, and nearly two-thirds of his law practice concerned commercial matters: breach of contract, debt, mortgage foreclosure, repossession or partition of property. So, Lincoln saw nothing unusual in focusing the actions government should take on the most routine of economic affairs—on "making and maintaining roads, bridges, and the like," facilitating the movement of goods to markets, "and disposing of deceased men's property."[1]

On the other hand, commerce was exactly what Lincoln understood to be the full partner of democracy. Commerce and merchandising were, like democracy itself, no respecters of aristocratic privilege. Dollars were the denomination of reason and logic, and property and freedom were two hands that washed each other. "The proposition that each man should do precisely as he pleases with all which is exclusively his own" is what lay "at the foundation of the sense of justice there is in me."

Lincoln had none of the sense of European socialists, from Wollstonecraft and Proudhon to Saint-Simon and Marx, of a world in which the interests of property and capital were arrayed against those of laborers, and where a sham form of democracy allowed capital to exert an inescapable hegemony over the vast mass of laborers. The liberal celebration of individual rights in democratic politics fostered a corresponding liberal individualism in national economies; hence, the best way to "protect labor" was to "facilitate commerce by cheap and safe exchanges," and especially between the laborers who produced and those who owned the means of production. There was, Lincoln said, "a certain relation between capital and labor," but it was one of harmony, not conflict, and his own career proved it. Labor had precedence over capital because labor was what created capital in the first place. "Capital is only the fruit of labor, and could never have existed if Labor had not first existed," Lincoln said in 1861. "Labor is the superior of capital, and deserves much the higher consideration."

But if Lincoln embraced a "labor theory of value," it was one drawn from John Locke (in chapter 5 of the *Second Treatise on Government*) rather than Karl Marx. "Property is the fruit of labor," but not its contradiction. "Property is desirable—is a positive good in the world." Few things irked him as angrily as the assertion that society was nothing more than a fixed division of "mud-sill" workers whose sole task in life was to create property for others and a landowning elite who appropriated that property to pursue their own leisure. This was not democracy, but oligarchy.[2]

And it irked him because his own life was a refutation of the idea. "Twenty-five years ago, I was a hired laborer," Lincoln reflected in 1859. "The hired laborer of yesterday, labors on his own account to-day; and will hire others to labor for him to-morrow. Advancement—improvement in condition—is the order of things in a society of equals." Rather than declaring "any war upon capital, we…wish to allow the humblest man an equal chance to get rich with everybody else." Against every notion of a static, rooted society of inalterably polarized classes, Lincoln saw economic self-transformation as the great gift of democracy. He had no illusions that this guaranteed equal outcomes for everyone, but he had no illusions, either, about where the fault for unsuccess lay. "If any continue through life in the condition of the hired laborer, it is not the fault of the system," he declared, "but because of either a dependent nature which prefers it, or improvidence, folly, or singular misfortune."

There was even a degree of callousness in Lincoln's dismissal of unsuccess. "Some of you will be successful…others will be disappointed, and will be in a less happy mood. To such, let it be said, 'Lay it not too much to heart.' Let them adopt the maxim, 'Better luck next time;' and then, by renewed exertion, make that better luck for themselves." But for Lincoln, the objection that the absence of economic equality was evidence of no equality at all—that "no one shall have any, for fear all shall not have some"—was simply a "pernicious" idea.[3]

Abraham Lincoln was born in 1809, while Thomas Jefferson was still president and while George III was still king. It was a world lit by candlelight (the kerosene lamp would not be invented until 1855), a world in which travel and information proceeded no faster than horse or sail could carry it. Out of the total American workforce in 1820, 97 percent labored on farms. And given that no technology for preserving farm produce existed (the Mason jar was not invented till 1859), farmers did not buy and sell to producers, processors, or distant consumers; they consumed what they produced or swapped with each other.

Anywhere beyond the reach of American towns, a subsistence economy prevailed rather than a market economy (where people bought and exchanged goods with others at a distance for cash or credit). Crops were grown for home consumption, and anything remaining could be bartered for liquor, tea, or other goods. "There was very little time spent in what deserves the name of business as now understood," remembered an octogenarian survivor of those times in Lincoln's Illinois. "Trade, barter, and exchange of commodities, and swapping work in corn planting and harvest time for work back in corn-husking and hay-making time, were the only commerce known in very early times." No "ledger… recorded balances of money and labor due," only memory, and economic exchange in remote areas might amount to nothing more than non-cash swapping of goods or produce, exchange of work (a day helping with a barn-raising in exchange for a day helping with harvest), and informal indebtedness along kinship and neighbor networks, with little or no interest asked or given. "There were no large places, no manufacturing, but little capital," recalled Henry Clay Whitney, no way to create substantial accumulations of capital, and especially "no men who understood the peculiar and recondite science and art of finance… to use and get money."[4]

But a new liberal economic world was already being born

at the same moment as Lincoln and the new liberal democratic one. Just as the idea of political hierarchy was overthrown by the seventeenth century's scientific revolution, the idea of economic hierarchy soon came tumbling down after it. As Adam Smith declared in *The Wealth of Nations,* the "propensity to truck, barter and exchange one thing for another" was as natural a law of human nature as gravity was of physical nature, and Smith branded restrictive economic laws as akin to laws against witchcraft.[5] Suddenly, a market economy acquired respectability, and with it cash exchange, finance, and inventions. "Commerce," wrote the French Enlightenment *philosophe* Montesquieu, cures "destructive prejudices" and "produces in men a certain feeling for exact justice." Likewise Montesquieu's contemporary, the Scottish historian William Robertson: "Commerce tends to wear off those prejudices which maintain distinction and animosity between nations." And between classes. "The antient families" are "worn out by time and family misfortunes," and their estates now pass into the hands of an enterprising "new race of tradesmen" whose "immense wealth" sprang into their hands "in the shop, the warehouse, and the counting-house."[6]

In no place was commerce better fitted for dominance than in the new American republic, which had no European-sized hierarchies to slough off. The problem was that America also had little in the way of interior market networks, largely because of three obstacles peculiar to the American environment: the sheer physical size and disconnectedness of the American nation, the resistance of an agrarian mentality which treated markets with suspicion and disdain (and whose chief voice belonged to Thomas Jefferson), and slavery. The answer to all three would, in varying degrees, be provided by Abraham Lincoln.

—

Even as Lincoln grew to maturity, the first obstacle to the spread of markets—time and distance—was already being leveraged out of the way by three dramatic technological innovations: the steamboat, the railroad, and the telegraph. Lincoln met the steamboat—and the easy connection to markets it carried—when he was only a boy on a raft, paddling passengers from the Ohio River shore to intercept steamboats on the river. "Two men came down to the shore in carriages with trunks," quickly hired him to row out to the steamboat in midstream, then each flipped him "a silver half dollar." Lincoln was astonished. "I could scarcely credit that I, a poor boy, had earned a dollar in less than a day and that I had earned it by honest work." From that moment, "the world seemed wider and fairer before me."[7] In 1832, after he had moved to New Salem, Illinois, Lincoln helped pilot the steamer *Talisman* up the Sangamon River in a bid to open up central Illinois to the Mississippi River traffic. And in his first bid for elected office in the Illinois legislature that year, he campaigned on building avenues for markets through the "opening of good roads, and...the clearing of navigable streams within their limits."[8]

Lincoln's eagerness to push a liberal economy over the hump of distance contrasted sharply with the attitudes of his family and its agrarian outlook. His father, Thomas, was a simple subsistence farmer with no particular thought for economic advancement, and even less comprehension of his son's ambitions. Thomas Lincoln "was like the other people in that country. None of them worked to get ahead. There wasn't no market for nothing.... The people raised just what they needed."[9] And they did so with the energetic encouragement of Thomas Jefferson, who imagined that real wealth was imbedded in land ownership, and real independence for Americans lay in supporting themselves entirely from that land. "The agriculturalist has his property, his land, his all," complained the ultra-Jeffersonian John Randolph of Roa-noke, "while the commercial speculators live in opulence, whirling in coaches and indulging in palaces." In that light, slavery could be construed by the owners of land as a species of noblesse oblige, a reversion to a kind of feudalism that Romantic intellectuals had begun to celebrate as the antith-esis of rationalized markets.[10]

It was true, Jefferson admitted, that such neo-feudal agrar-ianism might mean that America would never develop great merchant cities or manufacturing centers. But that might be for the best, warned Jefferson. "The mobs of great cities add just so much to the support of pure government, as sores do to the strength of the human body," whereas "those who labour in the earth are the chosen people of God, if ever he had a chosen people." Nothing in that attitude had changed by 1829, when a New England agricultural newspaper warned farmers that "the market is a canker that will, by degrees, eat you out, while you are eating upon it."[11]

Thomas Lincoln's son, however, was of a different mind. The next year, as soon as he turned twenty-one and could legally keep what he earned, Abraham Lincoln left his father's farm in central Illinois and never looked back. Setting up in New Salem, he hired himself out as a farmworker, ferryman, clerk, and flatboater, twice went into business—and twice failed—and then became a lawyer and one of the oilers of the machinery of debt, commerce, and property. His name appears in court records for the first time in 1830, drawing up documents (probably from a form book) for debt, prop-erty transfer, bonds, and wills—and all before he was actu-ally licensed by the Illinois state supreme court to practice law in 1836. By the time he appeared for the last time in a courtroom—in June 1860—the Illinois Central Railroad was his second-biggest client, and he had litigated hundreds of bridge, tax, real estate, and mechanical-reaper cases in state and federal courts.[12]

It was not in the courtroom, however, but in the Illinois state legislature, where he served four terms between 1834 and 1842, that Lincoln's interest in commercial development found its largest outlet. "Trade and exchange," he wrote for a legislative committee in 1840, are, as they were for Adam Smith, part of an "irresistible law." In his first campaign for the state legislature in 1832, Lincoln took for granted that no Illinois farmer wanted merely to idle away his advantages of "its fertile soil," but would want some pathway to market-places where his produce could be sold for cash or for store credit and could become capital. We need, Lincoln claimed, "some more easy means of communication than we now possess, for the purpose of facilitating the task of exporting the surplus products... and importing necessary articles from abroad." That, he proposed, would come by the application of "art" to the shallow waterways of central Illinois—meaning canals—and he boasted to his friend Joshua Speed that he hoped the public promotion of canal projects modeled on DeWitt Clinton's great Erie Canal would make him "the De Witt Clinton of Ills."

Once elected to the legislature in 1834, Lincoln became an eager proponent of "internal improvements" to "enable our state, in common with others, to dig canals and construct rail roads," and a state banking system which would bring the state and commerce into partnership by doubling "the prices of the products of" Illinois farmers and issuing a reliable paper currency that would fill "their pockets with a sound circulating medium." Commerce, as much as law, was the enemy of passion. "Commerce brings us together, and makes us better friends," Lincoln insisted. "We like one another the more for it."[13]

When Lincoln finally wangled a seat in Congress in 1847, his first moves were to advocate the construction of a railroad "from Alton to Springfield" as part of "a great chain of rail road communication," then to speak "briefly and happily" at the Northwestern River and Harbor Convention in Chicago on "internal improvements," and finally to draft an elaborate defense of tariffs for American manufacturing. "The question of internal improvements is now more distinctly made—has become more intense—than at any former period," Lincoln declared. No one would question funding the navy to clear pirates from the sea-lanes, but that was no different "in principle" from funding river clearance and canal construction, since both smoothed the path for trade. Nor was there any reason to worry about whether expenditures for commercial uplift were strictly constitutional. No one "who is satisfied of the expediency of making improvements, needs be much uneasy in his conscience about its constitutionality."

He was already using yet another commercial innovation, the electrical telegraph, in the summer of 1849 (just five years after Samuel F. B. Morse had tapped out the first message between Washington and Baltimore), and his boost to national notice in the Lincoln-Douglas Debates of 1858 was largely the result of the telegraph's ability to wire complete transcripts of each debate to East Coast newspapers within forty-eight hours.[14]

Lincoln's interest in commerce and infrastructure provided yet another point of intersection with his political model, Henry Clay. Although Clay had once been a fiery Jeffersonian Democrat in the House of Representatives, the War of 1812 taught him painful lessons about an economy built entirely on subsistence farmers. The agrarian economy, remembered John Pendleton Kennedy, "found us without the most ordinary resources of an independent people." There were no factories to manufacture uniforms, no suppliers of the "munitions of war" except "as chance supplied them from the four quarters of the earth." Overconfident Democrats like Kennedy and Clay awoke to the virtue of "extending more efficient protection...to those manufactures which were essential to the defence of the nation" and the creation of "a national currency." For Clay that meant three things: tariffs, a national bank, and a government-funded system of "internal improvements."[15]

To orthodox Jeffersonians and unpersuaded Democrats, this was political heresy. Thirty years before, at the beginning of the republic, Alexander Hamilton had persuaded George Washington and Congress to green-light a national Bank of the United States, along with tariffs and support for manufacturing. But the election of Thomas Jefferson in 1800 spelled doom to Hamilton's plans. Although Jefferson was frustrated at his inability to rip up everything Hamiltonian by the roots, Jefferson did enough damage to leave the United States utterly unprepared for the crisis of 1812: its navy was too feeble to do more than poke an occasional hole in a British naval blockade of the North American coast; its army was minuscule in size, and was expected to rely too much on untrained and poorly armed state militia. Even the national capital at Washington could not defend itself from British attack and occupation. The narrow margin by which the United States survived the War of 1812 convinced Clay that the republic needed a "great work...of internal improvement"—a "chain of turnpikes, roads and canals from Passamaquoddy to New Orleans," and tariffs to "effectually protect our manufacturers"—which in time of war would allow its army to move troops rapidly to counter invasion, and equip its industries to produce the munitions the army and navy needed.

Clay succeeded in reviving Hamilton's banking plan with a Second Bank of the United States, and in squeezing funding for infrastructure and new tariffs from Congress. Unrepentant agrarian Democrats, led by the solitary military hero of the War of 1812, Andrew Jackson, blocked Clay's path at every turn, and once Jackson was elected president in 1828, the stage was set for a sensational showdown in which Jackson vetoed the rechartering of the Second Bank of the United States, and Clay, now the "stanch friend of American Industry," walked away from the Democratic Party. Unchastened, he proceeded to organize a new party, the Whigs, and he laid down his platform for tariffs, national banking, and commercial infrastructure as the foundation for an "American System."[16]

Despite three attempts, Clay would never succeed in winning the presidency, but he gathered round him an eager following of disinherited Democrats who became the party of small-scale urban business and finance, allied with commercial farmers who were part of trade networks across states and regions that would prosper behind the shield of national tariffs. They believed that "the effect of the Tariff" would "raise wages," ensure a more productive economy, "lessen the prices of articles," and outsell unprotected, low-wage labor. Their banner was the independent free laborer, their economic pumping station was a national bank, and their ideal metropolis was Lowell, Massachusetts, "a manufacturing town" of "eleven great corporations with a united capital of more than Twelve millions of dollars" and "8,500 operatives."[17]

This opened the Whigs to the Democratic accusation that they were really just a party for the rich, the mill owners, the financiers. But the Whigs replied that all that such accusations really meant was that they were the party of true democratic self-transformation. "Who are the rich men of our country?"

asked the *New York American* in 1834. "They are the enterprising mechanic, who raises himself by his ingenious labors from the dust and turmoil of his workshop, to an abode of ease and elegance; the industrious tradesman, whose patient frugality enables him at last to accumulate enough to forego the duties of the counter and indulge a well-earned leisure." It also made the Whigs the party of national union, rather than state or region, since only a strong economic union could guarantee open access to markets. *"Protection,"* declared the National Home Industry Convention in 1842, *"was but another name for Independence."*[18]

Clay's Whigs could not have been better designed to appeal to the ambitions of Abraham Lincoln, and he would remain "an old line Whig" and "an old Henry Clay Whig" until the Whig party foundered in 1856, and then joined other Northern Whigs in the new Republican Party. On the other hand, embracing Clay's "System" positioned him as a member of the minority party in Illinois politics, and for much of his career as a Whig, Lincoln was a militantly partisan politician who organized Whig opposition to Illinois Democrats, wrote heated anti-Democratic political journalism, and in one embarrassing instance, almost fought a duel with a Democratic rival.

There was, however, more to Lincoln's Whiggish opposition to "the Democracy" than the stinking weed of party spirit. The hidden hand in Democratic and agrarian resistance to commerce and markets was slavery. Slavery depended on the stability that resulted from an immobilized and unconsenting workforce, and the principal product of that workforce was agricultural—the cotton grown by the Southern states of the Union. Capital formation scarcely existed as a goal; every ounce of profit was turned into more land and more slaves to satisfy the demand of the Liverpool cotton markets, and by the eve of the Civil War, the state of New York alone had more banking capital on its books than all the slave states that would make up the Southern Confederacy.

Since the Jeffersonian origins of the Democratic Party made "the Democracy" a natural home for agriculturalists, slave-owners flexed their political muscle largely through the Democratic Party. They joined hands with Northern Democrats who, in the Northeast, drew on marginalized urban "mechanics," immigrants, and artisans and in the West on farmers who were themselves migrants from the South and shared Southern agrarian racial antipathies. Opposed to the thousand-bale planters, there was always a vigorous Whig minority in the South until the 1850s, much of it rooted in the South's minuscule urban professional class. But otherwise, the planters easily bought off the South's large pool of lack-penny white farmers with visions of owning slaves themselves and reminders that they enjoyed a white racial identity with the plantation overlords—even if they enjoyed nothing more than that—and this unpleasant alliance formed the core of the Democrats' national political strength.

This was a world Lincoln loathed. From his earliest speeches in the Illinois legislature, Lincoln attacked slavery as "founded on both injustice and bad policy." It was "a great moral, social, and political evil" and "a foul blot on the Nation" which the founders of the republic had believed "would at some future day be removed." By the 1850s, he would declare that he hated slavery "because of the monstrous injustice of slavery itself. I hate it because it deprives our republican example of its just influence in the world." And he hated to see fugitives from slavery "hunted down, and caught, and carried back to their stripes, and unrewarded toils."[19]

Lincoln particularly resented the boast of the slaveholders and their apologists that slave labor was actually milder and more merciful to the slaves than "wage slavery" was to hired laborers like himself in the free states of the North. The Northern economy was already outstripping Southern agriculture in terms of production, net wealth, railroads, schools, and marketplaces. But the South's defenders looked away; worse than that, they convinced themselves that they, and not the free North, were the tide of the future. The Virginian George Fitzhugh insisted that "the unrestricted exploitation of so-called free society is more oppressive to the laborer than domestic slavery." After all, "the subsistence of a slave is safe; he cannot suffer from insufficient wages, or from want of employment; he has not to save for sickness or old age; he has not to provide for his family." This, Fitzhugh cheerfully admitted, was utterly at odds with free-labor capitalism. To the contrary, "a Southern farm is the beau ideal of Communism." In fact, it was "the only practicable form of socialism." Socialists were simply "afraid yet to pronounce the word."[20]

To this, Lincoln snorted angrily "that although volume upon volume is written to prove slavery a very good thing, we never hear of the man who wishes to take the good of it, by being a slave himself." Nor did they have any proof that Southern slave agriculture was prospering. Slavery apologists like Fitzhugh may "declare that their slaves are better off than hired laborers amongst us," but "how little they *know*..." Lincoln did. He "himself had been a hired man," and "he didn't think he was worse off than a slave." Those who started out working for wages and were "industrious and sober, and honest in the pursuit of their own interests" would in time "accumulate capital" and use that capital to "hire other people to labor for them." Free labor promised mobility, movement, aspiration; it was the entire opposite of a system in which one person literally owned the life and labor of another— *literally*, not just metaphorically. "The hired laborer with his ability to become an employer, must have every precedence over him who labors under the inducement of force," Lincoln said. And why? because "free labor has the inspiration of hope," while "pure slavery has no hope."[21]

The hope of labor translated for Lincoln, and for Whigs generally, into a redemptive pursuit. They loved "the *old Puritan character,*" not for its "theological doctrines," but for its strenuous commitment to work as a good in itself, "yielding nothing to luxury and nothing to idleness." Work, thought Horace Greeley, "may be rendered as attractive as play now is," and even become "a source of daily joy."[22] Lincoln liked to joke that "his father taught him to work but never learned him to love it." But what he meant by his father's work was agricultural labor—"farming—grubbing—hoeing—making fences." When it came to legal and political work, Lincoln's appetite seemed to have no terminus. To an aspiring lawyer he wrote, "Work, work, work, is the main thing." He criticized his stepbrother, John Johnston, not only because "you...very much dislike to work," but because of Johnston's habit of "uselessly wasting time" and especially for his indifference to earning cash. "You are now in need of some ready money," Lincoln advised him, "and what I propose is, that you shall go to work, 'tooth and nails' for some body who will give you money [for] it." When Johnston failed to heed his stepbrother's injunction, Lincoln became more blunt: "Go to work is the only cure for your case." Lincoln's son, Robert, recollected his father's "methods of office working were simply those of a very busy man who worked at all hours." Edward Neill, who was hired to work in the Lincoln White House, remembered that "the president's capacity for work was wonderful....Each hour he was busy." Lincoln had no sooner returned from Philadelphia in 1864 than "as soon as he had entered the house he went immediately to his office," where Neill found "a mulatto barber lathering his face" for a shave while talking to Edward Bates, his attorney general, "upon some matter of state."[23]

In Lincoln's world, there need be no slaves and no masters except the self-driven and the self-mastered. To see such a world prevail became the cause of his life.

Chapter Four

Political Economy
and the Nation

No independent science called *economics* existed in Lincoln's day. What we would call economics was understood in Lincoln's time as *political economy*. And for someone who believed that liberal economics and liberal politics proceeded hand in hand, Lincoln's natural intellectual curiosity fed on political economy more than on any other subject. "Lincoln I think liked political Economy—the study of it," recalled Lincoln's law partner, William Henry Herndon, a recollection echoed by Shelby Cullom, who served with Lincoln in the Illinois legislature and then in Congress. "Theoretically, Mr. Lincoln was strong on financial questions," Cullom remembered. "On political economy he was great." As Herndon remembered in 1886, the backbone of Lincoln's reading in the 1840s and 1850s was the basic texts of nineteenth-century liberal political economy: "[John Stuart] Mill's political economy, [Henry] Carey's political economy...[John Ramsay] McCullough's [McCulloch's] political economy, [Francis] Wayland, and some others." Nothing of the standard-issue works of liberalism's socialist critics: Proudhon, Saint-Simon, or Charles Fourier, much less Marx.[1]

This kind of reading surprised people whose first impression of Lincoln was a hollow-cheeked, drawly, "second-rate Illinois lawyer" and "genuine Sucker" who pronounced "heard" as *heerd* and scattered his conversation with provincialisms in a "homely way." His White House secretary, John Hay, was unprepared to discover that Lincoln "has a little-indulged inclination" for "philology." When the British barrister George Borrett showed up at the door of Lincoln's summer presidential retreat north of Washington in 1864, he was taken aback at how Lincoln "launched off into some shrewd remarks" on the comparative legal systems of Britain and the United States, and then spun into "English poetry" and Alexander Pope's *Essay on Man,* which Lincoln thought "contained all the religious instruction which it was necessary for a man to know."[2]

"I am slow to learn," Lincoln self-deprecatingly told his longtime friend Joshua Speed, but he then added more accurately that he was also "slow to forget that which I have learned. My mind is like a piece of steel, very hard to scratch any thing on it and almost impossible after you get it there to rub it out." And what he retained included an extraordinary amount of intellectual territory. Speed remembered in 1866 that Lincoln's reading sprawled across the English literary and philosophical terrain: "law History, [Thomas] Browns Philosophy or [William] Paley—Burns Byron Milton or Shakespeare."

His command of the Bible was like a ready-reference concordance. When he quoted a verse from Proverbs—*Accuse not a servant unto his master, lest he curse thee, and thou be found guilty*—to deflate a critic of Secretary of War Edwin Stanton, the man guffawed that there was no such verse. But Lincoln "soon reappeared with his Bible in his hand" and there it was: Proverbs, chapter 30, in the King James Version, verse 10. In June 1864, when four hundred dissident Republicans met in

Cleveland to nominate John Frémont for the presidency, Lincoln flipped through a Bible again and "read aloud...this verse": *And every one that was in distress, and every one that was in debt, and every one that was discontented, gathered themselves unto him; and he became a captain over them: and there were with him about four hundred men* (1 Samuel 22:2). Anyone, said Lincoln's fellow lawyer Leonard Swett, "who took Lincoln for a simple-minded man would very soon wake [up] with his back in a ditch."[3]

If Lincoln's grasp of what he read was tight, it was also narrow. "Shakespeare, of course, he always had by him," Robert Todd Lincoln remembered of his father. But that was far from uncommon among educated Americans in the nineteenth century, and even that was limited for Lincoln to the history plays and the tragedies. "Some of Shakspeare's plays I have never read; while others I have gone over perhaps as frequently as any unprofessional reader," Lincoln told the Shakespearian James Hackett in 1863. "Among the latter are Lear, Richard Third, Henry Eighth, Hamlet, and especially Macbeth." He read many of the minor nineteenth-century American poets—Fitz-Greene Halleck, Eliza Cook, Nathaniel Parker Willis—but scanted Longfellow, and there is only the vaguest suggestion from John Hay that Lincoln "read Bryant and Whittier with appreciation." Lincoln's religious skepticism attracted him to "Paine and Voltaire" and eventually to Robert Chambers's proto-Darwinian *Vestiges of the Natural History of Creation* (1844), but there are no traces that he read religious books with any seriousness, apart from James Smith's *The Christian's Defense* (1843) and even then only because Smith was close to the Lincoln family in Springfield. Lincoln did not read in the manner of a scholar or a student, but rather as a curious sympathizer with the milieu these works created, as a man who (as Herndon observed) "lived in the mind and...thought in his life and lived in his thought."[4]

The clearest and most unambiguous influence in Lincoln's reading came from that galaxy of authors Herndon identified on liberal political economy—Mill, McCulloch, Wayland, Carey. There are no direct references in Lincoln's speeches or writing to the ur-text of liberal economics, Adam Smith's *The Wealth of Nations* (1776). But when Lincoln spoke of labor as "the source from which human wants are mainly supplied," and therefore "prior to, and independent of, capital" and deserving of "much the higher consideration," he was certainly channeling not only Locke but Smith, who wrote at the very opening of *The Wealth of Nations* that "the annual labor of every nation is the fund which originally supplies it with all the necessaries and conveniences of life which it annually consumes." And like Lincoln, Smith lauded banks and the "circulating notes of banks and bankers" as "the great wheel of circulation and distribution." In 1847, Lincoln presented an analysis of the costs of transportation—"It appears to me, then, that all labor done directly and incidentally in carrying articles to their place of consumption, which could have been produced in sufficient abundance, with as little labour, at the place of consumption, as at the place they were carried from, is useless labour"—which directly parallels Smith's argument in favor of domestic manufacturing and against "the expence of land-carriage" which "increases very much both the real and nominal price of most manufactures." And it is difficult not to hear Smith in Lincoln's description of the "legitimate object of government," since Smith, like Lincoln, argued that government had "only three duties":

> *first, the duty of protecting the society from the violence and invasion of other independent societies; secondly, the duty of protecting, as far as possible, every member of the society from the injustice or oppression of every other member of it . . . and, thirdly, the duty of erecting and maintaining certain public*

works and certain public institutions, which it can never be for the interest of any individual, or small number of individuals, to erect and maintain; because the profit could never repay the expence to any individual, or small number of individuals, though it may frequently do much more than repay it to a great society.[5]

Much more than Smith, it was John Stuart Mill, the most famous voice of liberal democracy and liberal economics in America and England before the Civil War, whose hand reaches into Lincoln's thinking. It was Mill whom Lincoln singled out to the journalist Noah Brooks as one of the two most influential authors he had read, and it was Mill who contributed the passage that Lincoln cribbed for his own purposes in his notes for a series of speeches he gave in the fall of 1859 in Ohio, Indiana, and Wisconsin. "The hired laborer of yesterday, labors on his own account to-day; and will hire others to labor for him to-morrow," Lincoln announced. "Advancement—improvement in condition—is the order of things in a society of equals." This is plainly a borrowing from the 1848 American edition of Mill's *Principles of Political Economy:* "To begin as hired laborers, then after a few years to work on their own account, and finally employ others, is the normal condition of laborers in a new country, rapidly increasing in wealth and population, like America or Australia."[6]

Mill offered encouragement to Lincoln on several other points, too. Like Lincoln, Mill was "in favour of restricting to the narrowest compass the intervention of a public authority in the business of a community." But also like Lincoln, he was no libertarian: if government should do nothing "so long as a person practices no violence or deception, to the injury of others in person or property," why stop there? Why not require people "to protect themselves by their skill and courage even against force," or command someone to resist fraud by "the protection of his own wits" alone? Similarly, Lincoln's aversion to slavery was energetically paralleled in Mill, who denounced "property in human beings" as having no place whatsoever "in any society even pretending to be founded on justice, or on fellowship between human creatures"— although he certainly would have also fed Lincoln's caution in approaching the abolition of slavery by recognizing that "the state has expressly legalized it...for generations," and therefore should, at the moment of abolishing slavery, "make full compensation" to slave owners.[7]

But Lincoln's most immediate intellectual reliance was on the American Whig political economists, and especially Henry Carey. For Carey, as for Lincoln, the fundamental rule of economics was improvement, whether in the form of canals or social mobility. "The predominant desire of man... *to maintain and to improve his condition*" according to "the laws of nature." After all, Carey reasoned, "where there is nothing but agriculture, men must be idle for very much of their time," and when they are idle "they remain poor and weak, and they can have neither towns, nor roads, nor schools." But manufacturing can remedy this only when liberal democracy and liberal economics link arms and the "men of this country...advocate efficient protection" for "thought, speech, action, and trade"—things the slave South had not the slightest interest in promoting beyond cotton.[8]

Lincoln carried his Whiggish understanding of liberal political economy into the White House with his election as the first Republican president. Because Lincoln's most obvious problem was with slavery and the war triggered by the secession of the Southern states who sought to protect it, it has been easy to lose sight of the aggressive domestic agenda he and his fellow Republicans put into place. But aggressive it was: the Republican national platform called for tariffs that would frankly "encourage the development of the industrial interests" and permit the flourishing of American markets, and Lincoln had scarcely been inaugurated before Henry Carey met with him to remind him that if Clay's tariff policies had been enacted, "there could have been no secession," because "the southern mineral region would long since have obtained control of the planting one."

A new tariff bill, designed by Vermont Republican senator Justin Smith Morrill, fixed import duties, eventually averaging over 46 percent, on over 1,500 products. In 1862, Morrill introduced a second tariff bill to protect "American labor, American skill, and American soil," followed by yet a third tariff bill in 1864. All these, Lincoln signed without a demurrer. "In the days of Henry Clay I was a Henry Clay-tariff man," he wrote, "and my views have undergone no material change upon that subject." New York City, which lived and thrived by imports, responded by hanging Lincoln in effigy from a ship's masthead, and New York newspapers huffily predicted that "the Morrill Tariff will compel Northern merchants to do their importing" through the new Southern Confederacy "at Charleston, Savannah, and other Southern cities." Lincoln was unmoved. "A tariff is to the government what meat is to the family," he replied. "If there be any article of necessity which can be produced at home, with as little or nearly the same labor as abroad, it would be better to protect that article."[9]

Nothing had changed, either, in his views about banks. The dead hand of Andrew Jackson still had enough weight to make impossible any proposal to re-create a Hamilton-style Bank of the United States. But in 1861, Lincoln's treasury secretary, Salmon P. Chase (a onetime Democrat and a very reluctant convert to banking), unveiled a proposal to control the "circulation" of paper money "which enters so largely into the transactions of commerce" through a "system of notes prepared for circulation under national direction." The federal government would not create a bank, but it would do what private and state banks had been doing for decades by issuing a federal currency which existing banks would deal in, and thus "relieve the national from the competition of local circulation." The advantages would seem obvious: American commerce would get a "circulation of notes bearing a common impression and authenticated by a common authority," and the American people would be bound more tightly to a national loyalty by "the common interest" a common currency would promote "in its preservation."

This generated "a good deal of antagonism" from "some of the more prominent representatives" of the existing "bank system." But in February 1863, the Republican Congress adopted a National Banking Act which would bring the North's 1,400 banks (and the plethora of private paper money they issued) into a single system, replacing the private money issues (which Chase warned might actually be "prohibited by the national Constitution") with federally printed currency, and in turn, capitalize the banks with federal deposits. Lincoln was "cautious... about saying or doing anything which can be construed as Executive interference" with Congress, but he did not hesitate to commission members of his administration to lobby congressmen with the threat that a *no* vote would be published as a vote "cutting off pay and supplies to the army in the field." In the end, Lincoln not only signed the bill, but issued a special statement to support its passage, asking "the special attention of Congress" to the creation of "banking associations, organized under a general act of Congress."[10]

Even farming would be transformed. The first Republican Congress to assemble after Lincoln's election had hardly been gaveled to order before Lincoln's strongest political ally in the House, Owen Lovejoy, introduced a Homestead Act that opened vast stretches of government-owned public lands in the West to any claimant willing, for little more than a filing fee, to occupy and improve up to 160 acres of land. For twenty years, various bills had emerged in Congress for opening the public lands to homesteading. They had been just as routinely stopped cold by Southern Democrats, who feared that opening the public lands to homesteading would lead only to an influx of free settlers, and exclude slavery from the West. As the garrulous pro-slavery senator Louis Wigfall had once remarked, while a homestead bill would indeed provide "land for the landless, homes for the homeless," it would not offer slaves for the slaveless. But in 1862, Wigfall and his allies were gone, and the dream of free homesteads offered the ultimate fulfillment of Lincoln's vision of the hired laborer turning into his own self-employer, and the employer of others. Lincoln described the public lands as "our abundant room—our broad national homestead" and the nation's "ample resource," and he signed the Homestead Act into law on May 20, 1862. In less than twenty years, nearly half a million homestead claims had been filed, embracing over 55 million acres, representing the greatest privatization of government-owned property in American history.[11]

The apex of Lincoln's economic agenda was the railroads. In November 1861, Henry Carey described to Lincoln a system of railroads that would unite the interior of the continent "with the cities of the Atlantic coast." Railroads would encourage commerce, and commerce would unite the hill country of "Kentucky and West Virginia" to the Union and cause slaves to "become few in number." Following Carey's lead, Lincoln urged Congress to fund new railroad construction in North Carolina, Kentucky, and Tennessee as "a valuable permanent improvement" that would create a new north–south economic connection. Then, in 1862, Lincoln and Congress plunged into the grandest "internal improvements" project of them all, an east–west transcontinental railroad that would link the flood of homesteaders to markets and suppliers across the continent.[12]

"It is obvious," lamented Iowa Republican Samuel Curtis, "that no private enterprise will take hold of a work of such magnitude, without some demonstration on the part of Government to lend aid and assistance to the project." But that enablement was precisely what Lincoln had always associated with "internal improvements," and legislation was introduced to support the construction of the great east–west railroad with grants to the Union Pacific and Central Pacific Railroads from the public lands and installments of U.S. bonds ranging from $16,000 to $48,000 per mile. Lincoln signed the railroad legislation on July 1, 1862—and then proceeded to set a uniform gauge (of five feet), to recommend civil engineers whom he had known to the builders, and to designate Omaha and Sacramento as the jumping-off points for construction. Had he lived to see the completion of the railroad at Promontory Point, Utah, on May 10, 1869, it might have been Abraham Lincoln rather than Leland Stanford, the president of the Central Pacific, who drove the ceremonial golden spike that linked the continent.[13]

Lincoln's assassination in April 1865 cut short his life, but not the trajectory of his economic reconstruction of the Union. Even had there been no civil war, it is safe to say that Lincoln's administration would still be regarded as a hinge presidency in American history, if only for the way his economic policies inaugurated a new political generation that glorified free labor, protective tariffs, and federal encouragement for infrastructure while pushing back against the Jeffersonian glorification of agriculture and its animus against commerce.

Yet, Lincoln was uneasy about too great a resort to loosely backed paper money. He feared that "continued issues of United States notes," without sufficient insurance from loans or gold, "must soon produce disastrous consequences." And he was not entirely free from the anxiety that "finances"— and not commerce—"will rule the country for the next fifty years." Lincoln's image of a market economy was a system of small producers where the transition from hired laborer to employer seemed to have few obstacles. It was an economy that (for instance) in western Massachusetts rested on woolen factories that employed all of eighteen "hands" or a chair factory that produced "8,000 chairs a year" or a town with "a meetinghouse, academy, the Housatonic bank, a tavern, post-office, 4 merchant stores, various mechanic shops, and 45 houses, inhabited by 55 families." Protecting that small-producer economy made him suspicious "alike… of crowned-kings, money-kings, and land-kings." When he suspected Wall Street financiers of betting against Northern victory, he wished "every one of them had his devilish head shot off!"[14]

Lincoln's reservations did not keep him from being denounced, then and now, as the architect of a new, more expanded and intrusive federal government, or at least as the prophet of a "highly centralized (i.e., monopolistic) form of government that can better expand the welfare state, regulate the economy, or adopt socialism." This new denial of Lincoln blends the old Jeffersonian agrarianism (casting Lincoln as the new Hamilton) with the contentions of the postwar Lost Cause (who insisted that Lincoln's invasion of state rights must necessarily introduce an infinitely magnified federal government) and with a voluble and streamlined libertarianism, which identified Lincoln as the Trojan horse who made possible the New Deal in the twentieth century. After all, complained the libertarian economist Murray Rothbard, the driving lever of the New Deal and its massive expansion of government was a "strong central government, large-scale public works, and cheap credit spurred by government." Wasn't Lincoln's administration also built on "high tariffs, huge subsidies to railroads, public works"? Wasn't the war on the Southern Confederacy an excuse for blowing up the balloon of an over-mighty national establishment while crushing the air out of genuine federalism? Thus, Lincoln becomes a clone, not of Mill or Henry Carey, but of Otto von Bismarck, the ruthless manufacturer of a modern bureaucratic *Wohlfahrtsstaat* (welfare state). "Lincoln," concludes libertarian writer David Gordon, "like his Prussian contemporary Otto von Bismarck ... sought a powerful, centralizing state."[15]

But looked at carefully, even at the apex of the Civil War, the government that Lincoln presided over was surprisingly small in scope. Factor for inflation over time, and the 1865 federal budget would translate into only $26 billion and would account for only 1.8 percent of real GDP, while federal civilian employment would represent only 0.08 percent of the Northern wartime population. The entire federal bureaucracy under Lincoln was composed of just 22 agencies (compared to over 500 today), and Lincoln's White House staff consisted of just six persons. The entire State Department was staffed by thirty-three people in 1863, including the secretary of state, William Seward, and the department's four security guards; Attorney General Edward Bates managed the legal affairs of the Lincoln administration with exactly nine employees. Moreover, as Mark Neely writes, whatever expansion the federal government saw during Lincoln's presidency quickly evaporated once the Civil War was over. "The minimal enhancement of executive power in the Civil War had no lasting effect," Neely argues, and, in fact, Lincoln's wartime administration was followed in the Reconstruction years by an era in which "the powers of the legislative branch were as great as they had ever been."[16]

The other powers Lincoln ascribed to government were vastly overshadowed in his mind by government's obligation to promote economic enablement. Everything government should do, in Lincoln's mind, was geared toward an economy of democracy for upwardly aspiring free laborers, rather than regulation of their lives. He was, as Ralph Waldo Emerson eulogized him on April 27, 1865, "a middle-class president" for a "middle-class country . . . This man wrought incessantly, with all his might and all his honesty, laboring to find what the people wanted, and how to obtain that." That enablement was what ran through every piece of his administration's legislation, and even through the Emancipation Proclamation, where he urged freed slaves to "labor faithfully for reasonable wages." One of his favorite examples of this enablement was the governmental monopoly of the granting of patents, which Lincoln elevated to a plane equal to the invention of "the arts of writing and of printing" and "the discovery of America." Absent patent laws, "any man might instantly use what another had invented." But with the protection government threw around new inventions through patents, "the inventor" enjoyed "for a limited time, the exclusive use of his invention . . . in the discovery and production of new and useful things." (Not surprisingly, Lincoln took out a patent himself in 1849, for a flotation device to enable steamboats like the *Talisman* to free themselves from shoals in the inland rivers.)[17]

This is an understanding of economics and democracy—of political economy—which it is easy now to dismiss as antique. In Lincoln's lifetime, only in Rhode Island did workers in American factories amount to more than 20 percent of the population (although Massachusetts was a close second at 19 percent); in the West, the numbers rarely topped one percent. Even then, fully half of American manufacturing in the 1860s was still powered by water rather than steam, and the number of workers one could expect to meet in any given mill or factory hovered between eight and fourteen.

By the beginning of the twentieth century, Lincoln's free-labor economy increasingly began to feel dated against the background of rapid, large-scale industrialization and what Herbert Croly in 1909 called "the aggrandizement of corporate and individual wealth" and the need for "the regulation of commerce, the organization of labor, and the increasing control over property in the public interest." Helen Nicolay, the daughter of Lincoln's head of staff, believed in 1913 that Lincoln's "heart and mind were ... essentially of the old era," and by the 1920s, frustrated biographers of Lincoln began criticizing him as "strongly conservative and in firm support of vested interests and the conduct of business, unmolested as far as possible, by legislative or any kind of governmental interference," certainly "no knight errant" as a lawyer, and interested in the anti-slavery cause only as a vehicle for his own advancement. In his 1948 essay, "Abraham Lincoln and the Self-Made Myth," the great Columbia University historian Richard Hofstadter scorned Lincoln as "thoroughly middle-class in his ideas ... intensely and at times inhumanly individualistic." Lincoln's vision of self-transformation has become (as one recent *New York Times* letter writer complained) a "false foundation" and "only a myth."[18]

But it is also possible to exaggerate the scale of economic change as the United States entered the twentieth century, and with it the possibilities in Lincoln's liberal economics. Even as Americans move through the first quarter of the twenty-first century, three-fourths of the nation's towns are homes to fewer than 5,000 people; nearly half of those towns number fewer than five hundred. There remain over 30 million small businesses in America, as opposed to just 18,500 large ones (*large*, in this case, meaning 500 or more employees), and of those 30 million, an astonishing 73 percent are sole proprietorships. In 2021, Americans filed applications to begin 5.4 million new businesses, and followed that a year later with another 5 million. After a century and a half, Americans still look overwhelmingly like the free laborers Lincoln described, who "saved means to buy land of his own, a shop of his own, and to increase his property." This, Abraham Lincoln believed, "was the true, genuine principle of free labor," of neither slaves nor master, "and so it may go on and on in one ceaseless round so long as man exists on the face of the earth!"[19]

Chapter Five

Democratic Culture

L aw is the formal expression of the will of the people; it is, so to speak, democracy out of session, and its restraints are what prevent a democracy from careening into self-willed anarchy.

Underlying the laws are currents of something more volatile and less easily glimpsed: Alexis de Tocqueville's *mores,* the cultural assumptions that help to predispose a people to democracy in the first place. Long ago, Socrates warned that constitutions are not hewn from rock, but from "the characters of the people who live in the cities governed by them," and those "characters" were shaped by the implicit concepts Tocqueville called *mores.* Laws may "do more to maintain a democratic republic in the United States than physical causes do," but "*mores* do more than laws."[1] You can have a democracy without the underpinnings of culture, but you will probably not have it for very long, and even while you have it, it will be disappointing in its results.

Nothing illustrated more vividly how disconnected formal law could become from cultural realities than the slave South. Madison feared that slavery would be the cultural snake in the American republic, since the classical republics whose vices he studied demonstrated all too well that "in proportion as slavery prevails in a State, the Government, however democratic in name, must be aristocratic in fact." He was right. Slavery carried with it its own cultural code, which was not friendly to the aspirations of democracy. The South, complained Albion Tourgée, "was a republic in name, but an oligarchy in fact," where, as James Blaine acidly commented, "the slave-holders ruled their states more positively than ever the aristocratic classes ruled England." In the South, wrote Frederick Douglass, "Slavery is so strong that it could exist, not only without law, but even against law. Custom, manners, morals, religion, are all on its side everywhere in the South."[2]

Lincoln heard the advancing echoes of slavery's *mores* from a United States senator—and one from a Northern state, no less—who announced that Jefferson's declaration of the natural equality of all humanity was "a self-evident lie." And he was afraid he would hear it soon enough from Americans who allowed culture, prejudice, and greed to so "familiarize" them with "the chains of bondage" that they would be ready to offer their "own limbs to wear them...and become the fit subjects of the first cunning tyrant who rises."[3]

If the *mores* of slavery represented a threat to democracy, it would be useful to know just what *mores* encouraged and supported democracy. Four of these had particular force for Lincoln: property ownership, religious morality, toleration, and electioneering.

John Locke, as the first great theorist of liberal democracy, understood the preservation of property—of what someone had earned by their labor—to be the primary reason people bothered to create governments in the first place. In the largest sense, widespread ownership of property was the physical embodiment of the Constitution's prohibition of "titles of nobility," since the vast majority of Americans were freeholders, not tenants of aristocratic landlords. (By the 1760s, between three-quarters and four-fifths of settlers from Massachusetts to Virginia owned their own land.) Property provided the basis on which one gave consent *and* the reason for consenting at all. "We look with entire complacency on large accumulations of property by individuals," declared the *North American Review* in 1853. These "accumulations" did not always (or even mostly) extend to women, and they never extended to slaves in any legal sense. But at least in theory, "accumulations" were the goal of everyone.[4]

The second cultural underpinning of democracy was religion, since nothing struck observers of the American scene more forcibly than the pervasiveness of Protestant Christianity throughout American life. The most famous Americans of the republic's first political generation—Franklin, Washington, Jefferson, Madison—might have sat lightly by religion as "the imposture of priestcraft." But by the time Tocqueville undertook his famous tour of America, he found that "there is no country in the whole world in which the Christian religion retains a greater influence over the souls of men than in America." There might be no official church establishment in America (or, after 1833, in any of the states); there might even be an "entire separation between civil power and religious" and "perfect freedom in religious faith and worship," and a vast dispersal of religious organizations among a dozen major denominations. But one European visitor during the Civil War was surprised to find that "these great churches recognise each other as members of the same body and respect and honour each other...having between them no other tie than that of Christian love." It was religion which structured the life of its families and set down a severe rule of personal and public virtue. Even if "one cannot say that in the United States religion exerts an influence on the laws or on the details of political opinions," it nevertheless "directs *mores*," especially by "regulating the family," and instilling in the American family "the love of order" which the American then "brings into affairs of state."[5]

Toleration emerges as a third component of the *mores* of Lincoln's democracy, inspired largely by what Tocqueville thought was the American passion for equality, since in a society of equals, mutual tolerance and forbearance were natural concomitants. Religious toleration was the most obvious form toleration took in America, and in many ways, it was the most ingenious achievement of the American democracy, disarming the power of religious prejudices which had cast a long shadow of murderous warfare over Europe. American religious toleration was also more than the condescending indifference of the great for the few; it sprang directly from the assumption of liberal democratic equality, and a respect for the liberal individual that did not occlude disagreement. George Washington assured the Jews of Newport, Rhode Island, in 1790 that religious freedom in America was not the conventional "indulgence of one-class of people" by an enfranchised class; rather, it was a recognition of the equal standing of citizens, as individuals, who simply happen to be of one religious persuasion out of many. It gives "to bigotry no sanction ... and requires only that they who live under its protection should demean themselves as good citizens."

That attitude underlay the liberty that embraced many other sorts of toleration that would have been unthinkable in the European environment. The indifference of the laws to personal convictions was one foundation for democratic tolerance; but another part was just as surely the sheer impossibility of imposing top-down uniformity on social spaces as broad as the American ones. In America, announced Hector St. John de Crèvecoeur, "a perfect freedom of thought, a latitude of opinion" prevails because there are not enough authorities available to suppress it. "Be not afraid of tumult, sedition, and broil," he counseled. "The great and immense room" in which Americans "expand themselves prevents them from producing those evil consequences which opposition and contracted limits formerly occasioned."[6]

At its weakest, the spirit of toleration did not prevent nativist riots or the shameful creation of the Know-Nothing political party. What it restrained was the interposition of government assistance in suppressing the ideas or identities the nativists were attacking. At its best, like Nathaniel Hawthorne's narrator in *The Blithedale Romance,* Americans "were of all creeds and opinions, and generally tolerant of all, on every imaginable subject." An Episcopal bishop might splutter that it was "preposterous to suppose that a band of Hindoos could settle in any part of our territories, and claim a right, under the Constitution, to set up the public worship of Braham, Vishnu, or Juggernaut," or "for the Chinese to introduce the worship of Fo or Buddha, in California." But this was, in fact, what happened, even before the bishop had denied it could occur. Even racism, at its most lethally onerous, could not entirely wipe out family formation under slavery, or even suppress (despite "warm and almost indignant opposition") tiny enclaves of black enfranchisement in the North.[7]

Nothing, however, so stamped American culture as democratic as its passion for elections. In the normal sense, elections are simply a formal tool of a democracy. But for Americans of the nineteenth century, elections became totems of America itself, the instinctive solution to all questions. And it showed by the way Americans celebrated elections—as holidays, as entertainments, as political theater. Polling places teemed with "processions, the band-playings and the cheers and applause," alcohol flowed freely, rowdies fought in the streets, and people "bet a good deal of money on the result" of an election. The staggered calendar of American elections in Lincoln's day ensured that electioneering of this sort was in a constant froth; in 1844, states voted for members of Congress on nine different days in October and November and held state elections from March to November. A French visitor—an admirer of the "wise and profound Tocqueville"—watched in mixed amusement and disbelief before the 1864 elections as "a band of music played under my windows followed by a wagon full of women dressed in flags," accompanied by showers of lurid election leaflets and an endless succession of political orators.

Elections became what Charles Fried called "the festival of democracy," what Walt Whitman praised as "your power-fulest scene and show"—the "ballot-shower" that "foams and ferments the wine" of democracy. They were the wind that "swell'd Washington's, Jefferson's, Lincoln's sails." To fail in elections, Lincoln said, "would "practically put an end to free government upon the earth." He did not "deny the possibility that the people may err in an election," he said after his own election as president, but the solution is not in illegal riot. If the people "err," then "the true cure is in the next election."[8]

Lincoln was not a man who liked to talk about hearts; his guiding stars all belonged in the constellation of reason. But he was also not unaware of the emotional power of *mores* and the unexamined "prejudices" that composed them. He understood that it was "the torrent of party prejudices" which swept away judicial wisdom before his eyes as a state legislator in 1841; the biggest obstacles he faced in building up the new Republican Party in 1857 were "old differences, prejudices, and animosities" among "influential leaders"; and his deadly enemy as president was "the force of habit" and "the prejudices of the past" stoked by the Democratic opposition. They were cloaked in noble "sentiments" and in angry emotion, but they were all the more powerful for being out of reason's sight.[9]

Take, for instance, the slogan "popular sovereignty." This was the rallying cry of Lincoln's great rival, Stephen Arnold Douglas, who proposed to open the spigots of settlement and development in the western territories by allowing the people who settled those territories to decide for themselves whether or not to legalize slavery. Lincoln had serious difficulty opposing it, if only because "popular sovereignty" had a certain enchantment to American ears; it sounded like the very spirit of democracy itself. "What does Popular Sovereignty mean?" he had to ask in 1851. "Strictly and literally it means the sovereignty of the people over their own affairs— in other words, the right of the people of every nation and community to govern themselves." Never mind that in practical terms it meant opening the gate to slavery. In the face of such a lovely generality, Lincoln could only try to chip at the ways Douglas proposed to bask in its reflection.[10]

Lincoln navigated the shoals of American "sentiments" and *mores,* partly because he had no choice, and partly because they were intrinsic to American democracy itself. In a democracy, "where the voice of all the men of the country, enter substantially into the execution,—or administration, rather—of the Government—in such a Government, what lies at the bottom of it all, is public opinion," no matter what it was formed around. This "public sentiment is everything," he replied to Douglas in 1858. "Whoever can change public opinion can change the government."[11] Whether it was relocating the state capital in Illinois and or deciding the legitimacy of national policy, no politician dared trifle with the *mores* of the American public. "The people" were the "great tribunal" of American life, and their habits, prejudices, inclinations, and folkways had to be reckoned with, whether they concerned property, religion, toleration, or elections."[12]

Certainly there was nothing in Lincoln which challenged the assumption that property owning was the *summum bonum* of American desires, especially since so much of his political economy was founded on the primacy of free labor. "If a hired laborer worked as a true man" and "saved means to buy land of his own, a shop of his own," he would simultaneously "increase his property" *and* demonstrate "the true, genuine principle of free labor." Owning property, even if that property was only a patent, added "the fuel of interest to the fire of genius." No wonder, then, that Lincoln understood property-loving to be the first of American *mores*. "Public opinion is formed relative to a property basis," so that whatever "lessens the value of property is opposed, what enhances its value is favored." Property was the great equalizer in a democracy; even the slave, "in the right to put into his mouth the bread that his own hands have earned ... is the equal of every other man, white or black."[13]

Lincoln had a much more cagey relationship with American religion. Born into a devout Calvinist family, he never embraced his family's religion, or anyone else's. But he was also wary of publicly challenging the cultural power of American religion. "I do not think I could myself, be brought to support a man for office, whom I knew to be an open enemy of, and scoffer at, religion," he replied to his critics in 1846. "No one has the right thus to insult the feelings, and injure the morals, of the community in which he may live," and he insisted (not entirely convincingly) that he had "never spoken with intentional disrespect of religion in general, or of any denomination of Christians in particular." He maintained the same circumspection two decades later when he told Connecticut congressman Henry Champion Deming that although it was true that "he had never united himself to any church," nevertheless "when any church will inscribe over its altar, as its sole qualification for membership, the Savior's condensed statement of the substance of both law and gospel, 'Thou shalt love the Lord thy God with all thy heart, and with all thy soul, and with all thy mind, and thy neighbor as thyself,' that church will I join with all my heart and all my soul"—knowing full well that no such church existed.[14]

Yet, Lincoln did embrace natural law, and the mysterious course of the Civil War raised so many questions in Lincoln's mind about the purpose and meaning of the war that he gradually began speculating more deeply on the existence of the God who ordered that law and God's direction of human affairs. "The will of God prevails," he wrote in 1862, as though he was beginning a geometrical proof—for surely, everyone had to admit that if God really *is* God, his will *must* prevail, or else he would not be God. In this war, he continued, both sides claim "to act in accordance with the will of God." Yet the course of the war gave no encouragement to either side to believe that God was favoring their immediate demand, for either independence or union. There remained, however, the possibility that God intended something in the war which neither side had contemplated at its beginning—and for Lincoln, that meant emancipation. "I am almost ready to say this is probably true." By the time he wrote his second inaugural address, Lincoln was prepared to turn that speech into something that walked at a tremendous distance from the religious clichés that permeated the inaugurals of previous presidents.[15] And yet, for all the intensity of his religious musings during the war, he never did join a church, or make any other kind of formal religious profession.

It was easier for Lincoln to embrace the *mores* of toleration. He had none of the American nativists' or Romantic nationalists' obsession with ethnicity, tribe, or soil. He believed there was an "electric cord" in the Declaration of Independence which linked every human consciousness. America's immigrants may be "men who have come from Europe—German, Irish, French and Scandinavian men—that have come from Europe themselves, or whose ancestors have come hither and settled here," but when they "look through that old Declaration of Independence they find that those old men say that 'We hold these truths to be self-evident, that all men are created equal,'" and that gives them a right to claim it as though they were blood of the blood, and flesh of the flesh of the men who wrote that Declaration, and so they are." Not blood or throne or altar, but a reasoned perception of natural law, and respect for the moral goods natural law identified, bound them to America as much as any descendant of the Revolution.[16]

Simply in practical terms, "how can any one who abhors the oppression of negroes, be in favor of degrading classes of white people?" Campaigning for Henry Clay in 1844, Lincoln distanced Clay from a major anti-Catholic riot in Philadelphia by expressing "the kindest and most benevolent feelings toward foreigners" and claiming that "the whigs were as much the friends of foreigners as democrats." No doubt, Lincoln said in 1852, Clay loved his country "because it was his own country," but much more because "he burned with a zeal for...human liberty" and yearned to see the success of the American experiment "show to the world" that democracies were not doomed to anarchy or poverty, but instead "that freemen could be prosperous." Clay had no concept of an America whose liberties were merely an inheritance from British law or the expression of some organic folk unity. Clay was a statesman who had a "strong sympathy with the oppressed every where, and an ardent wish for their elevation," and the success of the American democracy would light the path that showed how all others might enjoy that same elevation.[17]

More even than property or religion or toleration, it was the whirl of elections which defined Lincoln. His adult life is a ledger of election days, from his first run for the Illinois state legislature in 1832 to his re-election to the presidency in 1864. And not merely on those election days, either: Lincoln lived in the entire electoral process, from giving stump speeches for other candidates to setting up a campaign newspaper to organizing party conventions. In those conventions, matters had to be settled by popular vote in just the same way, and with almost the same amount of work, as any election, and Lincoln never held himself aloof from the mechanisms of the most petty vote calls. "A convention, or common consent, are the only legitimate party tribunals to decide" party affairs, and had to be attended to, and he knew how to do the attending. "As you go along," Lincoln advised William Herndon, "gather up all the shrewd wild boys about town, whether just of age, or little under age" and "let every one play the part he can play best—some speak, some sing, and all hollow [holler]." He had no particular fixation on his own claim to office. "No, if we should all be turned out tomorrow and could come back here in a week, we should find our places filled by a lot of fellows doing just as well as we did," he told Lucius Chittenden in the White House, "and in many instances better." It was elections themselves that excited him, and for all the offices he held during his life, no political moment mattered more to him than the day the New Salem militia company elected him as their captain, "a success which" in 1859 "gave me more pleasure than any I have had since."

He found it saddeningly "singular" that the elections he thrived upon were also moments of great public viciousness. "I...am not a vindictive man," yet he always seemed "except once" to "have been before the people for election in canvasses marked for their bitterness." But "the strife of the election is but human nature practically applied." When, in August of 1864, it appeared "exceedingly probable that this Administration will not be re-elected," he still maintained that "it will be my duty to so cooperate with the President elect," even if it meant that the election of an anti-war president would doom all the sacrifices made to save the Union.[18]

Like Adam Smith's man of "public spirit," Lincoln sought to "accommodate…his public arrangements to the confirmed habits and prejudices of his people." Yet, for all of Lincoln's attentiveness to American *mores,* he did not intend to be their slave, or to use them as populist vehicles to ride to political victory. Populism, to the extent that it sets passion against property, laws, and elections, had its most flamboyant American exponent in Andrew Jackson, the "towering genius" whose "paramount object" was "distinction," and who would willingly "set boldly to the task of pulling down" the laws.[19]

Carl Schurz believed that Lincoln "had a thorough knowledge of the plain people," and relied "upon the popular feeling, in great measure, for his guidance." But Lincoln did not hesitate to stand apart from that "feeling," to cajole it, persuade it, and sometimes ignore it. There was, as Horace White, Jesse Weik, and William Herndon all discerned, "a certain degree of moral obtuseness in Abraham Lincoln" which, for all his wary deference to popular assumptions, "cared nothing for public opinion." Newspapers might have been, as Herndon wrote about Lincoln's Illinois days, Lincoln's "food," which brought him everything he needed to know about the currents that flowed beneath American politics. But as president, he had other sources of direction. "For newspaper public opinion he cared but little," one of his White House staffers, William O. Stoddard, recalled, and

John Nicolay actually thought that, apart from the Washington dailies, "the President rarely ever looks at any papers."[20]

It was Lincoln's great complaint against Stephen Douglas that Douglas cared entirely too much for public opinion, and had no inner moral gyroscope of his own. "There was danger to this country—danger of the avenging justice of God in that little unimportant popular sovereignty question of Judge Douglas," Lincoln snapped. And that was what made Douglas despicable in his eyes. Douglas "will tell a lie to ten thousand people one day, even though he knows he may have to deny it to five thousand the next." Lincoln wanted to be guided by "a sense of right," whereas "the modern Democratic idea" is that "slavery is as good as freedom, and ought to have room for expansion all over the continent, if people can be found to carry it." It was typical of Lincoln to insist that "moral principle is all, or nearly all, that unites us of the North," and if that put the anti-slavery cause at odds with popular prejudice, popular prejudice had to go down. "Moral Principle," he admitted, "is a looser bond, than pecuniary interest," but it trumps all other considerations.[21]

That included property. As sacrosanct as property rights were in a democracy, Lincoln was swift to condemn any justification of slavery on the grounds that human beings could be construed as property. "To us," he said in 1860, "it appears natural to think that slaves are human beings; men, not property; that some of the things, at least, stated about men in the Declaration of Independence apply to them as well as to us." But the slaveowner argued that slaves *were* property, and that slaveowning deserved to share all the cultural sympathies Americans had for property ownership. The "property view that Slavery is right ... demands that we shall do everything for it that we ought to do if it were right." Instead of undergirding democracy, "property has persuaded the owner to believe that Slavery is morally right and socially elevating" and that we should "regard slavery as one of the common matters of property, and speak of negroes as we do of our horses and cattle." Lincoln denied that "we will in any violent way disturb the rights of property," but he would not agree to call something *property* which wasn't. "This new proposition" had no other purpose than "to dehumanize the negro" and "to prepare the public mind to make property, and nothing but property of the negro in all the States of this Union."[22]

Like property, religion had also not proven itself immune to corruption. If the slaveholding theologian "decides that God Wills Sambo to continue a slave, he thereby retains his own comfortable position." But if he "decides that God wills Sambo to be free, he thereby has to walk out of the shade, throw off his gloves, and delve for his own bread." How much godly "impartiality" is then to be expected from the theologian? So, as much as Lincoln would welcome whatever allies he could find among the American churches during the Civil War, he would still hold them just beyond the lip of power. He would attend the New York Avenue Presbyterian Church in Washington (with at least becoming frequency), issue repeated calls for days of prayer and thanksgiving, endorse missions of "charity and humanity" by clergymen in the occupied Confederacy, and express thanks to "God, Who, in this our great trial, giveth us the churches." He nevertheless rebuffed the overtures of ministers offering him policy advice, and in 1864, he politely ignored the National Reform Association's proposal to amend the Constitution to recognize "the Lord Jesus Christ as the Governor among the nations."[23]

Lincoln inhabited America's democratic *mores*, but he negotiated them at the same time. He regarded them as both knowable and fundamental, and yet he regarded their self-proclaimed constituencies as unstable and occasionally prone to think more highly of themselves than they ought. He had his own course to steer, his own internal compass to mind. "I shall always try and preserve one friend within me, whoever else fails me, to tell me that I have not been a tyrant and that I have acted right," he assured one of his staffers.[24] His ideal was to master himself and to be mastered by no one else, and that expressed his idea of democratic culture, as well as democracy.

Chapter Six

Democracy and Civil Liberties

D efinitions of democracy are drawn for times of peace, reflecting the generous assumption that democracies are themselves agencies of peace. Especially in Lincoln's formula for democratic government, democracies assume conditions that permit citizens to go about their lives without serious interference from each other or their rulers, and they do likewise with the affairs of other nations.

In the political world before the Enlightenment, when hierarchy was the prevailing rule, societies were composed, not of citizens, but of subjects, and the subjects were layered, horizontally, one stacked upon another, ordered by custom and demanding obedience and reciprocity from each other. Governance was defined by the cultivation of style, the performance of honor, and the acquisition of power, all of which reached the highest expression in war. But in the new American republic, the lines of political life were drawn vertically, with the enjoyment of civil liberties and the self-direction of society left to one side, and the administration of the state left to the other, and with a middle band, created by law, separating the two. Governance was praised for exhibiting humility, resilience, and familiarity. There was no reward for style, honor, or power in a democracy as there was in the old pattern, and therefore little investment in the risk of war. That is, unless someone like the "towering genius" Lincoln criticized in 1838 could persuade people that honor, style, and power were more interesting or comforting patterns to applaud.

That last exception is a reminder that one of the embarrassing truths about democracies is that they can be stampeded easily into states of emergency and climates of crisis which, in turn, drag them into wars and near wars that erase the middle band of law and trample across civil liberties (and always in the name of *necessity*). And it is one of the great ironies of American history that the president most often accused of that erasure is Lincoln. This is an irony, not because necessities are all illusory; but because Lincoln himself was so suspicious of arguments from necessity, and claimed, even before his inauguration, that "it is not with any pleasure that I contemplate the possibility that a necessity may arise in this country for the use of the military arm" in suppressing the secessionists.

On the other hand, it is also true that as early as July of 1861, Lincoln began invoking "necessity" as the reason for calling "out the war power of the Government; and so to resist force," confident (or at least as confident as he dared to sound) that "Congress would readily ratify" what necessity seemed to demand. This was, he cautioned, only "yielding to partial, and temporary departures" from the letter of the Constitution; in fact, without those departures, he might be judged as guilty for doing too little as for doing too much. Still, in less than a year, he was warning that something more than partial and temporary "departures" might be in the offing. Emancipating Southern slaves might "become a necessity indispensable to the maintainance of the government," he warned in May 1862, and by August, he was explaining that

"Necessity knows no law." Sixty years later, Lincoln's first great academic biographer, James G. Randall, would conclude, almost in regret, that nothing was more "conspicuous" in Lincoln's presidency than "its irregular and extra-legal characteristics"—all in the name of necessity.[1]

Lincoln's predecessor in the presidency, James Buchanan, was so loath to reach for anything that looked like "necessity" in dealing with secession that he convinced himself that the Constitution literally prevented him from acting against secession. Buchanan had no actual sympathy with the secessionists. The problem was that, as Buchanan saw matters, the Constitution contained no enforcement mechanism to suppress secession. "The fact is that our Union...can never be cemented by the blood of its citizens shed in civil war. If it can not live in the affections of the people, it must one day perish. Congress possesses many means of preserving it by conciliation, but the sword was not placed in their hand to preserve it by force."[2]

Lincoln could not have disagreed more vehemently. True, the Union depended on "mystic chords of memory" to secure itself, but it did not depend on them alone. The notion that because the Constitution contains no reversion clause, it therefore permits, or even *authorizes*, reversion, is silly. "I hold that in contemplation of universal law and of the Constitution the Union of these States is perpetual. Perpetuity is implied, if not expressed, in the fundamental law of all national governments. It is safe to assert that no government proper ever had a provision in its organic law for its own termination." What the rebels were calling "secession" was actually insurrection, and in times of insurrection there are definite constitutional remedies. The federal government had taken direct military action to deal with the threat of insurrection from the Whiskey Rebellion, Aaron Burr, and John Brown; it would do so once again, and if insurrection did not justify measures that were demanded by necessity, there was some question about the meaning of the word. "The power in me vested by the Constitution and the laws"—specifically the Militia Acts of 1792 and 1795—allowed him to "call forth, the militia of the several States of the Union to the aggregate number of 75,000." Congress would also join him in hugely expanding the recruitment of the Regular Army and the U.S. Volunteers and imposing a naval blockade of the Confederate coastline.[3]

Beyond that, however, there was not much in the way of example provided by the "necessities" of the Whiskey Rebellion, which had collapsed almost as soon it was pushed, or by Burr and Brown, who had barely gotten armed conspiracies and hare-brained plans for alternative governments in motion before they were shut down. The Constitution itself is vague about how to deal with "necessity," including war. It designates the president as the commander in chief of the army, navy, and the militia of the states "when called into the actual Service of the United States," but it divides the overall war power by giving Congress the authority to declare war, issue letters of marque, appropriate funds, and ratify concluding treaties. Alexander Hamilton, in *The Federalist,* had suspected that if an "insurrection" engulfed "a whole state," the employment of large-scale military force would be certainly necessary. But his notion of the "commander-in-chief" role was marginal: he would have "occasional command" of the state militias, and offer "direction" to "the military and naval forces."[4]

Lincoln was staring at something which dwarfed Burr, Brown, and the Whiskey rebels, so there must be, Lincoln reasoned, "certain proceedings" which become justified by his "commander-in-chief" responsibilities at moments of high crisis, since the Constitution cannot be "in all respects the same, in cases of Rebellion or invasion... as it is in times of profound peace and public security." Otherwise, the Constitution would be what Buchanan understood it to be: a document incapable of defending itself (or as Justice Robert Jackson would say in 1949, "a suicide pact"). But Lincoln's question ran deeper than simply wondering about the adequacy of his constitutional powers. The crisis of the Civil War forced him to ask out loud whether liberal democracy itself, and its confidence that law could safely occupy a zone between state and society, was flawed. It forces us to ask, Lincoln said, if democracies suffer from an incurable systemic flaw. "'Must a government, of necessity, be too strong for the liberties of its own people, or too weak to maintain its own existence?'"[5]

Lincoln's struggle to answer these questions would begin almost at once after his inaugural, in April 1861, after riots in the streets of Baltimore attempted to obstruct the passage of federalized militia to Washington. The civil authorities in Baltimore proved to be unable—and perhaps even unwilling—to deal with the rioters. So, Lincoln issued an authorization to the federal military to suspend the writ of habeas corpus along the railroad corridor linking Washington and Philadelphia, allowing his generals to arrest and imprison suspected saboteurs without trials or charges. Two weeks later, he issued another suspension authorization, covering the Florida coast, and two months later issued yet a third suspension order, extending the scope of his original suspension to include the rail lines between Philadelphia and New York. He would follow this with a comprehensive suspension order "within the United States" in September 1862.

The Constitution does indeed provide for a suspension of habeas corpus in Article 1, section 9 ("The privilege of the Writ of Habeas Corpus shall not be suspended, unless when in Cases of Rebellion or Invasion the public Safety may require it"), but it is cast in the negative and situated in the article governing the powers of Congress. Lincoln's suspension of the writ, and the arrests by the military which followed, certainly damped down Confederate efforts to rouse Maryland into joining the secession movement, and thus surrounding the capital on all sides with secession territory. But it also triggered an eruption which accused Lincoln of unconstitutional dictatorship—not just a mild "departure" on the plea of necessity, but a flagrant trampling on the Constitution's intent. Anti-Lincoln newspapers raged that the republic had reached the "point in our history when men on mere suspicion of political opponents, are deprived of their liberty, and incarcerated in our jails, or held by military power." The *Brooklyn Daily Eagle* called the suspension "a conflict between law and illegal violence, in which law suffered total defeat."[6]

For a century and a half thereafter, the song of the Lincoln-haters has recited verse after verse of horror at the crimes of Abraham Lincoln against the restraints of habeas corpus in particular and law in general. These emerged, not from necessity, but from a lust for power; not as slight deviations, but determined subversions, as though the "towering genius" Lincoln had condemned in 1838 was a sort of Freudian slip for describing himself. These crimes include the use of the State Department to conduct arrests for suspected treason, the purging of government employees through the use of loyalty oaths, the creation of military commissions to conduct trials of those arrested in defiance of habeas corpus, the creation of networks of special agents and officers to spy on civilians, the use of the military to influence elections, the silencing of the courts, and even emancipation, all of which presumably set the American republic on the road to statism and tyranny.

The difficulty that covers the Lincoln-haters with confusion is this quiet fact: *if* the horrors visited upon the nation by its sixteenth president really had any substance, then what magical powder, sometime between 1865 and now, allowed Americans to resume the use of their democratic faculties? It was one thing to fear that the Civil War might erase the rule of law. Wartime exigencies always pose such problems. The practical truth is that Lincoln's management of the war was a major factor which explains why the various threats to that rule gained as little ground as they did and faded almost as quickly as the ending of the war that caused them. True: what Lincoln sanctioned really were more than "departures," and their invocation as "necessity" sometimes strained credulity; but they were not civil cataclysms, and they really did turn out to be "temporary."

Lincoln did not disagree about the need or the validity of the constitutional limitations on his presidency. When his ambitious treasury secretary, Salmon Chase, agitated for him to expand the terms of the Emancipation Proclamation to include all slaves in America, and not just those in the rebellious states, Lincoln's reply was a model of legal self-restraint. He had issued the Proclamation on the strength of his constitutional role as commander in chief, which implied that he could use emancipation as "a military necessity" to undermine the military resistance of the rebellion. But he could not do more than that, and he certainly could not, by simple decree, emancipate slaves in the states which had not joined the rebellion or even in those jurisdictions which had been returned to federal control. "If I take the step," Lincoln replied, "must I not do so, without the argument of military necessity, and so, without any argument, except the one that I think the measure politically expedient, and morally right? Would I not thus give up all footing upon constitution or law? Would I not thus be in the boundless field of absolutism? ... Would it not lose us ... the very cause we seek to advance?"[7]

The challenge for Lincoln lay in balancing constitutional restraint against the threat of anarchy, which was no less a threat to law for coming from the direction of society rather than from government. Just as a lynch mob responds with violence when the law does not provide it with the results the mob desires, and has to be dispersed with weapons deadlier than truncheons or police whistles, so a political mob—in this case, the secessionists—which has responded with "acts of violence…against the authority of the United States," requires more than merely a wave of the disapproving finger. A democratic order cannot survive if large parts of society conclude that they will walk away whenever they are displeased with a result—or, in this case, not even walk away, but assault federal property (namely, Fort Sumter) or federal troops (meaning the militia who were attacked in the streets of Baltimore five days after Sumter's surrender). As he had warned the Springfield Lyceum a quarter century before, the temporary euphoria of mob rule will make for a brief period of political exhilaration, but such societies will sooner or later seek some means of re-imposing order, and no longer by law.[8]

Nor can the citizens of a democracy merely stand by in time of war and adopt a neutral wait-and-see attitude toward the war's outcome. Neutrality "recognizes no fidelity to the Constitution, or obligation to maintain the Union; and while the very men who have favored it are, doubtless, loyal citizens, it is, nevertheless, treason in effect." Secession's basic principle is "one of disintegration, and upon which no government can possibly endure," and disintegration is no respecter of intentions. Anarchy, whether it arises from hostility or indifference, alienates "the attachment of the People" to law and sends them in search of some other power which will restore order. By the time some alt-Napoleon provides that cure, the last remains of a democratic order will have crumbled away.

The Confederacy was already an example of this disintegration. It purported to be a republic of some sort, but it turned rapidly into a military state, partly because so many of its people (or so Lincoln believed) had no real enthusiasm for it, and had to be dragooned or intimidated into supporting it. The Confederacy is "a Power existing in pronunciamento only." Its real strength, Lincoln had concluded by the summer of 1863, "is its military—its army. That army dominates all the country, and all the people, within its range." This was what made peace talks with a Confederate government pointless, because for all practical purposes, there *was* no Confederate government. "Any offer of terms made by any man or men within that range, in opposition to that army, is simply nothing for the present; because such man or men, have no power whatever to enforce their side of a compromise, if one were made with them."[9] The state, representing compulsion, posed one threat to the liberal order; society, by fleeing into anarchy, became a threat just as great; and both were enemies to democracy.

However, Lincoln did not hold back the forces of anarchy without putting some dents of his own in the laws. For in every one of the complaints of the Lincoln-haters, stretching back to 1861, there is invariably an element of truth.

Union soldiers did interfere with elections, especially in contested districts in the Midwest and the border states. In September 1861, nineteen members of the Maryland legislature were arrested before the legislature was due to meet for fear that their votes would tip the state over into secession. In 1862, Illinois Republican governor Richard Yates stationed draft enrollment officers at the polls, ostensibly to create accurate listings of those eligible for the draft, but in reality, complained Democrats, to suppress Democratic votes. Democrats in Indiana fumed that Lincoln had pumped the state with "a thousand spies or detectives" for the 1864 elections. "No man feels safe. Terror spreads over the land."[10]

Some of this had Lincoln's own thumbprint on it. Lincoln directly ordered the expulsion of former Ohio congressman Clement Laird Vallandigham from Ohio to the Confederacy, after Vallandigham's sensational arrest and imprisonment by military district commander Ambrose Burnside for an anti-draft speech Vallandigham gave at Mount Vernon, Ohio, on May 1, 1863, and then did likewise to Indiana state senator Alexander Douglas. Vallandigham and Douglas were only the most prominent among the dissenters arrested for criticizing Lincoln at public rallies and forums, and they included Philadelphia lawyer Charles Ingersoll, New York judge Francis Flanders, former Kentucky governor Charles Morehead, former Ohio congressman Edson Olds, and Baltimore newspaper editor Frank Key Howard, the grandson of Francis Scott Key, in addition to the ninety-six others whose thumbnail biographies are included in John Marshall's political martyrology of the Lincoln administration, *American Bastille*, in 1869.[11]

Lincoln also ordered the shutdown of two New York newspapers, the *New York World* and the *New York Journal of Commerce*, on May 18, 1864, and imprisonment of the papers' "editors, proprietors and publishers" for having published what turned out to be a bogus presidential proclamation of "an immediate and preemptory draft" call. Wilbur Storey's *Chicago Times*, a vigorous defender of Vallandigham and critic of Burnside, was shut down by Burnside's order on June 3, 1863, ignoring an injunction from a federal judge. Other generals did likewise: Milo Hascall, in command of the District of Indiana, stopped the presses of the *Plymouth Weekly Democrat*, the *Pulaski Democrat*, the *Columbia City News*, and the *South Bend Forum*, and would have done likewise to the *Huntington*

Democrat had not a crowd of armed men halted a squad of soldiers from arresting the paper's owners.[12]

What has to be said, however, is that none of this followed any sort of plan on Lincoln's part—or much of any plan, since no one had ever contemplated the size and threat of a domestic insurrection on the scale of the Confederacy—and frequently had no direction from Lincoln at all. Nor were the threats to civil liberties made by the Lincoln administration consistent, or consistently enforced. Marcus "Brick" Pomeroy of the *LaCrosse Democrat* abused Lincoln with frightful energy all through the war, culminating in his wish that if Lincoln should be re-elected in 1864, "we trust some bold hand will pierce his heart with dagger point for the public good"—yet Pomeroy was never arrested. Henry Hamilton of the *Los Angeles Star,* who had bitterly criticized the Lincoln administration for its wartime taxes and Lincoln as a "tool of Abolitionism," was arrested in the fall of 1862, imprisoned for ten days, then returned to edit the *Star* and get elected to the California legislature. Dennis A. Mahony, the editor of the *Dubuque Herald,* was arrested in August 1862 as a "political adversary," only to be released in November, greeted on his "return home with the most enthusiastic demonstrations," and promptly elected county sheriff.

They were far from alone. In the spring of 1864, a draft riot in Illinois led to the military arrests of sixteen civilians, and when an attempt was made to obtain a writ of habeas corpus for their release, Lincoln issued a direct suspension of the writ in their case—and then, after an intervention by David Davis, Lincoln ordered all of them freed. The Marylanders detained under Lincoln's suspensions of the writ in 1861 could "be released by taking a full oath of allegiance to the Government of the United States," and Lincoln specifically replied to a plea for the release of three pro-secession Kentuckians on the grounds that "the Kentucky arrests were not made by special direction from here, and I am willing if you are that any of the parties may be released." Lincoln also brushed back his own officers. The unhappy General Hascall was relieved of his command, and his district's boundaries redrawn. Even in 1861, Lincoln had no sooner authorized suspension of the writ of habeas corpus than he was urging military officers, "Unless the necessity for these arbitrary arrests is manifest, and urgent, I prefer they should cease." There was simply no pattern, much less a nefarious plan.[13]

Not all of those arrested were political innocents, either. Union soldiers were far from the only ones busy manipulating the results of elections. In the 1864 elections, the *New-York Tribune* howled that Democrats had mobilized "some Twenty-five to Thirty Thousand" illegal voters "all of whom went of course for [Lincoln's rival, George B.] McClellan"; New Jersey Republicans complained vociferously that "as soon as the Polls were opened...the Democrats had been colonizing [i.e., shipping voters from one polling place to another to cast multiple votes] pretty extensively"; and in Philadelphia, Republicans cheered "a number of arrests... made for illegal voting, and, strange to say, all were engaged in voting the Copperhead ticket."[14]

What is surprising in the case of Lincoln's presidency is how *few* such dents were made in civil liberties, especially compared to what he might otherwise have done, and in the context of four years of bloody civil war. He was no Cromwell, telling Congress they were no Congress, and he was no Robespierre sending Danton to the guillotine in the name of virtue. He rebuked his longtime friend, Orville Hickman Browning, when Browning supported Major General John Charles Frémont's imposition of martial law across the whole state of Missouri, saying that "I cannot assume this reckless position; nor allow others to assume it on my responsibility." Browning and Frémont might think of martial law as "the only means of saving the government," but Lincoln was just as sure that "it is itself the surrender of the government."[15] Despite the sensational arrests of Ingersoll, Olds, Howard, Flanders, and the other occupants of the "American Bastille," no mass roundups occurred. Overall, between 13,500 and 14,400 civilian arrests were made under the Lincoln administration—which, in a Northern population of 22 million did not exactly represent a Night of the Long Knives. Of these, 866 can be considered "political" arrests, and nearly half (40.8%) occurred in the border states, which were riven by guerrilla warfare. Few of them, apart from Vallandigham, represented well-known figures of opposition; many had simply antagonized local military commandants or provost marshals by draft-resistance. Others appear to have been smugglers and blockade-runners who were being detained as witnesses for hearings in maritime blockade capture cases. Even the detentions of foreign nationals apprehended while blockade-running amounted, in total, to less than 3,000, all of whom were eventually released on the appeal of their diplomatic representatives. And the arrests of the Maryland legislators in 1861 were actually carried out—and defended—by Lincoln's Democratic rival in the 1864 elections, George B. McClellan.[16]

In particular, Lincoln made no move toward jailing the people who were in a position to cause him the greatest harm politically, the Northern Democratic state governors, and especially Horatio Seymour of New York and Joel Parker of New Jersey. They went unmolested, and when Vallandigham slipped back into Ohio in 1864, so did Vallandigham. Lincoln told military officials to "watch Vallandigham and others closely," but unless there were signs of "any palpable injury, or eminent danger to the Military," they should leave him alone, not "arrest without further order." Lincoln did not defy Congress, nor did he close all courts or make everything into military tribunals. Writs of habeas corpus continued to be issued until Lincoln expanded suspension of the writ nationally in 1863, but by then, habeas corpus had fallen into becoming a tool for obtaining military discharges for underage recruits and draftees.[17]

The crowning irony of Lincoln's maintenance of law actually concerns, not the civil liberties of individuals, but the standing of the states within the federal system. Far from the federal government swallowing up state sovereignty, Lincoln's management of the war was actually a boon to federalism. In 1861, the Northern governors presided over their states with staffs so minuscule that they usually included no more than a state treasurer, a superintendent of public education, a secretary of state, an attorney general, and an auditor. By the end of the war, they had metamorphosed into networks of state agents, adjutants-general and aides-de-camp, camps of rendezvous and instruction, hospitals, and veterans' homes and orphanages where "the destitute orphans of our brave soldiers are to be the children of the State." In Massachusetts, over $8 million in aid to soldiers' families was disbursed during the war, almost twice the entire state budget for 1858. The postwar era became the golden era of state government activism—in education, in municipal reform, and even in women's voting rights. Alas! It also became the era of state-managed Jim Crow.[18]

Lincoln was neither an aristocrat nor a soldier, and if Lincoln committed offenses against civil liberties in the midst of civil war, it should be remembered that no handbook on how to wage such a civil war existed to warn him in advance. "In using the strong" methods which his administration has been "compelled to do," Lincoln admitted that he "had a difficult duty to perform," and even at "the very best, it will by turns do both too little and too much." But in exercising that "duty," the offenses occurred haphazardly, and with Lincoln intervening frequently to remove them. "Those who stress Lincoln's willingness to disregard constitutional limitations in the Civil War crisis have it wrong," writes Michael Les Benedict. "Lincoln did exercise the war powers of the presidency aggressively, but he never claimed the right to transcend constitutional limitations or to escape democratic control. Indeed, he was constrained by the very popular commitment to the rule of law that he had identified as the only security against presidential despotism."[19]

Benedict's judgment is an echo of a contemporary estimate of Lincoln, from William H. Smith, who met Lincoln first as a cub reporter for the *Indianapolis Argus* and who went on to become a major business figure in Indianapolis. "I first saw Mr. Lincoln in August or September of 1859," Smith wrote. "I noticed that he never used the term *obedience* to the law, but always *reverence,* seeming to regard that term higher and more comprehensive than the other.... I remember very distinctly that he spoke of this reverence for the law as the 'palladium of our liberties, our shield, buckler and high tower.' "[20] For all that we today laud Abraham Lincoln for his other virtues, it is this fundamental hesitation to quash law and democratic liberties which is the most important gift we inherit from him. As he was not a slave, so he was not a master.

Chapter Seven

Democracy and Race

Democracy should not be about race. Democracy is a regime of reason, debate, persuasion, or at least reasonable self-interest, while race is a non-rational factor that thrives on ineffable intuitions of group qualities and appeals to the basest of political passions. It is not even clear, in the first place, exactly what a *race* is, unless it can be defined by the arrangement of certain parts of one's DNA (so that particular diseases, like sickle-cell anemia, will follow the path of a particular "race"). On the other hand, it *is* certainly clear that there is no fixed boundary for a "race," since those same DNA strands record, in each individual, a myriad of tribal and "racial" histories, from the Neanderthal to the Denisovan.

Race accounts for so minuscule a portion of what makes us human that it cannot be said even to affect or alter the basic definition of humanity, much less the natural rights that are hardwired into every human being and form the basis of democratic politics and culture. Moreover, liberal democracy is based on assumptions about individuals and the rights they possess *as* individuals, not on group identities. (In classical terms, democracy is about participating in a *demos,* not an *ethnos.*) In a democracy, nothing ought to be less relevant than considerations attached to *race.*[1]

Yet race insists on intruding itself into democracy. The Athenians persisted in linking citizenship in their democracy to those possessing an Attic bloodline.[2] Two thousand years later, Tocqueville feared that notions of racial superiority and hierarchy might undo all the good liberal democracy had done for Americans by inducing them to withhold "almost all the privileges of humanity" from other races. Americans had wrought a near miracle in disarming religious prejudice through toleration; they were now proceeding to replicate all the original intolerances when they came in the form of race. The "Indian races" had been "condemned...to a wandering and vagabond life, full of inexpressible miseries," and even when "the Negro is free," he will be admitted to neither the "rights, nor the pleasures, not the labors, nor the grief, nor even the tomb" of white Americans. So much for liberal democracy.[3]

It had not started out that way. Although, at the outbreak of the Revolution, every one of the newly independent American states legalized black slavery, the first steps toward a new republican order signaled a drawing-back from approvals of race-based enslavement. As early as June of 1775, the Massachusetts Provincial Convention adopted a resolution deploring "the enslaving of any of the human race, and particularly of the Negroes in this country." George Washington originally banned black recruitment for the Continental Army, but was forced to back down, to the point where German officers in the British service were surprised that in the American army "you do not see a regiment in which there is not a large number of blacks." In 1787, the Constitutional Convention diplomatically suppressed all direct references to slavery to avoid acknowledging "men to be property," and made no allusion in the federal Constitution to race, white or otherwise.[4]

Not only slavery, but civil inequality based on race seemed on its way to the dustbin. When Massachusetts considered limiting its voting rights only to whites in 1778, one writer jeered, "Would it not be ridiculous, inconsistent and unjust, to exclude freemen from voting for representatives and senators, though otherwise qualified, because their skins are black, tawny or reddish? Why not disqualified for being long-nosed, short-faced, or higher or lower than five feet nine?" Two years later, the new Massachusetts state constitution declared that "all men are born free and equal" and with equal access to "acquiring, possessing and protecting property." Once independent, less than a quarter of the new American states limited voting rights to whites only.[5]

What was also true, however, is that as Americans advanced into the nineteenth century, much of what had been gained against slavery and inequality was rolled back. With the emergence of cotton as a major American export, slave-based cotton agriculture became wildly profitable, and along with the profits came disingenuous rationalizations for slavery. And as a Jacksonian white working class claimed an increasing share of power in the American democracy, white legislatures sought to solidify those gains by depriving black Americans of any access to the franchise. At the same time as New Jersey adopted a gradual emancipation plan and dropped its property requirements for voting, it also eliminated black voting rights. New laws in New York in 1811 set in place a pattern of slowly disfranchising "any black or mulatto person," while in 1818, a new Connecticut state constitution erased black voting. By the 1850s, even those who vocally opposed slavery did it less out of a concern for black humanity than for preserving the North American continent exclusively for white settlement. "The poor white man" moved into the western territories "to get a free home for himself"; there was no "talk about the sinfulness of slavery," because he "despised the negro."[6]

For two generations after the Civil War, Abraham Lincoln was revered as the American who led the way, not only out of slavery, but toward racial equality. When the black Chicago lawyer William Lilly set out to write a serialized biography of Lincoln in the 1930s for the *Chicago Defender*, he began the series with the headline, "Abraham Lincoln: Never Was a Man More Worthy of the Love of a People." After its dedication in 1922, the Lincoln Memorial became a black rallying point: Marian Anderson delivered her celebrated recital from its steps in 1939, and E. W. D. Jones, the bishop of the African Methodist Episcopal Zion Church, promised at the Memorial that "the immortality of Lincoln will cluster around his emancipation of the slaves."[7]

That adulation has now all but evaporated. Instead of the Great Emancipator, Lincoln is more often condemned as a racist whose interest in freeing American slaves was dictated purely and cynically by his desire to reunite the American Union and who included not just blacks but "Indians and Mexican greasers" in his catalogue of unwanteds. In *Forced into Glory: Abraham Lincoln's White Dream*, Lerone Bennett, the editor of *Ebony* magazine, indicted Lincoln as a calculating bigot.

> *He believed until his death that the Negro was the ... inferior, the subhuman, who had to be ... subordinated, enslaved, quarantined to protect the sexual, social, political, and economic interests of Whites. Everything he did ... everything he said,*

even the speeches his defenders are always praising, was based on this racist idea, which defined his life [and] his politics....

We are now arrived at "Thirteentherism," where even the 13th Amendment, which Lincoln navigated through Congress to abolish slavery once and for all, is castigated for having done nothing of the sort.[8]

This represents one of the greatest shifts in historical self-consciousness that has occurred in American life. But deposing Lincoln from his pedestal as the Great Emancipator is only one example of the rise of an Afro-pessimism which questions whether the entire premise of democratic government has failed on the doorstep of race. "Theft, seizure and abduction," writes Jared Sexton, "should be understood as the paradigmatic conditions of black existence in America," not democracy. Even Barack Obama is condemned for selling black Americans "the snake oil of hope and change." The "value gap" guarantees that "no matter the form of our system, it will always produce the same results: racial inequality."[9]

In Lincoln's defense, his admirers plead that the criticisms of Bennett, Nikole Hannah-Jones, Ibram X. Kendi, and others are an example of *presentism*—measuring people and situations from the past by the standards and sensibilities of the present. But wrapping Lincoln in the tissue of context also runs the risk of making Lincoln irrelevant; if he can be judged by only the reckoning of his own time, then he has meaning only for that time, too. Besides, a number of Lincoln's contemporaries did see the issue of racism with fully as much clarity and urgency as anyone today, and that seems to leave precious little excuse for him, or for democracy itself. If it turns out that Lincoln was a racist—a white supremacist with no confidence in the possibility of liberty and justice for all—then everything which connects Lincoln and democracy is suspect.

The term *racism* was first coined in the 1930s by Magnus Hirschfeld, who made it the title of his critique of the racial philosophy of the Nazis. In the ninety years since the Nazis came to power in Germany, the word has undergone a significant expansion, and sometimes even inflation. No longer do we confine *racist* to a political philosophy. Instead, we use *racist* to describe an attitude, which can be said to have two fundamental parts:

> *dishonor*—the idea that members of a certain race are (or possess characteristics which are) biologically, intellectually and permanently inferior to one's own race; and inferior to the point that it justifies what Glenn Loury calls "racial stigma," which in turn causes psychological and social harm.

> *enmity*—that it is permissible, or even necessary, to practice exploitation, disrespect (or inadequate respect, compared to one's own race), condescension and manipulation toward members of another race, often by employing anger, derision, self-seeking advantage, contempt, or worse, real physical damage to persons and property.

Racism can also exist as *social* racism, where racist beliefs are widely shared but only as a sort of social assumption, without clear targets or definition, and as *institutional* racism, which describes racism as practiced as policy by specific institutions, such as schools or governments. Finally, racism can exist on a spectrum of malevolence. It may be little more than exaggeration of *racialism,* which talks about differences without implying dishonor, or it may give rise to a militant genocidal hatred which takes serious, even hideous, public form.[10]

Opposing slavery is not the same thing as opposing racism, although the two are often confused in Lincoln's case, since slavery was an exclusive application of racism to African Americans and their offspring. Lincoln lived all but the earliest years of his life in Northern states which were technically "free" (in that they outlawed permanent enslavement). Nevertheless, the social and institutional world of Lincoln's Illinois in the 1830s through the 1850s was so pervasively racist that the state's "Black Laws" required free blacks to file certificates of freedom, proscribed "sexual intermixture," and finally, in 1848, flatly prohibited the immigration of free blacks.

With that distinction in view, there is no reason to doubt Lincoln's claim in 1864 that he had "always" hated *slavery* and could not "remember when I did not so think, and feel." It was an opposition which surfaced early in his career as a lawyer when, in 1836, he assisted Mary Turner, "an indentured slave under the Illinois laws," to gain her freedom, and in his earliest record in the Illinois state legislature when, on March 3, 1837 (in his second term as a member of the legislature), he declared that "the institution of slavery is founded on both injustice and bad policy," and that Illinois should repeal resolutions it had adopted commending the silencing of abolitionist protests.

In his recollection of a "tedious low-water" steamboat passage on the Ohio River which Lincoln took with Joshua Speed in 1841, the sight of a coffle of chained slaves, "shackled together with irons," was "a continued torment to me," and he warned Speed that any willingness he showed toward tolerating legalized slavery in the South should not be read as indifference. "It is not fair for you to assume that I have no interest in a thing which has, and continually exercises, the power of making me miserable," he wrote. "You ought rather to appreciate how much the great body of the Northern people do crucify their feelings, in order to maintain their loyalty to the Constitution and the Union." In his solitary term in Congress, from 1847 to 1849, he endorsed every anti-slavery measure that came before the House of Representatives, and in January 1849 he drafted a bill to abolish the slave trade in the District of Columbia, until, "abandoned by my former backers and having little personal influence, I dropped the matter."[11]

But Lincoln is also an unhappy example of how opposition to slavery did not necessarily guarantee any sort of enlightenment on race, and there is an uncomfortable zigzag in much of Lincoln's thinking on racial issues. In 1839, he voted to table a Democratic resolution that defended the Black Laws, but in 1858, the black abolitionist H. Ford Douglass could not coax him to sign a petition "to give me the right to testify in a court of justice." In 1845, he successfully defended Marvin Pond (the son of the ineptly named abolitionist minister, Billious Pond) when Pond was accused of harboring a fugitive Kentucky slave, John Hauley, and he acquired a reputation among Illinois lawyers for his willingness to take up "an arrested fugitive slave." Yet he rebuked Salmon Chase fourteen years later for allowing the Ohio state Republican convention to include a plank in its platform condemning the Fugitive Slave Law of 1850, arguing that "the cause of Republicanism is hopeless in Illinois, if it be in any way made responsible for that plank."

Out of the more than five thousand cases in which he participated as a lawyer, as few as three dozen may have involved African Americans, and even in those cases, he showed little overt dissent from the prevailing patterns of racism in Illinois. On the one hand, he negotiated the freedom of "a Negro girl" named Nance Legins in *Bailey v. Crom-*

well in 1841 in the Illinois Supreme Court (a decision which was then in turn cited in other anti-slavery cases); handled the legal affairs of his Haitian barber, William de Fleurville; lived in an unsegregated neighborhood in Springfield; and extended himself in 1857 to obtain the freedom of an Illinois black youth, John Shelby, who had been imprisoned in New Orleans for lacking a certificate attesting to his free status. On the other hand, he represented slaveowner Robert Matson in a dubious suit (under Illinois's transit laws) which would have returned Jane Bryant and her four children to Matson's grasp.[12]

As much as Lincoln opposed slavery, he often explained that opposition as no more than opposing the extension of legalized slavery outside the South, not the destruction of slavery in the South itself. When he campaigned for Zachary Taylor's presidential bid in 1848, he puzzled "his free-negro friends" by insisting that "promoting freedom would be easier and better attained by voting for Taylor, the owner of three hundred negro slaves." He puzzled them still more just before the election when "he scored" abolitionists "with the most scathing language." This was not because he necessarily opposed abolition; he opposed the abolitionists for demanding too much, too quickly, and with too little prospect of success. Abolitionists declared "that they would 'do their duty and leave the consequences to God.'" That was simply exalting passion over reason, and

> *merely gave an excuse for taking a course that they were not able to maintain by a fair and full argument. To make this declaration did not show what their duty was. If it did we should have no use for judgment, we might as well be made without intellect, and when divine or human law does not clearly point out what is our duty, we have no means of finding out what it is by using our most intelligent judgment of the consequences.*

His own "first impulse would be to free all the slaves" but then send them "to Liberia," because to "free them, and make them politically and socially, our equals" ran directly across "my own feelings" and "those of the great mass of white people." But expulsion to Liberia was not really worth considering, either, because "whatever of high hope, (as I think there is) there may be in this, in the long run, its sudden execution is impossible." Black people, he believed, were incapable of managing their affairs, and "if they were all landed there in a day, they would all perish in the next ten days." To Kentucky chief justice George Robertson, Lincoln admitted that "our political problem now is 'Can we, as a nation, continue together permanently—forever—half slave, and half free?'" When he asked that question in 1855, he had no answer. "The problem is too mighty for me."[13]

The zigzag became persistent. Though he was "troubled and grieved" over the annexation of Texas as a slave state "as far back as 1836–40," Lincoln nevertheless "gave it up." Much as he revered Henry Clay's Missouri Compromise of 1820, he was at first inclined to believe that "the Missouri Compromise had nothing to do" with legalizing slavery in the New Mexico territory acquired in the Mexican War. He voted "above forty times" for the Wilmot Proviso, which *would* have banned slavery there, but eventually he yielded to legalizing slavery in New Mexico as a special case under the Compromise of 1850, and largely because many Americans had no idea of settling in what was usually regarded as a barren desert, useful only for establishing a right-of-way for future railroads to the Pacific. As much as he was "inflexible" on "the question of extending slavery under the national auspices," he was willing to be flexible "about New Mexico, if further extension were hedged against."

What Lincoln seemed to find most objectionable about Southern demands to admit slavery to the rest of the western territories was not their racial tyranny, but the likelihood that legalizing slavery there would cut off access to those territories—to Kansas, to Nebraska, to the Dakotas, to the Pacific coast—for white farmers who would not be able to rival the economies of scale enjoyed by slave-gang labor. "The mass of white men" are "injured by the effect of slave labor in the neighborhood of their own labor." Hence, "free white men had a right to claim that the new territories into which they and their children might go to seek a livelihood should be preserved free and clear of the incumbrance of slavery."[14]

He certainly had no desire in the 1850s to tamper with slavery in the existing slave states. Although Lincoln had often repeated his hope for the "ultimate extinction of the institution," he clarified "ultimate" to mean somewhere off in the far, far distance, and shortly after his election in 1860, he even authorized *New York Times* editor Henry J. Raymond to assert that "Mr. Lincoln is not pledged to the ultimate extinction of slavery." As president, Lincoln disciplined two of his generals, John Charles Frémont and David Hunter, and rebuked a cabinet secretary—Simon Cameron—who wanted to move toward emancipation in 1861 and early 1862. When he issued an Emancipation Proclamation of his own later in 1862, the document sounded remote and indifferent, and liberated only slaves in the rebellious Confederate states, not in the four upper South slave states—Missouri, Kentucky, Maryland, and Delaware.[15]

Lincoln seemed scarcely more encouraging to African Americans in the free states. Stumping Illinois in 1840 against Martin Van Buren, Lincoln condemned "Little Van" for "his votes in the New York Convention in allowing Free Negroes the right of suffrage," and in his debates with Douglas in 1858, Lincoln warned that

*anything that argues me into his idea of perfect social and
political equality with the negro, is but a specious and fantas-
tic arrangement of words, by which a man can prove a horse
chestnut to be a chestnut horse. I will say here, while upon this
subject, that I have no purpose directly or indirectly to interfere
with the institution of slavery in the States where it exists. I
believe I have no lawful right to do so, and I have no inclination to do so. I have no purpose to introduce political and social
equality between the white and the black races.*

In his post-election letter to Henry Raymond, he directed
the New York editor to assure his readers that he "does not
hold the black man to be the equal of the white"—at least not
"unqualifiedly"—and years later, William Herndon attested
that "Mr. Lincoln at no time in his life advocated the social
Equality of the White & Black races." (Of course, Herndon
added, Lincoln never believed there was "Social Equality
even in the white race themselves—never was & never will
be," since "a dishonest man . . . is never the Equal in society of
an honest man or a man of integrity.")

The oddest twist in Lincoln's racial imagination was his
enjoyment of blackface minstrelsy, with its "vulgar notion
of the negro as man-monkey,—a thing of tricks and antics."
He assured Leonard Grover, the proprietor of Grover's The-
atre in Washington, that "I really enjoy a minstrel show."
And not just as entertainment: the "immortal emancipator,"
recalled Herndon, enjoyed "mimicking the clownish antics
of the negro Minstrel." When Herndon and Henry C. Whitney accompanied Lincoln in March 1860 to a performance
of Rumsey & Newcomb's Minstrels at Metropolitan Hall in
Chicago, Whitney was surprised to see Lincoln "perfectly
'taken' with" a rousing rendition of "Dixie." Lincoln "clapped
his great hands, demanding an encore, louder than anyone. I
never saw him so enthusiastic." Lincoln "had an insatiable

fondness for negro minstrelsy and seemed to extract the greatest delight from the crude jokes."[16]

Lincoln was only marginally more respectful to the delegations of Cherokee, Cheyenne, Arapaho, Potawatomi, and other western tribes who waited on him as president. He addressed the Potawatomi representatives in the East Room of the White House in 1861 in a childish pidgin—"Where live now? When go back Iowa?"—and when another delegation of "nine chiefs of different nations" in the federal territories "asked the President to counsel his white children, who were annually encroaching more and more upon their tribes, to abstain from acts of violence and wrong towards them," Lincoln merely replied that he would "endeavor to have satisfactory treaties made with them." At the same time, he added, "there is no way in which your race is to become as numerous and prosperous as the white race except by living as they do, by the cultivation of the earth."

Lincoln's principal encounters with the tribes had not been happy ones, going as far back as his grandfather's murder by Shawnee in Kentucky in 1786 and his own service as a militia captain in the Black Hawk War. He signed death warrants for thirty-eight Sioux whose 1862 uprising in Minnesota was crushed by federal and state troops, while the savage Sand Creek massacre of Cheyenne and Arapaho by the 3rd Colorado Volunteer Cavalry in 1864 passed without any notice by Lincoln.[17]

Even if it is pleaded that this does not necessarily make Lincoln a *racist* within the definition laid out by Magnus Hirschfeld, it certainly appears that he condoned racism in others, and confined his opposition to slavery to the most minimal grade of opposition. The distance between this Lincoln and the author of the Emancipation Proclamation seems so great that Lincoln's defenders frequently resort to useless tropes like *growth* or *evolution* to argue that, over time, Lincoln changed for the better. But Lincoln's closest students have warned against trying to squeeze a new Lincoln out of the old one. "The conception of Lincoln as a man of very ordinary talents who became in five years of stress educated to a point of intellectual greatness cannot hold," wrote Roy Prentice Basler, the editor of the canonical edition of Lincoln's writings and speeches. "The essential elements of his greatness which were generally recognized after his death and canonization were, if they existed at all, present in the Lincoln of 1860."[18]

How, then, is it possible to take the measure of a Lincoln who seems to offer repeated images of the master? Is it possible now only to conclude that Lincoln really did prefer to keep at least some people, at least in some measure, as slaves?

Chapter Eight

Democracy and Emancipation

The modern age is a skeptical age. But it is a cheap skepticism, built not on wariness or prudence, but on what John Gardner called a "posturing misanthropy" which masquerades as the mark of genius.[1] Abraham Lincoln has been a particularly marked target for this misanthropy for his backwardness on race, and unnecessarily so, if the original definition of racism can be kept in view.

Watch Lincoln in the debates with Douglas, where he must deal with an undiluted white racial supremacist and nationalist, threading the needle in front of crowds of voters to whom he is appealing at election time: "Certainly the negro is not our equal in color" (which means *what*? That *white* is not the same color as *black*, or *black* the same as *white*? What does this do beyond stating the obvious?)... "perhaps not in many other respects" (which Lincoln never bothers to specify)... "still, in the right to put into his mouth the bread that his own hands have earned, he is the equal of every other man, white or black" (and isn't that the fundamental equality which, by contrast, renders enslavement an abomination?). "In pointing out that more has been given you"—and Lincoln did not specify what that *more* was, or given by *whom*—"you can not be justified in taking away the little which has been given him. All I ask for the negro is that if you do not like him, let him alone"—which was exactly what every slave-owner refused to do.[2]

One part of Lincoln's notion of equality was legal and con-stitutional, and while it had gradations, its gradations were those of the law itself. The most fundamental of these his-torical circumstances concerned the line between federal and state jurisdictions. Natural law called for legal respect for natural rights. But in a liberal democracy, there is always the risk that the positive laws a society enacts might fall short of what natural law demands. The great advantage of a liberal democracy is that, with the persistent application of reason, defective laws can be changed as majorities change. But in the meantime, there seemed, in Lincoln's mind, no choice, short of anarchy, but to wait calmly for the majorities, and the laws, to change.

In the American case, not only did the Constitution leave it to the states to determine voting rights; the states claimed vast defining powers over issues as various as whether banks should be allowed to incorporate and what constituted citi-zenship. These decisions about civil rights could be wrong, could differ from state to state, or could even be arbitrary, but they were what the people of a state wanted them to be, and in a democracy, Lincoln felt compelled to agree that the majority in those states had the majority's privilege to deter-mine those rights peacefully.[3]

Nevertheless, whatever any particular polity did about articulating the *civil* rights of its members, Lincoln believed that no political community—state or otherwise—should have the power to alter or disregard in any way the *natural* rights of its members. "Equality of natural rights" was the "gem" of the Declaration, and though the Declaration "does not declare that all men are equal in their attainments or social position, yet no sane man will attempt to deny that the African upon his own soil has all the natural rights that instrument vouchsafes to all mankind." It was not clear why *not* being "upon his own soil" should have made any difference in the enjoyment of those natural rights, especially since Lincoln would move at once to insisting that because he possesses all the *natural* rights that any other human being possesses, he could not be stripped of them and enslaved. "I have said that I do not understand the Declaration [of Independence] to mean that all men were created equal in all respects...but I suppose that it does mean to declare that all men...are equal in their right to life, liberty, and the pursuit of happiness. Certainly...in the right to put into his mouth the bread that his own hands have earned, he is the equal of every other man, white or black."[4]

That excluded from the outset any appeal from slavery or slaveholders. Slavery was, very simply, "a gross outrage on the law of nature." It trampled upon one of the great natural rights—the right to liberty—which Jefferson had spelled out in the Declaration of Independence, and that explained why a loathing for slavery amounted to human instinct. Even if Congress was not obligated to mandate "social and political equality between whites and blacks," still "the declaration of the equality of all men" must be "kept in view, as a great fundamental principle," and that would mean a future for the territories "strongly opposed to the incorporation of slavery among its elements." If "slavery is wrong," then "like every other wrong which some men will commit if left alone, it ought to be prohibited by law," especially in "a government like ours, professedly based on the equality of men."[5]

There are two further things to notice about Lincoln's handling of equality. While natural equality need not translate logically into *civil* or *social* equality, no one missed the likelihood that the distance between the two would logically, in the course of time, shrink. This was something Stephen Douglas, who may have been right about nothing else, saw with unerring clarity. "Lincoln maintains there that the Declaration of Independence asserts that the negro is equal to the white man," Douglas complained. That was only a step away from "negro citizenship, which, when allowed, puts the negro on an equality under the law." No one should be fooled by Lincoln's distinctions between natural and civil rights, Douglas insisted; grant Lincoln the first, and the second would come inevitably, and soon. So, Douglas roared, to the approval of his backers, "if you desire negro citizenship...then support Mr. Lincoln and the Black Republican party, who are in favor of the citizenship of the negro." Didn't Lincoln insist that "the Declaration of Independence asserts that the negro is equal to the white man, and that under Divine law"? After all, Douglas asked wickedly, "How can you deprive a negro of that equality which God and the Declaration of Independence awards to him?" Good lawyer, Douglas knew what the answer to his own question must be.[6]

There was even more practical slipperiness in Lincoln's idea of equality when it became an economic affair. However much democracy was defined by certain political features, equality of opportunities should be non-negotiable in the formation of a democracy, and on no point did he verge more closely on race equality than when it came to the unfettered opportunity to "toil, work and earn bread." He was convinced "by natural theology, apart from revelation" that "every man, black, white or yellow, has a mouth to be fed and two hands with which to feed it—and that bread should be allowed to go to that mouth without controversy." This was "the design of the Creator," drawn from "the deeps of natural theology," a system in which "every man" was to "have the chance" to "better his condition," to "look forward and hope to be a hired laborer this year and the next, work for himself afterward, and finally to hire men to work for him"—and, he interjected, "I believe a black man is entitled to it" as well.[7]

There need be no conflict between black and white in an environment of economic freedom. *Slave* labor might drive out free labor, but *black* labor had no such downwards tendency on white labor, so long as it was free. Free laborers competed simply as free individuals, with no advantage or disadvantage accruing to race, whereas slavery organized workers in labor gangs that enjoyed substantial economies of scale in competition with free individuals. "There is a falsehood," he maintained (and maintained much too confidently, as the ensuing century would demonstrate), in claiming that "the white man must enslave the negro or the negro must enslave the white"—because "there is no such struggle."

> *The idea that there was a conflict between the two races, or that the freedom of the white man was insecure unless the negro was reduced to a state of abject slavery, was false and that as long as his tongue could utter a word he would combat that infamous idea. There was room for all races, and as there was no conflict so there was no necessity of getting up an excitement in relation to it.*

In this world, the "good earth is plenty broad enough for white man and negro both, and there is no need of either pushing the other off." It was exactly this ineluctable triumph of a free-labor economy, hand in hand with the natural-law principles of the Declaration, which assured him of the eventual disappearance of slavery. "The time will come, and must come," he told the Hungarian freedom fighter Julian Kune (who had taken on the "hazardous" job of campaigning for Lincoln in southern Illinois in 1860), "when there will not be a single slave within the borders of this country." Far better, then, to "discard all this quibbling about...this race and that race and the other race being inferior, and therefore they must be placed in an inferior position."[8]

When his legal understanding of the slavery crisis and his economic gradualism are taken into the reckoning, they go some distance toward explaining why Lincoln manifested so little energy in demanding, like the outright abolitionists, the immediate and unconditional ending of slavery. "Gradual can be made better than immediate for both black and white," and so long as "neither the General Government, nor any other power outside of the slave states, can constitutionally or rightfully interfere with slaves or slavery where it already exists," there was no point to the abolitionist campaign.[9]

So long as slavery's expansion "shall be fairly headed off," Lincoln believed that the "conflict" over slavery "could have but one ending," and that was its extinction. But he was more inclined to think its death would take till the end of the century. (Believing that "there were plenty of people then living who would see the end of human slavery" was surely little consolation for those who would be condemned to stay enslaved till then; on the other hand, the example of gradual emancipation plans in the Northern states fifty years before had been that, once the first moves toward emancipation had been made, the process speeded up of its own urgency.) Until that moment, it was the "paramount duty of us in the free states, due to the Union of the states, and perhaps to liberty itself (paradox though it may seem) to let the slavery of the other states alone." That did not mean doing nothing. "On the other hand, I hold it to be equally clear, that we should never knowingly lend ourselves directly or indirectly, to prevent that slavery from dying a natural death—to find new places for it to live in, when it can no longer exist in the old."[10]

Yet, the doing-nothing was passive. He saw no good result

in active resistance, and contented self-satisfaction guided much of Lincoln's lack of aggressive opposition to slavery in the 1830s and 1840s. Slavery's death needed no more particular prodding from him than from any other anti-slavery Whig: "For that reason, it had been a minor question with me." All of that collapsed on him, as it did for so many others, with the passage of the Kansas-Nebraska bill in 1854, which cast aside the restraints on the expansion of slavery in the Missouri Compromise and opened the vast swath of the old Louisiana Purchase to legalized slavery on Stephen Douglas's "popular sovereignty" basis.[11]

Lincoln's new program was still not abolitionism. In the run-up to his election to the presidency, he affirmed that "we of the North certainly have no desire and never had to invade the South," and once in Washington, he assured Charles Morehead that he was even "willing to give a constitutional guarantee that slavery should not be molested in any way directly or indirectly in the States," an offer Lincoln repeated in his inaugural address. But in so saying, Lincoln was merely offering to the slaveholding states the protection of the same constitutional firewall between federal and state authority they had always enjoyed; they showed how little they trusted that firewall—and his likely intentions for slavery—by seceding anyway and triggering a civil war. They were right. Within six months of his inauguration, Lincoln had devised a federal buy-out plan for the four slave states that had not joined the Southern Confederacy—Kentucky, Maryland, Delaware, and Missouri—which dodged the firewall by inducing the state legislatures to act on their own, and "which should work the extinction of slavery in twenty years."

Even so, Lincoln's ultimate goal in managing the war was still not abolition, but the survival of democratic government itself, "whether a Representative republic, extended and aggrandized so much as to be safe against foreign enemies can save itself from the dangers of domestic faction." When *New-York Tribune* editor Horace Greeley chided him in 1862 for not pressing more vigorously to adopt an emancipation policy, Lincoln replied that his overall goal in the war was to "save the Union." If emancipating all the slaves—or some of them, or even none of them—would advance "the cause" of reunion, he would do that. But reunification was the primary goal, and whatever policy he adopted toward slavery had to be secondary to achieving that goal.[12]

For just that reason, Lincoln's reply to Greeley has appeared over and over again as prima facie evidence that Lincoln had no more interest in ending slavery than he had in intervening in France's invasion and occupation of Mexico in 1862, or, years before, in guaranteeing an independent Hungary for Lajos Kossuth. Fine talk, yes, but no real action, much less moral urgency over racial justice. What the criticism misses is that no president before Lincoln would have dared to suggest that he would consider *any* form of emancipation as a part of *any* national policy to preserve the American union or any form of democratic government. It was, ironically, exactly a war for the Union which offered him the opening a president would never have otherwise had available, and that was the "war power" that presumably inhered in his constitutional title of "commander in chief." A civilian president had no more authority to change state laws on slavery than to walk on water, and a federal judiciary at whose head sat Roger Taney would be only too pleased and too swift to remind him of it. But as a constitutional commander in chief, the rules changed (and so long as habeas corpus was in suspension, there was little the federal courts could do to change them back), and opened up an unexplored vista of "necessity" that he could explore for the first time. And it was on the strength of "military necessity" that, on September 22,

1862, he released his Emancipation Proclamation, declaring the slaves of the rebel states to be "thenceforward, and forever free," and signed it into law on January 1, 1863.

The Proclamation was not his ideal path to ending slavery. He told Greeley in the spring of 1862 that his preferred strategy had always involved "three main features—gradual—compensation—and vote of the people" (which is to say, buying out the slaveowners, creating a timetable based on age so that the elderly and the under-aged could not be thrown out of doors by their infuriated owners, and state legislative action to head off any constitutional challenges slaveowners might try to make in the federal courts). In this way, Lincoln hoped to find a means "by which the two races could gradually live themselves out of their old relation to each other, and both come out better prepared for the new." The attraction of gradualism lay, for Lincoln, mostly in producing "less confusion, and destitution." Significantly, he added that "education for young blacks should be included in the plan." Education, whether anyone noticed it or not, was an imperative for *citizens;* it was one of the limited list of priorities he believed that government was expected to undertake. So, even while he talked gradualism, he was at the same moment looking for a democratic, not a Jim Crow, future.[13]

One way to avoid Jim Crow would be to send Jim himself someplace else, and Lincoln has been severely faulted for trying to solve any problem a newly free black population might create for white Americans by deporting the freed people, to Central America, the Caribbean, or West Africa. He might deplore "quibbling" about race, but he then turned to quibbling himself and conceding that "what I would most desire would be the separation of the white and black races." His State of the Union message (although the president's "annual message to Congress" was not actually called the "State of the Union" until 1934) to the first regular session of Congress in his presidency recommended appropriations for colonization, and in 1862 his secretary of the interior, Caleb Blood Smith, submitted a plan for "the Transportation, Settlement, and Colonization of Persons of the African Race" to Central America for Congressional approval.[14]

It did not seem to occur to Lincoln that this would, in effect, punish African Americans for seeking freedom, in this case by expelling them from their country. But he then proceeded to aggravate the situation in August 1862, by summoning a delegation of Washington's African American clergy—all of them dissenters from colonization—for a less-than-subtle exhortation to join him in promoting a colonization scheme to someplace where they would find no difficulty in granting themselves the civil and political rights denied them in white America. "Your race are suffering, in my judgment, the greatest wrong inflicted on any people," Lincoln candidly admitted.[15] But even if slavery were to disappear, the sufferings inflicted by racism would not. "It is a fact, about which we all think and feel alike, I and you," he explained to the clergymen. "It is better for us both, therefore, to be separated." Lincoln could not argue with the determination "some of you" have to "remain within reach of the country of your nativity." But he would be the first to acknowledge that it was the land, and not the people, to which they owed loyalty. "I do not know how much attachment you may have toward our race. It does not strike me that you have the greatest reason to love them."

No other moment in Lincoln's dealings with race shows him to worse advantage. What is especially bizarre is that Lincoln was at the same time readying the release of the preliminary version of the Emancipation Proclamation (which would be announced a month later). That Lincoln expected colonization to play in tandem with a larger agenda of emancipation seems to argue for a sort of political schizophrenia. What may be the key to this harangue was the "tendency" Lincoln expected colonization would impart "to the ultimate emancipation of the slaves."

Lincoln, like his idol Henry Clay and most of the Whig Party, endorsed "colonization" largely as a strategy for inducing white Americans to acquiesce in the erasure of slavery. In his mind, anti-slavery people favored resettling slaves in Liberia ("their own native land"), while pro-slavery people favored selling slaves to Kansas. "The separation of the races" was the easiest way to make ending slavery palatable to white American society, and "such separation ... must be effected by colonization," especially since those who hated emancipation pure and simple also hated colonization as a trick to persuade the wavering. The obstreperous Dennis Mahony not only assaulted the prospect of emancipation, but the idea that colonization should go along with it. "I am opposed to paying for the colonization of these slaves" fully as much as he was opposed to "suffering them to run loose in the Northern States," and Mahony was suspicious from the start that "no statesman of ordinary common sense would think seriously of getting rid of the black race in that way."[16]

But also Mahony knew that colonization was an argument with more than a little persuasive glitter for anti-emancipationists. In March 1862, Tammany Hall Democrats denounced "abolition rebels who seek rule or ruin in their blind zeal for the negro's welfare." They "are opposed to emancipating negro slaves, unless on some plan of colonization, in order that they may not come in contact with the white man's labor." If a public display of colonization sugar-coating was what was required to make the emancipation pill go down, Lincoln had no objections to such a display. And *display* seems to have been the important word. The English observer Frederick Milnes Edge chuckled over the "mis-construction" put on colonization by Europeans: "This was adopted to silence the weak-nerved, whose name is legion." Henry McNeal Turner assured readers of the African Methodist Episcopal Church weekly newspaper, *The Christian Recorder*, that, based on his own interview with Lincoln, talk about colonization is "a strategic move upon his part in contemplation of this emancipatory proclamation... a preparatory nucleus around which he intended to cluster the rain of objections while the proclamation went forth."

In the event, Lincoln took only one unenthusiastic step in the direction of creating a free-black American colony, sponsoring the settlement of 453 volunteers from the crowded "contraband" camps around Fortress Monroe to Haiti's deserted Île-à-Vache. The settlement lasted eight months, until Lincoln recalled the experiment in February 1864, and washed his hands of all further plans for colonization. John Hay believed that Lincoln "has sloughed off" the "hideous & barbarous humbug," and Congress repealed the legislation it had adopted supporting the plan.[17]

Ultimately, the greatest obstacle in the way of colonization was the simple fact of the black soldier, who had been freed and enlisted to fight in the Union army by the Emancipation Proclamation. A democracy cannot ask people to make the sacrifices of citizens without making them citizens, and Lincoln could not ask those who had fought to save the Union to leave it. "When you put a gun in his hands," Lincoln remarked to Josiah Grinnell, "it prophesies something more: it foretells that he is to have the full enjoyment of his liberty and manhood." Nor was Lincoln shy about telling these soldiers how to use their weapons. "Although you have been deprived of your God-given rights by your so-called masters," Lincoln told the black volunteers of the 29th Connecticut in 1865, "take the sword and the bayonet and teach them that you are; for God created all men free, giving to each the same rights of life, liberty and the pursuit of happiness."

Even before the colonization "humbug" had exhausted itself, Lincoln was nudging the governors of reconstructed Southern states to include voting rights for blacks as part of their new state constitutions. In the fall of 1864, he sent one of his White House staff, William O. Stoddard, to occupied Arkansas as the new U.S. marshal, and instructed him to "do all you can, in any and every way you can, to get the ballot into the hands of the freedmen!" Even more remarkably, he was willing to talk to black people about it: breaking precedent with every previous president, Lincoln welcomed a stream of black visitors to the White House. The cutting edge of American black leadership—Abraham Galloway, Martin Delany, Sojourner Truth, and Frederick Douglass— moved through Lincoln's office without let or hindrance, and in 1864, black missionary and fraternal organizations were even authorized to hold fundraising picnics on the White House lawn.[18]

Douglass was particularly surprised at Lincoln's openness, telling the American Anti-Slavery Society's convention in Philadelphia in December 1863 that Lincoln's greeting at the White House was how "you have seen one gentleman receive another. . . . I tell you I felt big there." Lincoln was "the first great man that I talked with in the United States freely, who in no single instance reminded me of the difference between himself and myself, of the difference of color, and I thought that all the more remarkable because he came from a State where there were black laws." John Eaton met Douglass at the home of "a wealthy colored man" of Washington shortly after Douglass's first meeting with Lincoln, and listened to Douglass "in a state of extreme agitation" exclaim that Lincoln "treated me as a man; he did not let me feel for a moment that there was a difference in the color of our skins!"

Douglass was not the only one to be thus surprised. Sojourner Truth, who was introduced to Lincoln at the White House in the fall of 1864, said, "I never was treated with more kindness and cordiality than were shown to me by that great and good man, Abraham Lincoln." "The President," wrote the French emissary Charles-Adolphe Pineton, the marquis de Chambrun, with a hint of amazement in March 1865, was "blinded by no prejudices against race or color," a freedom which Horace White echoed when he claimed that Lincoln "paid the same deference" to everyone and "never gave himself any airs of superiority over anybody, old or young, white or black." When the English-born Richard Hinton, representing the Haitian republic, interviewed Lincoln before his inauguration about diplomatic recognition for Haiti, Hinton was relieved that Lincoln "showed how little the prejudice against color affected his own conclusions."[19]

If it is necessary to give Lincoln some kind of grade on the score of racism, perhaps our simplest response is to remember the various shapes racism can take. If we are testing Lincoln on racism as *dishonor,* there are both large pluses (his one-on-one interactions with black Americans) and large minuses (his condescension, his vocabulary, and even strange enthusiasm for minstrelsy); if the test is *enmity,* the pluses are substantially larger. He tolerated social and institutional racism without demurrer, but then destroyed the single most racist institution in American history. His long indifference to black civil equality weighs heavily against him. But that indifference is not unmixed with a certain candor about the unfairness of inequality. Lincoln frankly admitted to the black ministers in August 1862, "The aspiration of men is to enjoy equality with the best when free, but on this broad continent, not a single man of your race is made the equal of a single man of ours."[20] And his underlying commitment to democracy, which made him oppose slavery from the start, as well as to natural rights, positioned him at a point strategically closer to black equality than even he was willing to admit, and which finally led him to equality's borders just as his life was cut short. Democracy, after all, is not about perfection. He can be judged too passive and acquiescent in the racism all around him. But that is another matter entirely from describing Lincoln as a racist himself. Lincoln may not have been an abolitionist *per se*, but, as he admitted to John Roll, he was "mighty near one." And in Douglass's estimate, he was "emphatically the black man's president."[21]

Racial distinctions should, by their very nature, be matters of indifference in a democracy. Democracy is the regime of reason and law, not unreason and passion, and race is no more a reasonable consideration in understanding either the natural rights that inhere in all human beings or the civil rights that define democratic laws than the color of one's hair or the length of one's inseam. And yet we are still within living memory of the last edition of the Green Book. Ironically, it was the most signal triumph of the American democracy that it found a way successfully to defuse what had been the single greatest obstacle to any form of equality in the preceding three hundred years, and that was religion, and so successfully that its success is now hardly noticed. Race has proven a harder and more unpredictable problem for democracy, and has demanded more confrontational and less democratic ways of dealing with it. Yet, who would suggest this as a solution to histories of religious discrimination in democracies? And let us not fool ourselves into thinking that religious discrimination has been any less toxic, or dismissing it as being of no importance to democratic societies. Can a democracy survive its departures from its ideals by imposing equal but opposite departures? And how many such departures can there be before the shadow of anarchy arises?

If Lincoln holds out to us anything instructive about liberal democracy, it is that liberal democracy can wear away even the irrationality of race. James Oakes has said that Lincoln was not (as he is sometimes understood to be) an emancipator who was restrained by his limited thinking on race, but a limited thinker on race whose limitations were overthrown by his passion for emancipation.[22] Lincoln had to reject race as a denominator in a liberal democracy because he had to make straight the path for self-transformation. He could not withhold that from anyone else without denying how it had worked for him.

He would not be a slave, *because* he would not be a master. Except of himself.

Chapter Nine

Democracy's Deficits

As pessimistic as modern writers about democracy can seem, they almost always, at some point, push back the clouds of popular misbehavior in democratic politics to reveal what can only sound like a peculiarly toothless optimism. Remove the temptations and irritations of the moment, they say, and liberal democracy will permit citizens to sort matters out and "reach mutually acceptable decisions." This is because (they say again) there is no fixed truth, and once people are willing to admit this, they learn that they can easily get along with each other. In the words of the famed Austrian jurist Hans Kelsen, "there is no such thing as an objectively ascertainable common good," and therefore democracy is simply a "procedure by which a social order is created." Justice, Kelsen added, "can be only a knowledge of relative justice," and so no one needs to raise their voice in an insistent way. The most influential liberal thinker of our times, John Rawls, believed that it was one of the jewels in democracy's crown that it promotes a "reasonable pluralism" which assumes that all can "affirm" a set of basic and common political conclusions "and join an overlapping consensus."[1]

But it is not clear that even the best of democracies can

count on disagreement always being held within the bounds of mutual political forbearance or producing untroubled outcomes. The American democracy has not managed to dispose either readily or easily of a number of disturbing demands within its boundaries. What it has demanded at those moments is a sense of motion toward moral resolution (rather than the immobility of Rawls's consensus), which may be the real core of democratic purpose.

Lincoln was not a moral purist, seeking to anathematize anyone who disagreed with every jot-and-tittle of his convictions. But he was also not a Rawlsian liberal. Natural law tethers democracy to certain conclusions toward which it aspires, and Lincoln certainly did not regard pro-slavery and anti-slavery arguments as being equally amenable to "consensus." There would always be a realm of everyday issues which could be settled by simple deliberation and statute; but there was also a core of non-negotiable goods which reason discovered in human nature, and these did not yield themselves to exhortations for consensus. Slavery was a deliberate trampling-down of one of those goods, and for the basest of reasons, while it was a fundamental orientation toward justice that warred against it. "Slavery is founded in the selfishness of man's nature—opposition to it, in his love of justice. These principles are an eternal antagonism; and when brought into collision so fiercely, as slavery extension brings them, shocks, and throes, and convulsions must ceaselessly follow." Slavery was not a conflict that was going to be talked away. "Do you think that the nature of man will be changed?" was the question he hurled at his opponent, Stephen Douglas, or "that the same causes that produced agitation at one time will not have the same effect at another?" That was why, in his most risky political utterance, he was willing to say that "this government cannot endure, permanently half slave and half free." On questions like slavery, there was no room for Kelsen's "relative" justice. "It will become all one thing, or all the other." However, the response given by Douglas could have been pure Kelsen, pure Rawls: the Union can stay divided because slavery is an issue everyone can decide for themselves personally and therefore don't need to argue about.[2]

In Lincoln's mind, the purpose of reason in government was to correct mistakes in public thinking, not to make concessions to them. He admired Henry Clay's talent for compromise in 1850, not because he believed that compromise was the only satisfactory democratic solution, but because he believed that an attempt to solve the slavery question by blunt political force was liable to be self-defeating, since time and space were wearing slavery away to the point of "ultimate extinction." But once the Kansas-Nebraska Act had jolted him into wakefulness of slaveholders' true intentions, then he became convinced that slavery had to be "fairly headed off" so that the route to "ultimate extinction" would remain open and inevitable.[3] Anything else would have resulted in simple moral oblivion (which is what liberal democracy's critics and enemies, from Patrick Deneen and Adrian Vermeule to Carl Schmitt and Wang Huning, have most often accused it of fostering). However much he might shun absolutist means, Lincoln still embraced some very absolutist ends.

Lincoln was not unaware of the deficits in a democracy, and the weak-willed fallback represented by Douglas's "popular sovereignty" was only the most obvious way in which democracy might show itself yielding to unthinking passion. There were plenty of everyday shortfalls as well. "A jury too frequently have at least one member, more ready to hang the panel than to hang" the guilty. He worried in 1858 that voter fraud "will introduce into the doubtful districts numbers of men who ... will swear falsely" that they are legal voters and warp an election, and even as late as 1865, he asked the army's judge advocate general, Joseph Holt, for the records of a case of ballot forgery by New York Democrats. He was fearful that democracy required habits of behavior that people simply could not sustain; that there were times when oppression could masquerade as democracy, mouth its formulas, and reduce its real operation to feebleness; that democracies might encounter crises which required sacrifices people would not make; that democracies could lapse into vengeance-seeking that would destroy them. But the worst fear, for Lincoln, was that a democracy might ignore a natural law which could not be glimpsed through the filter of "two hundred million of dollars." He was not an illusionist. "The world has never had a good definition of the word liberty," Lincoln acknowledged in 1864, "and the American people, just now, are much in want of one."[4]

Americans began the nineteenth century by swilling immense amounts of alcohol. The estimates on consumption vary per year from five and a half to fifteen gallons of hard liquor for every American. In Lincoln's youth, "the ladies of maturer years drank whiskey toddy, while the men took the whiskey straight," and the song they sang was a tipsy bowdlerization of Joseph Hopkinson's national anthem:

Hail Columbia, happy land
If you ain't drunk I will be damned.

Lincoln, however, "hated drunkenness," and an early acquaintance "never knew him to drink a drop of liquor—or get drunk." If the mobs he condemned in 1838 at the Springfield Lyceum were an illustration of how the wrong people—the passionate—gained control of a democracy, then alcohol was one explanation of how good people lost it.[5]

Almost exactly four years after the Lyceum address, Lincoln accepted an invitation to address the local chapter of the Washingtonian Temperance Society at the Second Presbyterian Church (a New Light reformer congregation) in Springfield.[6] Lincoln began his speech confident that the abolition of drunkenness would prove almost as great a monument to self-government as the Revolution. "What a noble ally this, to the cause of political freedom," Lincoln rhapsodized. "With such an aid, its march cannot fail to be on and on, till every son of earth shall drink in rich fruition, the sorrow quenching draughts of perfect liberty."

But the temperance movement's successes had come at a price. Its early advocates had been perfectionists, "Preachers, Lawyers, and hired agents" who demanded the "fanatic" price of absolute abstinence and alienated drinkers, and drunks, rather than persuading them. The genius of the Washingtonian Temperance Society was that the WTS dropped the perfectionist tactics. It treated drunkenness as a problem, not a moral catastrophe, and employed "entreaty and persuasion, diffidently addressed by erring man to an erring brother." By treating alcoholism with "rational causes," Lincoln was sure Americans would see a "stronger bondage broken; a viler slavery, manumitted; a greater tyrant deposed" than even the Revolution had achieved. "Glorious consummation!" he concludes, borrowing the salutations of *Macbeth*. "Hail fall of Fury! Reign of Reason, all hail!"[7]

Both slavery and addiction were elements that would poison a democracy. He had no doubt that the enemies of both were on the side of truth, and that ultimately both would have to be expelled. But the conquest would have to come through reason, not fury, and without any demand for a total proscription. Temperance, after all, was not an absolute moral issue (since alcohol itself was not an evil, like slavery), but a practical one (that could be made evil by recklessness). A democracy could not survive by choosing absolutist means to solve every problem. But neither could it survive by com-promising the absolutist ends demanded by other issues, in the blandly liberal expectation that freedom and deliberation would work out some peaceful resolution on their own. Who, then, was to tell the difference?[8]

A dozen years later, Lincoln had less cause to hope for the fall of fury, and the principal irritant was the Kansas-Nebraska Act of 1854. Instead of slavery gliding smoothly and patiently toward its "ultimate extinction," Stephen A. Douglas and the "popular sovereignty" principle gave slavery a new and aggressive lease on life in the western territories.[9]

By mid-summer of 1854, Lincoln was sketching out notes on slavery and government which contained more anti-slavery vigor than anything he had previously composed. "I have ever been opposed to slavery," Lincoln claimed, although that had never been translated into serious politi-cal action because of his confidence in "ultimate extinction." But with the Kansas-Nebraska bill, "the institution was being placed on a new basis ... for making it perpetual, national and universal."

Not that everyone would see it that way at first. The genius of Stephen A. Douglas had been to use the "lullaby" of "popular sovereignty" to "tranquilize the whole country," promising that "there would be no more slavery agitation in or out of Congress, and the vexed question would be left entirely to the people of the territories." The real damage came from the implication that "popular sovereignty" *was* real democracy, that democracy had no bedrock of principle beyond the mechanics of democratic process. If a territory, declared Douglas, "wants a slave-State constitution she has a right to it ... I do not care whether it is voted down or voted up," so long as the voting was done decently and in order.[10]

Lincoln suspected another agenda was at work, and he brought those suspicions to Peoria, Illinois, on October 16, 1854, in what amounted to the greatest speech he had yet uttered. Democracy could not survive, he warned, by leaving fundamental moral issues to be decided by majority vote. Speaking from the portico of the county courthouse in Peoria, Lincoln dismissed "popular sovereignty" as "wrong; wrong in its direct effect, letting slavery into Kansas and Nebraska— and wrong in its prospective principle."[11] Lincoln had no quarrel with majority rule in every instance where simple process was relevant, but slavery was not a legitimate subject for process. It was a violation of natural law and natural right, and no majority vote, or any vote, could blur that violation. Furthermore, Lincoln argued, neatly inverting the logic of popular sovereignty, "if it is a sacred right for the people of Nebraska to take and hold slaves there," then it should be equally their right to re-open the African slave trade as well. The "future use" of Douglas's indifference argument will "be the planting of slavery wherever in the wide world, local and unorganized opposition cannot prevent it." And that, in turn, would exhibit the American experiment as a fraud. People around the world could take courage from the American democracy and hope by its example to strive for their own democracy, if slavery was simply the by-product of an earlier regime from which Americans were struggling to disentangle themselves. But not if those same Americans claimed to be an example of democracy while renewing, reinforcing, and even exporting slavery.

The real surprise of the Peoria speech was Lincoln's on-the-other-hand caution that there were, in fact, "so many really good men" supporting Douglas. "I have no prejudice," he insisted, against the slaveholding South. Slaveholders and alcoholics were alike in this respect, that they were obeying what they perceived as their self-interest, and like the Washingtonians, he could not convince himself that demonizing Southern slaveholders would accomplish anything, except rip the American democracy still further apart. Even when the ends were absolute, he remained chary of embracing absolutist means.[12]

Lincoln would, that winter, draft resolutions for amending the Kansas-Nebraska Act, but they died, stillborn. "When we were the political slaves of King George, and wanted to be free, we called the maxim that 'all men are created equal' a self evident truth," Lincoln sighed wearily to Kentucky judge George Robertson. "But now when we have grown fat, and have lost all dread of being slaves ourselves... may God, in his mercy, superintend the solution."[13]

Democracy is a government for humanity, not angels, and it has to be content to be aspirational, yet to live with the pace of aspiration. The Revolution had been a moment of greatness in human history, but it, too, left many aspirations as yet unfulfilled in 1842. "It had its evils," Lincoln said to the Washingtonians; "it breathed forth famine, swam in blood and rode on fire; and long, long after, the orphan's cry, and the widow's wail, continued to break the sad silence that ensued." No good thing ever came without a mixture of evil, and no evil could be walked away from with a tidy and small-souled sense of self-righteous purity. Even in the case of the Revolution, these mixtures "were the price, the inevitable price, paid for the blessings it bought."

There would be an inevitable price for eradicating slavery, too, but it would come in the form of a civil war which would complicate the very survival of democracy. As president, Lincoln was called upon to preside as the chief elected officer over generals who didn't know how to win, over draftees who didn't want to fight, over financiers who feared risk, over journalists who indulged in hysterical invective, and over whites who didn't want freed slaves to compete with them in the marketplace. Lincoln's staffer William O. Stoddard remembered how people "rose in anger to remind Lincoln that... they never, never told him that he might set the negroes free, and, now that he has done so... they tell him that the army will fight no more, and that the hosts of the Union will indignantly disband rather than be sacrificed upon the bloody altar of fanatical Abolitionism."[14]

Despite the disheartening circumstances of the war's first two years, Lincoln tried to appear serenely confident in ultimate victory. "I believe there was never a day," Ulysses Grant recalled, "when the president did not think that, in some way or other, a cause so just as ours would come out triumphant."[15] But there were many more moments when Lincoln's confidence ebbed to a trickle. In January 1862, he complained that the Treasury "has no money, the General of the Army has typhoid fever," and "The bottom is out of the tub. What shall I do?" After the debacle at Fredericksburg, he "walked the floor, wringing his hands" and raging that "if there was any worse hell than he had been in for two days, he would like to know it." After Chancellorsville, Lincoln ("a picture of despair... ashen in hue") could only pace the White House, moaning, "Our cause is lost."[16]

Then, at the midpoint of the war, Lincoln glimpsed something in the victories at Gettysburg (on July 3, 1863) and the surrender of Vicksburg (on July 4) which appeared almost as a sign in the heavens for the future of democracy. "How long ago is it? eighty odd years?" he asked a crowd of well-wishers who had gathered outside the White House on July 7, "since on the Fourth of July for the first time in the history of the world a nation by its representatives, assembled and declared as a self-evident truth that 'all men are created equal'"? Was there not something more than mere accident in how "on the

4th the cohorts of those who opposed the declaration that all men are created equal, 'turned tail' and run"?[17]

Four months later, delivering the dedication sentences at the creation of the Soldiers National Cemetery at Gettysburg, Lincoln refined that language to become *Fourscore and seven years ago, our fathers brought forth on this continent a new nation, conceived in liberty and dedicated to the proposition that all men are created equal.* But this time, he injected a note of caution. From the tremendous baseline of the Declaration, Americans had fumbled away democracy's promise, to the point where they had descended into *a great civil war* that raised the ominous question whether *any nation so conceived and so dedicated can long endure.* Lincoln could not dodge the terrible fact that the Civil War was a moment of failure, and so serious as to cast a shadow of doubt over the viability of democracy itself. That was clearly how observers overseas read it. "In America they saw democracy on its trial, and they saw how it failed," announced an overeager Earl of Shrewsbury in November 1861, "the result would show that the separation of the two great sections of that country was inevitable, and those who lived long enough would, in his opinion, see an aristocracy established in America."[18]

There was a sign at Gettysburg, but in his November address, that sign came, not through the coincidences of the calendar, but in the sacrifices of the soldiers—*the brave men, living and dead, who struggled here*—for *that cause which they have thus far so nobly advanced.* The Union men who fell and were buried there were not professional mercenaries, nor were they dispirited peasants, driven into battle by the whips of their betters. They were the same people whom the German poet Heinrich Heine dismissed in 1834 as "dolts" living in "that big outhouse of freedom," whom Sydney Smith sneered at for having "given no indications of genius, and made no approaches to the heroic, either in their morality or character," whom Charles Dickens attacked as "maimed and lame . . . full of sores and ulcers, foul to the eye and almost hopeless to the sense"—these had risen up and offered everything they had, present and future, *that that nation might live.*[19] They had, as one New Jersey veteran of the fighting exclaimed, "exhibited to the world the sublime spectacle of a nation of freemen determined that everyone within its borders should have that liberty which the Declaration of Independence had proclaimed to be the inalienable right of all men."[20]

Exactly for that reason, *the world will little note, nor long remember what we say here, but it can never forget what they did here.* And in that never-forgetting, he glimpsed something all Americans could borrow: a renewed enthusiasm for *that cause for which they gave the last full measure of devotion,* for *government of the people* (that vital spark of consent), *by the people* (that giddy involvement in election after election), *for the people* (that essential focus on the welfare of the people themselves, not the self-service of aristocrats or bureaucrats or plutocrats).

Civil war "environed" Lincoln "with difficulties." Yet, he counted them as straw compared to the price being paid "upon the battle field" by those who "are endeavoring to purchase with their blood and their lives the future happiness and prosperity of this country." *From these honored dead* there could arise *increased devotion* to the original vision of the American democracy, and the result would be *a new birth of freedom,* a renewal like the "new birth" of the revival preachers. Not some curious new departure, as though democracy had indeed (as the Earl of Shrewsbury believed) betrayed its shortcomings and required an entirely different departure, but a revitalization of the original purpose of the American Founding that would, as Lincoln said in 1858, "turn this government back into the channel in which the framers of the Constitution originally placed it."[21]

But there remained one abiding anxiety for Lincoln in the last months of the war, and that was his fear that democracy might be as easily torn apart by triumph as by disaster. Demagogues feast on revenge, and the venom of revenge was exactly what Lincoln feared might, at the moment of democracy's triumph, undo all the good democracy had done against slavery and needed to do for the future. "I wish you to do nothing merely for revenge," he instructed one of his generals in the fall of 1864.[22]

No one would have been surprised if he had said something more angrily thunderous. Lincoln had not hesitated to threaten retaliations of various sorts against the Confederates for the massacre of black soldiers at Fort Pillow and the re-enslaving of black prisoners of war, and he refused to reprieve the sentence of high-seas slave trader Nathaniel Gordon to die on the scaffold in 1862. When he stood up on the east portico of the Capitol to deliver his second inaugural address on March 4, 1865, he was the survivor of a war that was now nearly won, a re-election that he had feared would be hugely lost, and political scoffers within his own party who had dismissed him. If anyone in American political history had earned the right to demand an eye for an eye and a tooth for a tooth on the day of his triumphant second inauguration, Abraham Lincoln had.[23]

His guiding rule, however, was that "blood can not restore blood." *I shall do nothing in malice,* he had written more than two years before, and his advice to his generals in the closing weeks of the war was that "as soon as the Rebel armies laid down their arms... they would at once be guaranteed all their rights as citizens of a common country; and that to avoid anarchy the State governments then in existence, with their civil functionaries, would be recognized by him as the government *de facto* till Congress could provide others."[24] As for the Confederate leaders, Lincoln hoped they "ought to clear out, 'escape the country,'" and so avoid a tempest of hoarse rage in the land. He wanted no part in "hanging or killing" the rebel generals and politicians, "even the worst of them," and would rather "let down the bars, scare them off" (and to illustrate this, he waved "his hands as if scaring sheep"). When he walked through the streets of the conquered Confederate capital of Richmond, it was without a particle of anger, as "if he were only a private citizen ... not as a conqueror—not with bitterness in his heart, but with kindness." It was as though he was tempting some unbalanced Richmonder to ambush him and to prove him wrong—and after failing to do him violence, prove to the victors that he was right not to demand pounds upon pounds of retributive flesh.[25]

The weather on that inauguration morning had been overcast and rainy, but as he took the oath and delivered his inaugural address, the clouds suddenly thinned, a glorious column of light descended on the Capitol portico, and there was "a tremendous outburst of enthusiastic cheers" from the "thirty to forty thousand persons" present. The "brief address" was surprisingly short—only 662 words, far shorter than his first inaugural four years previously—and the section devoted to reviewing the carnage of four years of civil war was marvelously brief. "Each looked for an easier triumph and a result less fundamental and astounding." Each side had even prayed "to the same God" and "invoke[d] His aid against the other." He had been toying with these ideas for a year, and in almost the same words in a short speech in Baltimore. And if he had stopped there, Lincoln's observation might have seemed merely ironic, and offered "no information as to his future policy."[26]

But those words were the pivot on which Lincoln turned

to a far larger question. Both North and South, Union and Confederate, abolitionist and slaveholder had had opposing expectations and made opposing demands of God. And both were wrong. In one long sentence, he inverted the triumphalism that could have exalted one side beyond reason and inflamed the other beyond hope. "If" (and he was careful to pose what was coming as a hypothetical, even when he clearly intended it as a sober statement of the truth) "we shall suppose that American slavery is one of those offenses which in the providence of God must needs come" and if we teach ourselves to realize that God, in his mysterious providence, has given "to both North and South this terrible war as the woe due to those by whom the offense came," will we not understand the purpose of the war in its deepest moral sense?

Saying this would be of no consolation whatsoever to the triumphalists, and would probably enrage them. He let it. As uncompromising as he must be about slavery as a violation of natural law, he was the greatest of compromisers when it came to the weaknesses and foibles of natural law's violators. The problem with the triumphalists was not that they were in error, but that they were not triumphal enough— they did not include themselves. The fact was that both North *and* South had been complicit in slavery, and the war was the price both paid for that complicity, and that fact had to mean something about the divine purpose. If suffering in the South meant God's judgment, could it mean less for the North? Upright Northern souls might rise up in dismay and declare that any suggestion that they, too, were under divine judgment was offensive. Wasn't this calling, not sinners, but the righteous to repentance? But Lincoln countered: had not Northerners imbrued their hands in the slave trade? Had not Northerners turned a blind eye to Southern accounts in their banks, and Southern shipments in their steamers? Shall we not see that God judges every sin? "Shall we discern therein any departure from those divine attributes which the believers in a Living God always ascribe to Him?" Obviously not.[27]

This was not Rawlsian relativism. He was inviting, not the descent of a veil of ignorance about the right or wrong of slavery, but a pure confession of guilt from the limited, stumbling, blind, and wrong-headed folly of all parties. It is from this silencing realization—that *all* Americans had been invested in the evils of slavery, that *all* had suffered in the war that ended it—that Lincoln could hope for a democracy that rose above the giddiness of venom. "With malice toward none" (because, in the long view of divine providence, no one ever acts independently of the will of God, and therefore no one must be burdened more than others with the consequences of that providence) and "with charity for all" (because the human spirit that embodies natural right must reach out with one hand to the God who created it and with the other to its neighbor), let the American democracy finish the work of dedication Lincoln had described at Gettysburg, "to bind up the nation's wounds, to care for him who shall have borne the battle and for his widow and his orphan— to do all which may achieve and cherish a just and lasting peace among ourselves and with all nations."[28] There was no question that slavery was beyond some "consensus"; but that did not mean that its human perpetrators were beyond forgiveness.

The vengeance-mongers were not amused by Lincoln's "short moral lecture." They "were openly hostile to Mr. Lincoln's scheme," and Benjamin Wade frankly urged the hanging of "ten or twelve" of the Confederate leadership, or even "make it thirteen, just a baker's dozen." But they were not at the helm of the government, while Lincoln was willing to bring American democracy to some surprising conclusions, especially about justice and mercy, and without cheapening the meaning of either of those words. "Men are not flattered by being shown that there has been a difference of purpose between the Almighty and them," Lincoln replied to Thurlow Weed, who had written to compliment him. But "it is a truth which I thought needed to be told; and as whatever of humiliation there is in it, falls most directly on myself, I thought others might afford for me to tell it."[29]

He had helped abolish slavery; it was now time to lay aside mastership as well.

What If Lincoln Had Lived?

The round, lead .41-caliber bullet which John Wilkes Booth fired into the head of Abraham Lincoln on the night of April 14, 1865, was the most lethal gunshot in American history. Lincoln's vice president, Andrew Johnson, took the presidential oath within hours of Lincoln's death. But Johnson had none of Lincoln's political skills, much less Lincoln's notions of a future for the four million slaves whom the Civil War had freed. A Tennessean who had remained loyal to the Union, Johnson saw his mission only in terms of punishing the Confederate elites whom he despised. He had no similar animosity toward the larger body of poor whites (whom he described as "poor, quiet, unoffending, harmless"), and no brief for the freed slaves.

Defeated Southerners soon turned from despairing submission to arrogant defiance. Christopher Memminger, the former Confederate secretary of the treasury, said that Johnson "held up before us the hope of a 'white man's government,' and this led us to set aside negro suffrage…It was natural that we should yield to our old prejudices." By the time Johnson left office in 1869, the pace of Reconstruction was already faltering, and Johnson had become so despised that he barely survived an impeachment. The victorious North sank down into Reconstruction fatigue, while the former Confederates simply substituted Jim Crow for slavery.[1]

Would it have been different if Booth's bullet had missed? Having guided the nation through a wartime valley of shadows, could Lincoln have found the path to a new height upon which the American democracy could stand?

Lincoln never laid out a final, definitive plan for Reconstruction. In his last public speech on April 11, 1865, Lincoln hinted broadly that he had "some new announcement" to make "to the people of the South" about Reconstruction, which would include voting rights for the freedmen. But Lincoln had nothing more specific than that to offer as yet; if anything, he was trying as hard as he could *not* to be too specific. "So great peculiarities pertain to each state," he warned, "and such important and sudden changes occur in the same state; and, withal, so new and unprecedented is the whole case, that no exclusive, and inflexible plan can safely be prescribed as to details and colatterals. Such exclusive, and inflexible plan, would surely become a new entanglement."[2]

Still, there is no question that nags more often at American memory than *what if Lincoln had lived?* And there are at least four paths to reconstructing the Union which it seems likely Lincoln would have pursued, starting with voting rights. If there was any emotional guiding star in Lincoln's life, it was loyalty, and it was that admiration of loyalty in the black soldier more than anything else which persuaded Lincoln that there was no real alternative, especially for those blacks who had worn the Union blue, but to reward that service with voting rights. "Why should they do any thing for us, if we will do nothing for them?" Lincoln asked in his letter to James Conkling in September 1863. By January of 1864, Lincoln had come to see this as the condition of any peace terms. If the Confederates wanted amnesty, Lincoln could not "avoid exacting in return universal suffrage, or, at least, suffrage on the basis of intelligence and military service."[3]

There was also a practical political motive in promoting black voting rights, since only the voting power of the newly freed slaves could offset the political dominance of unbowed whites in the South. Purely on numbers alone, the freedmen could (promised Frederick Douglass) "raise up a party in the Southern States among the poor," and establish a long-term Republican political hegemony in the formerly Democratic South. "Give the negro the elective franchise," said Douglass, "and you at once...wheel the Southern States into line with national interests and national objects."[4] Had Lincoln lived, both his own sense of fairness and the political needs of his own administration would have made black voting rights an imperative they never were for Andrew Johnson.

But voting rights detached from economic leverage often drift away into nothingness. Economic independence is what gives heft to political aspiration, something Lincoln understood from his own struggle to rise from poverty. One aspect of economic integration would be education—"giving the benefit of public schools equally to black and white"—which in his last speech, he raised to a level equal in importance to that of voting. "Free labor insists on universal education," and he looked forward to a day "for the profitable and agreeable combination of labor with cultivated thought."

But in Lincoln's world, economic opportunity was also tied overwhelmingly to the ownership of land, and the newly freed slaves owned none. The most direct means for redressing this imbalance lay in the Bureau of Refugees, Freedmen and Abandoned Lands (known simply as the Freedmen's Bureau) which was launched on March 3, 1865, with a mandate to claim land which had been abandoned by plantation owners, or which had been forfeited by non-payment of taxes during the war, and divide it up into forty-acre plots for ex-slaves to farm as their own. This redistribution was bound to be challenged in the postwar courts (as indeed wartime property confiscations were, in a series of cases before the Supreme Court). But especially in South Carolina and Georgia, the land already being farmed by freed slaves on their own initiative was substantial, and if the white owners of such lands had taken themselves into exile under threat of prosecution for treason, they would be in a poor position to contest the transfer of title, especially if it was helped along by some adroit legislative action in Congress.[5]

Lincoln, in his career as an attorney for the Illinois Central Railroad, had no qualms about asserting the primacy of occupancy in ownership. "In equal right, better is the condition of him in possession," he wrote in a legal opinion in 1856, and if the lands had been vacated by slaveowners, there was no one better to put in ownership than the ex-slaves who had once worked them. Labor, once again, had precedence over capital, and capital of their own, in turn, would be created by their labor. To encourage "persons, formerly held as slaves, to labor as freedmen in insurrectionary states" and "become self-supporting," Lincoln ordered his generals to "suspend" any attempts to "interfere with the transportation of supplies to, or products from, any plantation worked by free labor," and those who dragged their heels in observing this "will be deemed guilty of a military offence and punished accordingly."[6]

The difference here between Lincoln and Andrew Johnson is stark. Johnson could not imagine a world in which ownership-in-fact had any appeal against ownership-in-law, even if the law had now been circumscribed by abandonment and treason. When he issued a preliminary Reconstruction plan on May 29, 1865, Johnson offered amnesty "to all persons who have, directly or indirectly, participated in the existing rebellion," except for a small class of Confederate leaders, "with restoration of all rights of property, except as to slaves." No compensatory concession on black voting rights was demanded, or even mentioned.[7] This effectively pulled both the political and the economic rugs from under the freed slaves, allowed newly reconstituted Southern state legislatures to pass "Black Codes" that sharply circumscribed blacks' economic liberty, and threw them onto the untender mercies of their former owners as agricultural workers, sharecroppers, and menials. As a result, land ownership by blacks lagged far behind that of whites in the postwar decades, and only a determined push by the federal government in using the federal lands in the West privatized by the Homestead Act for the resettlement of freed slaves could have changed that. From Johnson, no initiative of that sort could be expected.

Even if these moves had been frustrated in the federal courts, Lincoln might still have opened a wider path to the future simply by cleaning the white leadership slate in the former Confederate states. Lincoln may have had no wish to hunt down the Confederacy's leaders as the war ended. But he also had no wish to stop them leaving for exile. When he was asked whether federal authorities should seek the extradition of Jacob Thompson, a Confederate official and diplomat in Canada, Lincoln only said, "Well, I rather guess not. When you have an elephant on hand, and he wants to run away, better let him run." His staffer Edward D. Neill heard Lincoln sigh that he preferred to hear nothing more about Jefferson Davis, the Confederate president. "I hope he will mount a fleet horse, reach the shores of the Gulf of Mexico, and drive so far into its waters that we shall never see him again." This would clear the way for a new leadership in the South, a leadership of Unionist whites and their natural allies, the freed slaves, and it would free him from the burden of signing death warrants. Charles Sumner remembered that when one of his cabinet secretaries "insisted" that Davis "must not be spared, the Presdt said ... 'Judge not that ye be not judged,' & when still further pressed on this point, he repeated these words again." He even offered a certain measure of indulgence to them, and in 1865 authorized defeated Virginians to "allow members of the body claiming to be legislature of Virginia to meet here for purpose of recalling Virginia soldiers from rebel armies, with safe conduct to them, so long as they do and say nothing hostile to the United States." But his indulgence had its limits. When the Virginians proposed to function as though they were the legitimate "Legislature of Virginia" on "the assumption that I was recognizing them as a rightful body," Lincoln cancelled the authorization.[8]

Andrew Johnson's pardon policies, however, had a very different effect. The Georgia legislature elected as its two new senators Alexander Stephens, the former Confederate vice president, and Herschel V. Johnson, a former Confederate congressman; in the House of Representatives, thirteen Confederate generals arrived to represent the supposedly reconstructed Southern states. Not surprisingly, this attempted restoration of white power was attended by an upsurge of mob violence against the freed slaves, much of it organized and led by former Confederate officers and politicians. "You have doubtless heard a great deal of the Reconstructed South, of their acceptance of the results of the war," wrote a Freedmen's Bureau agent in South Carolina. "This may all be true, but if a man ... had the list of Negroes murdered in a single county in this most loyal and Christian state, he would think it a strange way of demonstrating his kindly feelings toward them."[9]

Appalled at the barefaced conceit of electing to Congress men who had only months before been trying to destroy the government, Republicans in Congress refused to seat the quondam rebels, and instead passed legislation which returned the Southern states to military occupation. But they did so at the price of a fearful political contest with Andrew Johnson which allowed disgruntled Southerners to realize that they could play the ends off against the middle to their advantage. Trying to outmaneuver Johnson, Congress resorted to the cumbersome mechanism of amending the Constitution, not once but twice (in the 14th and 15th Amendments) to prevent a white restoration in the South. But the Supreme Court bent over backwards to limit the application of the amendments, and so the restoration happened anyway.

The speed with which this restoration of white racial supremacy occurred in the former Confederacy is a reminder that, even if Lincoln *had* lived to finish out his second term *and* put an active presidential shoulder to black voting rights, to black economic integration, and to the scattering of the old Confederate leadership, the results might not have been hugely different from what they were. Lincoln would still have faced stiff opposition, as much from the Northern Democrats as from their quondam allies in the white South.[10] Similarly, Lincoln could scarcely have guaranteed the operation of any "practical system" of racial reunion without an ongoing military presence in the South to enforce it. "Any man of Northern opinions must use much circumspection of language" while touring the South, wrote Sidney Andrews, who did in fact tour the defeated Confederacy for the *Atlantic Monthly* in 1865. "In many counties of South Carolina and Georgia, the life of an avowed Northern radical would hardly be worth a straw but for the presence of the military."[11] Yet, Americans were chronically unwilling, in times of peace, to foot large military budgets, and in 1865 the soldiers themselves were mostly civilians in uniform who wanted nothing more than to go home at war's end. Above all, Lincoln would have occupied the Executive Mansion only until 1869, which is not a long time to implement the vast programs his version of Reconstruction would have required. In the end, not even Abraham Lincoln might have been able to wrench success out of Reconstruction.

And yet, it is hard to imagine how we could have done worse. "Had Mr. Lincoln lived," said Frederick Douglass in December 1865, "the negro of the South would have more than a hope of enfranchisement and no rebels would hold the reins of government in any one of the rebellious states."[12] Even Lincoln hoped so. Only days before his death, a jubilant Lincoln told New Jersey politician James Scovel that "if God gives me four years more to rule this country, I believe it will become what it ought to be... no longer one vast plantation for breeding human beings for the purpose of lust and bondage, but it will become a new valley of Jehosaphat, where all nations of the earth will assemble together under one flag worshipping the common God, and they will celebrate the resurrection of human freedom." We can only say *perhaps.*

It must seem uncanny that so many of our current frustrations with democracy were actually encountered by Abraham Lincoln more than a century and a half ago. He, too, had to absorb complaints that he was using the presidential office to subvert civil and constitutional liberties. He, too, endured a political environment polarized between extremes that had little hope of reconciliation. Uncanny, yes, but also comforting that these frustrations are not novelties, however much they feel like them, and that the American democracy has endured, risen, and surmounted them once, and will do so again.

Perhaps the most lasting lesson here is that democracies worry too much and too little. "Democracies are not good at recognizing crisis situations," says David Runciman, because "all the surface noise of democratic politics makes them insensitive to genuine turning points." Just as often as democracies predict doom, they rejoice in reprieves, and then fail to recognize the real crises when they materialize. Even Lincoln failed to recognize the likelihood of war in 1861, despite the secession of seven Southern states in the weeks after his election. "There will be no war, no violence," he claimed in 1858, and was still claiming that to the throngs that gathered along his journey to inauguration in 1861. "There is really no crisis except an artificial one!" Democracies tend to wait until a situation gets completely out of hand, and only then gather their full strength for a solution, and that puts them in danger from autocracies and dictators that can strike quickly and forcefully. Yet, remarkably, they possess a resilience which allows them to spring back from catastrophes in ways totalitarians have shown over and over again that they cannot.[13]

There are, nevertheless, certain features of the democratic landscape today which Lincoln never encountered, and which pose threats for which his example yields little in the way of direction. Suzanne Mettler and Robert Lieberman, in diagnosing four historic dangers to democracy in America (starting with the Hamiltonian-Jeffersonian standoff of the 1790s and continuing through the Civil War), worry that the "executive aggrandizement" begun during the Great Depression has mushroomed into a bureaucratic nightmare at odds with the fundamentals of democracy. "The exertion of presidential power," together with the multiplication of executive agencies, the willingness of Congress to offload responsibility for governance, and the technical capacity for creating a "surveillance state," aided by "surveillance capitalism," have together allowed virtually a fourth branch of government to emerge, protected by near-permanent tenure and internal administrative law.[14]

How Lincoln might have dealt with the bureaucratic miasma that afflicts, not only the American democracy, but democracies around the world, is a mystery. In 1861, Lincoln found "the various Departments of the Government filled with unfaithful clerks and officers, whose sympathies were with the South, who had been placed in their positions for the purpose of paralyzing his administration." Gideon Welles, Lincoln's secretary of the navy, was exasperated in 1864 to discover that "a majority of the men in the [Brooklyn Navy Yard] are...opposed to the Administration," and were being sheltered by "Mr. Davidson, the Assistant Naval Constructor," who "would not dismiss, or give permission to dismiss" any anti-Lincoln employees. Lincoln's White House staffer William O. Stoddard remembered that Lincoln responded by hiring and firing federal officeholders with dizzying energy. "I doubt if ever before there was so general displacement as at the beginning of Mr. Lincoln's term." Of the 1,520 executive branch positions immediately under Lincoln's oversight, Lincoln dismissed 1,195 of their occupants, which amounted to "the most sweeping removal of federal officeholders in the country's history up to that time."[15]

In the State Department, Lincoln not only replaced the secretary and assistant secretary, but the disbursing clerk and all five territorial governors; in the Treasury Department, he appointed not only a new secretary and assistant secretary, but the 1st comptroller, treasurer, register, solicitor, chief of the Bureau of Construction, and the director, treasurer, and chief coiner of the U.S. Mint; the Interior Department also got a new secretary and assistant secretary, and also a new chief clerk, new administrators of the General Land Office, the Indian Office, and the Pension Office, the superintendent of the Census, and commissioner of public buildings. As Emanuel Hertz wrote in *The Wizardry of Lincoln's Political Appointments and Party Management,* "Lincoln never abdicated his power of appointing and filling the appointive position in his administration.... He looked into every appointment himself and no matter how low were the fortunes of war he was always ready to consider the strengthening of the party in one place or another by judicious distribution of patronage."[16]

But Lincoln only attempted to restaff the federal bureaucracy, not dismantle it. And in the decades following the Civil War, the increasing social and economic complexity of American life rendered bureaucratization inevitable. Despite all protests to the contrary, Max Weber believed that Americans would eventually create a ruling bureaucracy of "lifelong pensionable posts" filled by "university educated officials... as in Germany." And they did so by what Tocqueville had feared would be the end of all democracies, a despotism which appeared benevolently and professionally as "the mender of all ills suffered."[17] Lincoln feared the subversion of democracy by mobs; modern democracy may have more to fear from technicians, and especially technicians who do not even have to occupy public office to threaten the infrastructure of democracy.

Lincoln might have been closer to another problem, which is the increasingly problematic role of the federal judiciary in a modern democracy. In the 1830s, he had feared mobs and how easily they would overthrow "the sober judgment of Courts." Twenty years later, he had a serious taste of how readily those courts might overthrow what John Quincy Adams called "the sober judgment of the People of these United States" when Chief Justice Roger Taney wrote the infamous *Dred Scott* decision. Taney dismissed the appeal of a Missouri slave, Dred Scott, who had claimed freedom on the grounds that his master had taken him into one of the federal territories (and a free state) where slavery had been banned, thus rendering Scott a free man. Taney dismissed Scott's plea for lack of standing—Scott was black, Taney reasoned, and since blacks could not be citizens, only citizens could plead in federal courts—and then added that the federal government had no authority to ban slavery in federally owned territories.

Even before the decision was released, Lincoln anticipated that the federal judiciary would claim a unilateral authority for that opinion across the entire federal government, to "be obeyed, and enforced by all the departments." He agreed that the Court's "decisions on Constitutional questions, when fully settled, should control, not only the particular cases decided, but the general policy of the country." The uncertainty lay in what made something *settled*. In the first place, *Dred Scott* was simply "erroneous." Taney's announcement that blacks had never been, and could never be, considered citizens was contradicted by the numerous instances of states granting citizenship to free blacks, which (by the "privileges and immunities" clause of the Constitution) should guarantee national citizenship as well. What was more, *Dred Scott* "was made by a divided court—dividing differently on the different points"—and on erroneous historical evidence. On those grounds, Lincoln declared that "it is not resistance, it is not factious, it is not even disrespectful, to treat it as not having yet quite established a settled doctrine for the country." He did not propose "to disturb or resist the decision," and he would certainly "excite no mobs." But slavishly bowing to the chief justice's dictum without demurrer "would reduce us to the despotism of an oligarchy" and "the people will have ceased, to be their own rulers."[18]

This impulse of the federal courts to magnify their office was put on pause during the course of the Civil War. But once the war ended, Lincoln feared that judicial high-mightiness would re-assert itself, even over the Emancipation Proclamation. "I think it is valid in law, and will be so held by the courts," he told Stephen Hurlbut in mid-1863, but he could not be sure. "What the courts might ultimately decide was beyond his knowledge as well as beyond his control." And high-mightiness did indeed reappear, negating much of the effect of the 14th and 15th Amendments through Supreme Court decisions beginning with *The Slaughterhouse Cases* in 1873 and running up through *Plessy v. Ferguson* in 1896.

Even more in modern times, as Robert Nisbet wrote, "the Supreme Court is the single most glittering prize to be had in America for activism, reform, or revolution-seized mentality...without having to go through the channels set up and favored by the Framers." What Lincoln might have said to the Warren, Burger, Rehnquist, and Roberts Courts is a matter of guesswork, but it is not likely to have sounded like tame acquiescence. Lincoln might have considered law to be supreme and would certainly have given no approval to civil disobedience, but he would also have been unwilling to assume that courts had the authority to convert mere impulse into law.[19]

What may be a more pressing question is whether Lincoln would have been as successful a politician today as he was in his time. Lincoln was not a charismatic leader, on the pattern of Weber's "leader of conviction." He more nearly resembles Weber's other model, the "leader of principle," or even Aristotle's "great soul," and there is some uncertainty whether, in a media-mad environment, Lincoln could have prevailed. He was no manner of populist, in the Jacksonian template, since populists assume that they already know the mind of a dissatisfied people and are authorized to speak for those people without the trouble of discussion, debate, or deliberation, and to discard any obligation to others whom they dismiss as unwanteds. Lincoln cultivated a "reserve of soul" and an "economy of words and deeds," a "distance" which has disappeared from modern democratic leadership over the last century.

Lincoln was conscious that people might not think well of him, and for a variety of reasons, ranging from political theory down to his awkward, cadaverous looks. "O, who will write this ignorant man's state papers," raved one journalist after his election in 1860, and it was not for some time that he was able to embarrass the journalists into silence. But far from this generating resentment, it led Lincoln to embrace an unusual measure of humility. "I have endured a great deal of ridicule without much malice," he wrote to the actor James Hackett, "and have received a great deal of kindness, not quite free from ridicule. I am used to it." He admitted to Noah Brooks that he considered himself "a great coward physically, and was sure that he should make a poor soldier, for, unless there was something in the excitement of a battle, he was sure that he would drop his gun and run at the first symptom of danger." And Cordelia Harvey, who very nearly pestered him beyond his limits for the funding of military hospitals, was shocked by how "the President bowed his head and with a look of sadness I never can forget he said, 'I shall never be glad any more.' All severity had passed from his face. He seemed looking backward, and heartward, and for a moment to forget he was not alone, a more than mortal anguish rested on his face."[20]

In a Lincolnian future, democracy will exhibit three characteristics. First, it will recover consent. If the people are genuinely the sovereigns of a democracy, then it is they who bestow stability on it, rather than having it imposed by a self-designated oligarchy. The amassing of bureaucratic and hierarchical structure which has stiffened the joints of American politics is antithetical to a democracy, and allows "offense's gilded hand to shove by justice" (Shakespeare's phrase, but from Lincoln's favorite soliloquy). It is a consent which can only thrive by reason—by "observation, reflection, and trial"—and reason grows out of a civic education which is now, more than at any time in the past, in danger of perishing in a flood of meaningless social media and the surrender of education to credential-mongering. But when it is recovered, it is a consent which will not make the mistake of Stephen Douglas—or Thrasymachus—and imagine that consent can be untethered from "the mountain-tops where is the throne of Truth."[21]

Democracy will then be able to recover and embrace an equality in which no privileged groups claim superior sanction for power, an equality which will understand that power is not, after all, its friend. A Lincolnian democracy in particular will remember the basics of an American system that protects American industry and productivity, empowers and organizes workers and small producers, encourages the re-shoring of American productivity, and begins the perilous and unpredictable work of leveling the dangerous cliffs of class alienation. "I am glad to know that there is a system of labor where the laborer can strike if he wants to!" Lincoln said in 1860, "where they are not obliged to work under all circumstances, and are not tied down and obliged to labor whether you pay them or not!...I would to God that such a system prevailed all over the world."[22] From this equality will emerge a conscious determination to relieve poverty and suppress the plague of crime and corruption, and our history will re-emerge from its neglect not as an ethnic or social monstrosity, but as the application of reason, collectively applied and at great sacrifice, so that we may do great things together and yearn to do more. We will not do these great things free from mistakes, but one mistake we will not make is to fail to try. It was Aristotle, and not just Lincoln in the Lyceum speech, who warned that we will get tyrants if we allow ourselves "to think small...to distrust one another completely" and to lapse into a powerlessness where "no one attempts impossible things."[23]

A Lincolnian democracy will also be a democracy of citizens, in which *citizen* is the highest title it can bestow. "Let us at all times remember that all American citizens are brothers of a common country," Lincoln said after his election in 1860, "and should dwell together in the bonds of fraternal feeling." It scandalized Stephen Douglas that, by Lincoln's logic, "he must be in favor of conferring the right and privilege of citizenship upon the negro!" But, sooner or later, it did. In his first inaugural address, Lincoln conceded the legitimacy of enforcing the Fugitive Slave Law of 1850, but then inverted its priorities by adding that "if the slave is to be surrendered" under the terms of the law, there should be safeguards, based on the "privileges and immunities of citizens," which ensured "that a free man be not, in any case, surrendered as a slave." But since the only "free man" liable to be snared by the law was a *black* free man, Lincoln had quietly attached citizenship to him—something which the *Dred Scott* decision's author, sitting immediately behind Lincoln, had declared an impossibility.

When Lincoln's black valet, William Henry Johnson (who had accompanied Lincoln to Washington from Springfield), died of smallpox in 1864, Lincoln paid for his funeral and settled his expenses. He may not be the same William H. Johnson who is buried in Arlington National Cemetery under a headstone with his name and the single description *Citizen,* but it would be boundlessly appropriate to Lincoln's purposes if it was. For in the prominence given that one word, the hierarchies of race, blood, and soil erected by the Romantic nineteenth century shrink to irrelevance. The

Lincolnian democracy is a democracy of citizens, or else the word is hollow.[24]

One more thing: a Lincolnian democracy is a democracy which embodies Lincoln's own virtues—resilience, humility, persistence, work, and dignity. Through the example of Lincoln, democracy can claim to offer people, not only order, but decency, even a kind of quiet and unostentatious grandeur. "I knew the man," wrote the Philadelphia poet George Henry Boker.

No king this man, by grace of God's intent;
No, something better, freeman,—President!
A nature modelled on a higher plan,
Lord of himself, an inborn gentleman!

Even in its faults, then and now, democracy is still the best method for people to live lives free from domination and exploitation, at peace with themselves and with others, embodying "a progressive improvement in the condition of all men... and augmenting the happiness and value of life to all peoples of all colors everywhere." Lincoln, then, was not wrong to trust that "our principle, however baffled, or delayed, will finally triumph.... Men will pass away—die—die, politically and naturally; but the principle will live, and live forever."[25]

And there would be neither slaves, nor masters.

Notes

Introduction: The Disposition of Democracy

1. Jason Brennan, *Against Democracy* (Princeton, NJ: Princeton University Press, 2016), x.
2. Jean-Francois Revel, *How Democracies Perish,* trans. W. Byron (Garden City, NY: Doubleday, 1984), 3; Francis Fukuyama, "The End of History?," *The National Interest* 16 (Summer 1989): 5.
3. Christopher H. Achen and Larry Bartels, *Democracy for Realists: Why Elections Do Not Produce Responsive Government* (Princeton, NJ: Princeton University Press, 2017), 7.
4. Ryszard Legutko, *The Demon in Democracy: Totalitarian Temptations in Free Societies,* trans. T. Adelson (New York: Encounter Books, 2016), 92, 122–23.
5. Daniel Levitsky and Steven Ziblatt, *How Democracies Die* (New York: Broadway Books, 2018), 5.
6. Freedom House, *Freedom in the World 2022: The Global Expansion of Authoritarian Rule* (Washington, DC: Freedom House, 2022), 4.
7. Donald Kagan, *Pericles of Athens and the Birth of Democracy* (New York: Free Press, 1991), 2.
8. James Madison, No. 55, *The Federalist Papers,* ed. G. W. Carey and J. McClellan (Indianapolis, IN: Liberty Fund, 2001), 288, 291.
9. Alexander Keyssar, *The Right to Vote: The Contested History of Democracy in the United States* (New York: Basic Books, 2000), 4–7; Bernard Bailyn, *The Ideological Origins of the American Revolution* (Cambridge, MA:

Harvard University Press, 1967), 51; David Ramsay, *The History of the American Revolution*, 2 vols. (Trenton, NJ: James J. Wilson, 1811), 1:44, 49.

10. François-René de Chateaubriand, *Travels in America and Italy*, 2 vols. (London: Henry Colburn, 1828), 2:124; William Livingston, "Number XXXIII" (July 12, 1753), in *The Independent Reflector*, ed. M. M. Klein (Cambridge, MA: Harvard University Press, 1963), 287.

11. Gordon S. Wood, *The Radicalism of the American Revolution: How a Revolution Transformed a Monarchical Society into a Democratic Order Unlike Any That Had Ever Existed* (New York: Knopf, 1992), 250; Sean Wilentz, *The Rise of American Democracy: Jefferson to Lincoln* (New York: W. W. Norton, 2005), 138, 178; Donald Ratcliffe, "The Right to Vote and the Rise of Democracy, 1787–1828," *Journal of the Early Republic* 33 (Summer 2013): 232, 241; Chilton Williamson, *American Suffrage: From Property to Democracy, 1760–1860* (Princeton, NJ: Princeton University Press, 1960), 174, 181; Keyssar, *The Right to Vote*, 23–28; Fisher Ames, "The Dangers of American Liberty," in *Works of Fisher Ames* (Boston: T. B. Wait, 1809), 429.

12. Alexander Hill Everett, *America: Or, A General Survey of the Political Situation of the Several Powers of the Western Continent* (Philadelphia: Carey & Lea, 1827), 81.

13. Francis Wayland, *The Duties of an American Citizen* (Boston: James Loring, 1825), 36.

14. John Gray, *Liberalism* (Minneapolis: University of Minnesota Press, 1995), xii; Pierre Manent, *An Intellectual History of Liberalism*, trans. R. Balinski (Princeton, NJ: Princeton University Press, 1995), 11–12, and *The City of Man*, trans. M. A. LePain (Princeton, NJ: Princeton University Press, 1998), 161–62.

15. Arend Lijphart, *Democracy in Plural Societies: A Comparative Exploration* (New Haven, CT: Yale University Press, 1977), 104–14; Francis Fukuyama, *Liberalism and Its Discontents* (New York: Farrar, Straus & Giroux, 2022), 3. Hans Kelsen, on the other hand, insisted that "modern democracy cannot be separated from political liberalism." See Kelsen, "Foundations of Democracy," *Ethics* 66 (October 1955): 27.

16. Harvey C. Mansfield, "Conservatism and the Common Good," *National Affairs* 55 (Spring 2023): 178.

17. Michael P. Zuckert, *A Nation So Conceived: Abraham Lincoln and the Paradox of Democratic Sovereignty* (Lawrence: University of Kansas Press, 2023), 270–71.

18. Ames, "Dangers of American Liberty," 392.

19. Thomas N. Mitchell, *Democracy's Beginning: The Athenian Story* (New

Haven, CT: Yale University Press, 2015), 111–12, 245–46, 260–69; James Miller, *Can Democracy Work? A Short History of a Radical Idea, from Ancient Athens to Our World* (New York: Farrar, Straus & Giroux, 2018), 236.

20. David Paul Nord, *Communities of Journalism: A History of American Newspapers and Their Readers* (Urbana: University of Illinois Press, 2001), 202; Harvey C. Mansfield, *Tocqueville: A Very Short Introduction* (New York: Oxford University Press, 2010), 39.

21. Alexis de Tocqueville, *Democracy in America*, ed. H. C. Mansfield and D. Winthrop (Chicago: University of Chicago Press, 2000), 166–67, 185; John Quincy Adams, *The Jubilee of the Constitution: A Discourse* (New York: Samuel Colman, 1839), 69; Frederick Grimke, *Considerations Upon the Nature and Tendency of Free Institutions* (Cincinnati: H. W. Derby, 1848), 93.

22. David Runciman, *The Confidence Trap: A History of Democracy in Crisis from World War I to the Present* (Princeton, NJ: Princeton University Press, 2013), xi; Theodore Sedgwick, *The American Citizen: His True Position, Character and Duties, a Discourse* (New York: Wiley & Putnam, 1847), 12–13.

23. Polybius, *The Histories*, book 6, chapter 4, trans. E. S. Shuckburgh (London: Macmillan, 1889), 1:460; Tocqueville, *Democracy in America*, 293, 295; Jan-Werner Müller, *Democracy Rules* (New York: Farrar, Straus & Giroux, 2021), 100.

24. Justin Buckley Dyer, *Natural Law and the Antislavery Constitutional Tradition* (New York: Cambridge University Press, 2012), 7; Johann Georg Hülsemann, in "History of Democracy in the United States," *North American Review* 23 (October 1826): 306; Karl Marx, "Critique of the Gotha Programme" (1875), in *Karl Marx: Selected Writings*, ed. David McClellan (New York: Oxford University Press, 1977), 565; Friedrich Nietzsche, *Thus Spake Zarathustra: A Book for All and None*, trans. A. Tille (New York: Macmillan, 1896), 11.

25. John Maynard Keynes, *The Economic Consequences of the Peace* (New York: Harcourt, Brace & Howe, 1920), 12; Jan-Werner Müller, *Contesting Democracy: Political Ideas in Twentieth-Century Europe* (New Haven, CT: Yale University Press, 2011), 10–11; Max Weber, *The Vocation Lectures*, ed. D. Owen and T. B. Strong (Indianapolis, IN: Hackett, 2004), 75.

26. Julian Waller, "Authoritarianism Here?," *American Affairs* 6 (Spring 2022): 159.

27. Thomas I. Palley, *Financialization: The Economics of Finance Capital Domination* (New York: Palgrave Macmillan, 2013), 7–30; David Graeber, *The Utopia of Rules: On Technology, Stupidity, and the Secret Joys of Bureau-*

cracy (Brooklyn, NY: Melville House, 2015), 10, 21–22; Sam Rosenfeld, *The Polarizers: Postwar Architects of Our Partisan Era* (Chicago: University of Chicago Press, 2018), 44.

28. Samuel Huntington (2004), in Miller, *Can Democracy Work?*, 226; Paul Berman, *Terror and Liberalism* (New York: W. W. Norton, 2003), 166; Jon Baskin, "Academia's Holy Warriors," *Chronicle of Higher Education* (September 12, 2019); Patrick Deneen, *Why Liberalism Failed* (New Haven, CT: Yale University Press, 2018), 149–53, 183, 191; Chilton Williamson, "What Happened to Liberalism?," *Modern Age* 64 (Spring 2022): 28. A great deal of the complaint of the integralists is a counsel of despair among conservatives, for their lack of success in prevailing over left-wing politics in the twenty-first century. All of this was, in a deadly irony, echoed by two intellectuals who wished America nothing but harm, Sayyid Qutb, the ideological sponsor of the Islamic revival, and Wang Huning, the éminence grise of the Chinese rulership's stride toward world economic domination. Qutb believed that democracy had rendered "intelligence and morality" null, reduced "sexual relations to a level lower than that of the beasts," and rendered democratic souls "inoperative, debilitated and atrophied" and beset by "monotony and weariness." Wang Huning, with just as hot an iron, branded liberalism as atomized and characterless. "Nihilism has become the American way, which is a fatal shock to cultural development and the American spirit," Wang wrote in 1991, after touring America like a latter-day Tocqueville. And he, too, asked Huntington's question: "If the value system collapses, how can the social system be sustained?" See Qutb, *Islam, The Religion of the Future* (Kuwait: International Islamic Federation of Student Organizations, 1971), 77; and N. S. Lyons, "The Triumph and Terror of Wang Huning," *Palladium* (October 11, 2021).

Chapter One: The Cause of Human Liberty

1. Lincoln, "Speech in U.S. House of Representatives on the Presidential Question" (July 27, 1848), and "Fifth Debate with Stephen A. Douglas, at Galesburg, Illinois" (October 7, 1858), in *Collected Works of Abraham Lincoln*, 9 vols., ed. R. P. Basler (New Brunswick, NJ: Rutgers University Press, 1953), 1:507 and 3:222 (henceforth *CW*). Hans Kelsen would describe this easy assumption as the embrace of "a generally recognized value." See Kelsen, "Foundations of Democracy" (1955), in *Verteidigung der Demokratie: Abhandlungen zur Demokratietheorie* (Tubingen: Moor Siebeck, 2006), 250.

2. Lincoln, "To Martin S. Morris" (March 26, 1843), "Speech at Kalama-zoo, Michigan" (August 27, 1856), "Speech at New Haven, Connecti-cut" (March 6, 1860), "Fragment on the Constitution and Union" (January 1861), and "Speech to One Hundred Sixty-sixth Ohio Regi-ment" (August 22, 1864), in *CW,* 1:320, 2:364, 4:24, 168, and 7:512; John Hall, in Eleanor Gridley, *The Story of Abraham Lincoln: Or, The Journey from the Log Cabin to the White House* (Juvenile Publishing, 1909), 108; J. Henry Shaw to William H. Herndon (August 22, 1866), in *Herndon's Informants: Letters, Interviews, and Statements About Abraham Lincoln,* ed. Douglas L. Wilson and Rodney O. Davis (Chicago: University of Illi-nois Press, 1998), 316; Daniel Walker Howe, *Making the American Self: Jonathan Edwards to Abraham Lincoln* (Cambridge, MA: Harvard Uni-versity Press, 1997), 138–49.

3. Lincoln, "Speech at Taunton, Massachusetts" (September 21, 1848), "Eulogy on Henry Clay (July 6, 1852), "Speech to the Springfield Scott Club" (August 14, 1852), and "Speech at Belleville, Illinois" (October 18, 1856), in *CW,* 2:7, 121–22, 137, 380; Rowan Herndon to William Henry Herndon (May 28, 1865), in *Herndon's Informants,* 8; Charles Maltby, *The Life and Public Services of Abraham Lincoln* (Los Angeles: Gilchrist Pub-lishing, 1884), 18; Edgar DeWitt Jones, *The Influence of Henry Clay upon Abraham Lincoln* (Lexington, KY: Henry Clay Memorial Foundation, 1952), 11, 19; Montgomery Blair to J. C. Frémont (August 24, 1861), in *New-York Tribune* (March 4, 1862).

4. Lincoln, "Eulogy on Henry Clay" (July 6, 1852) and "First Debate with Stephen A. Douglas at Ottawa, Illinois" (October 21, 1858), in *CW,* 2:121–22, 130, and 3:29; Drew R. McCoy, "Lincoln and the Founding Fathers," *Journal of the Abraham Lincoln Association* 16 (Winter 1995): 10–11 (hence-forth *JALA*); Kevin J. Portteus, "'My Beau Ideal of a Statesman': Abra-ham Lincoln's Eulogy on Henry Clay," *JALA* 41 (Summer 2020): 1–24; Michael Lind, *What Lincoln Believed: The Values and Convictions of Amer-ica's Greatest President* (New York: Doubleday, 2004), 88–92. In a curi-ous anticipation of Lincoln's famous "Lost Speech" at Bloomington, Illinois, in 1856, Lincoln described one of Clay's speeches as so beam-ing with eloquence that "the reporters forgot their vocations, dropped their pens, and sat enchanted from near the beginning to quite the close" (*CW,* 2:127).

5. Knud Haakonssen, "From Natural Law to the Rights of Man: A Euro-pean Perspective on American Debates," in *Natural Law and Moral Philosophy: From Grotius to the Scottish Enlightenment* (Cambridge: Cam-bridge University Press, 1996), 311; Herndon to Jesse Weik (January 1,

1886), in *Herndon on Lincoln: Letters,* ed. Douglas L. Wilson and Rodney O. Davis (Urbana: University of Illinois Press, 2016), 181; Francis Wayland, *University Sermons: Sermons Delivered in the Chapel of Brown University* (Boston: Gould, Kendall & Lincoln, 1849), 10; Mark Hopkins, *Lectures on Moral Science: Delivered Before the Lowell Institute, Boston* (Boston: Gould & Lincoln, 1863), 228; Noah Porter, *The Elements of Moral Science: Theoretical and Practical* (New York: Charles Scribner's, 1885), 113–14.

6. Lincoln, "Address Before the Young Men's Lyceum of Springfield, Illinois" (January 27, 1838), "Fragment on Slavery" (July 1, 1854), "Speech at Springfield, Illinois" (October 4, 1854), "First Debate with Stephen A. Douglas at Ottawa, Illinois" (August 21, 1858), "Speech at Carlinville, Illinois" (August 31, 1858), "Speech at Edwardsville, Illinois" (September 11, 1858), "Fifth Debate with Stephen A. Douglas, at Galesburg, Illinois" (October 7, 1858), "Seventh and Last Debate with Stephen A. Douglas at Alton, Illinois" (October 15, 1858), and "To Albert G. Hodges" (April 4, 1864), in *CW,* 1:113, 3:28, 80, 95, 222, 300, and 7:281; D. H. Meyer, *The Instructed Conscience: The Shaping of the American National Ethic* (Philadelphia: University of Pennsylvania Press, 1972), 27; Joseph R. Fornieri, *Abraham Lincoln's Political Faith* (DeKalb: Northern Illinois University Press, 2003), 49–50; James Oakes, "Natural Rights, Citizenship Rights, State Rights, and Black Rights," in *Our Lincoln: New Perspectives on Lincoln and His World,* ed. E. Foner (New York: W. W. Norton, 2008), 112.

7. "Speech of Wendell Phillips, Esq." (January 26, 1864), in *The Liberator* (February 5, 1864); Horace Porter, *Campaigning with Grant* (New York: Century, 1897), 408; Lincoln, "Speech in United States House of Representatives: The War with Mexico" (January 12, 1848), "Annual Message to Congress" (December 3, 1861), and "To James C. Conkling" (August 26, 1863), in *CW,* 1:437, 5:53, and 6:410. Lincoln could never have agreed with Herbert Croly's Progressive dictum in 1909, that "the average American individual is morally and intellectually inadequate to a serious and consistent conception of his responsibilities as a democrat," and must yield to "the march of a constructive national democracy." See Croly, *The Promise of American Life* (New York: Macmillan, 1914), 276.

8. Lincoln, "Speech at Peoria, Illinois" (October 16, 1854), "Speech at Cincinnati, Ohio" (September 17, 1859), "Fragment on the Constitution and the Union" (January 1861), "Address to the New Jersey Senate at Trenton, New Jersey" (February 21, 1861), "Speech in Independence Hall,

Philadelphia, Pennsylvania" (February 22, 1861), and "Message to Congress in Special Session" (July 4, 1861), in *CW*, 2:276, 3:453, and 4:169, 236, 240, 439; Lucas E. Morel, *Lincoln and the Founders*. On the imperative to recur to "first principles" in government, see Henry Clay, "On the Sub-Treasury" (February 19, 1838), in *The Life and Speeches of Henry Clay, of Kentucky* (New York: James B. Swain, 1843), 2:354; John Trenchard and Thomas Gordon, "The Leaders of Parties, their usual Views" (February 11, 1720), in *Cato's Letters: Or, Essays on Liberty, Civil and Religious, and Other Important Subjects*, ed. R. Hamowy (Indianapolis: Liberty Fund, 1995), 1:121; Granville Sharp, *The Legal Means of Political Reformation* (London: Gallabin & Baker, 1780), iv; Emmerich de Vattel, *The Law of Nations, Or, Principles of the Law of Nature: Applied to the Conduct and Affairs of Nations and Sovereigns* (London: G.G. Robinson, 1797), 81; Jonathan Dymond, *Essays on the Principles of Morality and on the Private and Political Rights and Obligations of Mankind* (New York: Robert B. Collins, 1854), 507; and Samuel Johnson, "The Rambler No. 156," in *Selected Essays*, ed. David Womersley (New York: Penguin Books, 2003), 255.

9. Lincoln, "Speech at Springfield" (July 17, 1858), in *CW*, 2:513; Henry Clay Whitney, Robert Wilson, and Sarah Bush Johnston Lincoln, in *Herndon's Informants*, 108, 202, 648; George C. Shepard, Ada Bailhache, and William L. Gross in *Concerning Mr. Lincoln*, ed. H. E. Pratt (Springfield, IL: Abraham Lincoln Association, 1944), 20, 32, 56; Jane Martin Johns, *Personal Recollections of Early Decatur, Abraham Lincoln, Richard J. Oglesby and the Civil War*, ed. Howard Schaub (Decatur, IL: Daughters of the American Revolution, 1912), 62; Henry Clay Whitney, *Lincoln the Citizen*, ed. Michael Burlingame (unpublished manuscript, forthcoming from the University of Illinois Press, 2023), 207; William Howard Russell, *My Diary North and South* (Boston: T.O.H.P. Burnham, 1863), 37, 480; Benton J. Lossing, *Pictorial History of the Civil War in the United States of America* (Hartford, CT: T. Belknap, 1868), 1:280; Louise L. Stevenson, *Lincoln in the Atlantic World* (New York: Cambridge University Press, 2015), 82–83.

10. Lincoln, "Speech at Bloomington, Illinois" (April 10, 1860), "To the Regent Captains of the Republic of San Marino" (May 7, 1861), and "Message to Congress in Special Session" (July 4, 1861), in *CW*, 4:42, 360, 426. Massachusetts Republican senator Henry Wilson used the phrase "this democratic republic," in *Democratic Leaders for Disunion: Speech of Hon. Henry Wilson of Massachusetts, Delivered in the Senate of the United States, January 25, 1860* (Albany, NY: *Albany Evening Journal*, 1860), 4.

11. Lincoln, "Definition of Democracy" (August 1, 1858), in *CW*, 2:532.

12. See the classic definition of slavery as "the permanent, violent domination of natally alienated and generally dishonored persons," in Orlando Patterson, *Slavery and Social Death: A Comparative Study* (Cambridge, MA: Harvard University Press, 1982), 13; but see also Joseph Miller, *The Problem of Slavery as History: A Global Approach* (New Haven, CT: Yale University Press, 2012), 32.

13. Lincoln, "'Spot' Resolutions in the United States House of Representatives" (December 22, 1847) and "To Henry L. Pierce and Others" (April 6, 1859), in *CW*, 1:421, 3:376.

14. Lincoln, "Speech at Peoria, Illinois" (October 16, 1854), in *CW* 2:265–66.

15. Lincoln, "Speech at Worcester, Massachusetts" (September 12, 1848), "Fragment: Notes for a Law Lecture" (July 1, 1850), "Speech at Bloomington, Illinois" (September 26, 1854), "Speech at Peoria, Illinois" (October 16, 1854), and "Speech at Springfield, Illinois" (June 26, 1857), in *CW*, 2:1, 82, 235, 247, 266, 270, 399.

16. Lincoln, "Speech at Bloomington, Illinois" (September 12, 1854), "Speech at Springfield, Illinois" (June 26, 1857), and "Speech at Edwardsville, Illinois" (May 18, 1858), in *CW*, 2:232–33, 408, 447.

17. John E. Roll (1895), in *Recollected Words of Abraham Lincoln*, ed. Don and Virginia Fehrenbacher (Stanford, CA: Stanford University Press, 1996), 383; Lincoln, "Speech at Chicago, Illinois" (July 10, 1858), "Fragment on Pro-Slavery Theology" (October 1858), "On Slavery" (March 22, 1864), and "Speech to the One Hundred and Fortieth Indiana Regiment" (March 17, 1865), in *CW*, 2:500, 3:205, 7:260, and 8:361; John C. Calhoun, in Justin Buckley Dyer, *Natural Law and the Antislavery Constitutional Tradition* (New York: Cambridge University Press, 2012), 94.

18. Lincoln, "To Henry L. Pierce and others" (April 6, 1859), in *CW*, 3:376.

19. Lincoln, "Speech at Peoria, Illinois," (October 16, 1854) and "Speech at New Haven, Connecticut" (March 5, 1860), in *CW*, 2:271 and 4:16; Peter Garnsey, *Ideas of Slavery from Aristotle to Augustine* (Cambridge: Cambridge University Press, 1996), 38.

20. Lincoln, "Message to Congress in Special Session" (July 4, 1861), "Reply to Emancipation Memorial Presented by Chicago Christians of All Denominations" (September 13, 1862), and "To James C. Conkling" (August 26, 1863), in *CW*, 4:437–38, 5:424, and 6:407; James G. Blaine, *Twenty Years of Congress: from Lincoln to Garfield, with a Review of the Events which led to the Political Revolution of 1860* (Norwich, CT: Henry Bill, 1884), 1:256; George Kateb, *Lincoln's Political Thought* (Cambridge, MA: Harvard University Press, 2015), 42.

21. John Hay, diary entry for May 7, 1861, in *Inside Lincoln's White House: The Complete Civil War Diary of John Hay*, ed. M. Burlingame and J. R. T. Ettlinger (Carbondale: Southern Illinois University Press, 1997), 20; Lincoln, "Notes for Speeches at Columbus and Cincinnati, Ohio" (September 16–17, 1859), "Message to Congress in Special Session" (July 4, 1861), "Reply to Edward Count Piper" (November 8, 1861), "Annual Message to Congress" (December 3, 1861), "Reply to Lorenzo Montufar" (April 24, 1862), and "To Henry W. Davis" (March 18, 1863), in *CW*, 3:435, 4:432, 5:18, 51, 198, and 6:140; Samarth P. Desai, "'Jackson Redivivus' in Lincoln's First Inaugural," *JALA* 43 (Spring 2022): 23–26.

22. Lincoln, "Fragment of a Speech" (May 18, 1858), "Speech at Leavenworth, Kansas" (December 3, 1859), "Reply to Governor Andrew J. Curtin at Harrisburg, Pennsylvania" (February 22, 1861), "Message to Congress in Special Session" (July 4, 1861), and "Fragment" [to the James C. Conkling letter] (August 26, 1863), in *CW*, 2:454, 3:501, 4:242, 437, and 6:410.

Chapter Two: Law, Reason, and Passion

1. John Lord Sheffield, *Observations on the Commerce of the American States* (London: J. Debrett, 1784), 198; "From the Cabinet of Versailles to Otto, Versailles, August 30, 1787," in George Bancroft, *History of the Formation of the Constitution of the United States of America* (New York: D. Appleton, 1883), 1:432.

2. David S. Brown, *The First Populist: The Defiant Life of Andrew Jackson* (New York: Scribner, 2022), 34–35; Douglas L. Wilson, *Honor's Voice: The Transformation of Abraham Lincoln* (New York: Knopf, 1998), 26; George R. Dekle, *Prairie Defender: The Murder Trials of Abraham Lincoln* (Carbondale: Southern Illinois University Press, 2017), 21, 102; Francis Parkman, "The Failure of Universal Suffrage," *North American Review* 127 (July-August 1878): 7; Richard Franklin Bensel, *The American Ballot Box in the Mid-Nineteenth Century* (Cambridge: Cambridge University Press, 2004), 21; Georges Fisch, *Nine Months in the United States During the Crisis* (London: James Nisbet, 1863), 9–10.

3. Alan Taylor, *The Civil War of 1812: American Citizens, British Subjects, Irish Rebels, & Indian Allies* (New York: Knopf, 2010), 81; Letters of Peter Cassel and Johan Johansson, in *The Scandinavians in America, 986–1970*, ed. H. B. Furer (Dobbs Ferry, NY: Oceana Publications, 1972), 104, 110; Cooper, *The American Democrat*, ed. G. Dekker and L. Johnston (New

York: Penguin Classics, 1989), 70, 227; Henry Clay, "On the Seminole War" (January 1819), in *The Speeches of Henry Clay*, ed. Calvin Colton (New York: A. S. Barnes, 1857), 1:203.

4. Abraham Lincoln, "Address Before the Young Men's Lyceum of Springfield, Illinois" (January 27, 1838), "Remarks in Illinois Legislature Concerning Appropriation for Building the State House" (January 7, 1839); "Speech at Kalamazoo, Michigan" (August 27, 1856), "Speech to Germans at Cincinnati, Ohio" (February 12, 1861), and "Speech to One Hundred Eighty-Ninth New York Volunteers" (October 24, 1864), in *CW*, 1:112, 126, 2:364, 4:202, and 8:75.

5. David Hoffman, *A Course of Legal Study* (Baltimore: Coale & Maxwell, 1817), viii; William Sampson, *Sampson's Discourse, and Correspondence with Various Learned Jurists* (Washington: Gales & Seaton, 1826), 5–6; Francis Wayland, *The Duties of an American Citizen: Two Discourses, Delivered in the First Baptist Meeting House in Boston, on Thursday, April 7, 1825* (Boston: James Loring, 1825), 14, 30, 37.

6. Robert V. Remini, *Andrew Jackson and the Course of American Democracy, 1833–1845* (Baltimore: Johns Hopkins University Press, 1984), 154–55; James Parton, *Life of Andrew Jackson* (New York: Mason Bros., 1860), vii. See also Robert Tracy McKenzie, *We the Fallen People: The Founders and the Future of American Democracy* (Downers Grove, IL: InterVarsity Press, 2021).

7. "The Riot of Last Evening," *New York Evening Post* (February 14, 1837); David Grimsted, *American Mobbing, 1828–1861* (New York: Oxford University Press, 1998), 4; William Ellery Channing, *A Letter to the Abolitionists* (Boston: Isaac Knapp, 1837), 7; William Hawkes Smith, *Letters on the State and Prospects of Society* (Birmingham, England: B. Hudson, 1838), 25; "Mob in New York," *Niles National Register* (February 18, 1837); "Outrage," *Baltimore Sun* (May 25, 1837); *Philadelphia Public Ledger* (December 18, 1837); "The Riot of Last Evening," *New York Evening Post* (February 14, 1837); "Letter of Dr. Wm. Channing, to James G. Birney," *New York Evening Post* (January 20, 1837).

8. Thomas F. Schwartz, "The Springfield Lyceums and Lincoln's 1838 Speech," *Illinois Historical Journal* 83 (Spring 1990): 48.

9. Michael P. Lynch, *In Praise of Reason: Why Rationality Matters for Democracy* (Cambridge, MA: MIT Press, 2012), 3.

10. Ritchie Robertson, *The Enlightenment: The Pursuit of Happiness, 1680–1790* (New York: HarperCollins, 2021), 21–31; Thomas Paine, "Common Sense" (1776), in *The Writings of Thomas Paine*, ed. M. D. Conway (New York: G. P. Putnam's, 1894), 1:75.

11. Tim Blanning, *The Romantic Revolution: A History* (New York: Modern Library, 2011), 16–24.
12. Immanuel Kant, *Prolegomena to Any Future Metaphysics*, ed. and trans. Gary Hatfield (Cambridge: Cambridge University Press, 2004), 66–67.
13. Alexander Pope, "An Essay on Man," in *The Complete Poetical Works of Alexander Pope* (Boston: Houghton, Mifflin, 1903), 143; Anthony Ashley Cooper, *Characteristics of Men, Manners, Opinions, Times, etc.*, ed. J. M. Robertson (London: Grant Richards, 1900), 1:18; Adam Smith, *The Theory of Moral Sentiments* (London: A. Millar, 1761), 278; Julien Benda, *The Treason of the Intellectuals*, trans. R. Aldington (1928; New York: Transaction Publishers, 2007), 46.
14. Caleb Bingham, *The Columbian Orator: Containing a Variety of Original and Selected Pieces* (Baltimore: Philip H. Nicklin, 1811), 203–4, 272. Dennis Hanks identified *The Columbian Orator* as one of two school texts that the young Lincoln read. See Hanks interview with Herndon (September 8, 1865) in *Herndon's Informants: Letters, Interviews, and Statements About Abraham Lincoln*, ed. Douglas L. Wilson and Rodney O. Davis (Chicago: University of Illinois Press, 1998), 105.
15. Abraham Lincoln, "Temperance Address" (February 22, 1842), in *CW*, 1:278.
16. Louis Gerteis, *Civil War St. Louis* (Lawrence: University Press of Kansas, 2001), 9–15; Neil Schmitz, "Murdered McIntosh, Murdered Lovejoy: Abraham Lincoln and the Problem of Jacksonian Address," *Arizona Quarterly* 44 (Autumn 1988): 22–29; Grimsted, *American Mobbing*, 104–15; David A. Bell, *Men on Horseback: The Power of Charisma in the Age of Revolution* (New York: Farrar, Straus & Giroux, 2020), 27–34.
17. Diana Schaub, *His Greatest Speeches: How Lincoln Moved the Nation* (New York: St. Martin's, 2021), 6, 25–56, 46–57; Michael Lind, *What Lincoln Believed: The Values and Convictions of America's Greatest President* (New York: Doubleday, 2004), 2–4, 285–89; William Miller, *Lincoln's Virtues: An Ethical Biography* (New York: Knopf, 2002), 114; Harry V. Jaffa, *A New Birth of Freedom: Abraham Lincoln and the Coming of the Civil War* (Lanham, MD: Rowman & Littlefield, 2000), 400; Clay, "On the Seminole War" (January 1819), *Speeches*, 1:203.
18. Lincoln, "Fragment on Slavery" (July 1, 1854), "Speech at Springfield, Illinois" (October 4, 1854), "Speech at Peoria, Illinois (October 16, 1854), "Speech at Bloomington, Illinois" (May 29, 1856); "Speech at Springfield, Illinois" (July 17, 1858), and "Speech at Edwardsville, Illinois" (September 11, 1858), in *CW*, 2:222, 245, 249, 341, 519 and 3:92.
19. Lincoln, "Fragment on Government" (July 1, 1854), "Speech at Peo-

ria, Illinois" (October 16, 1854), "Notes for Speeches at Columbus and Cincinnati, Ohio" (September 16–17, 1859), and "To Edwin M. Stanton" (March 18, 1864), in *CW,* 2:220, 266, 3:435, and 7:255.

20. Lincoln, "Communication to the People of Sangamo County" (March 9, 1832), "Portion of a Bill Introduced in Illinois Legislature Concerning Estrays" (December 6, 1834), "Notice to Illinois Legislature of a Bill to Authorize Samuel Musick to Build a Toll Bridge" (December 9, 1834), "Resolution Introduced in Illinois Legislature Revenue from the Sale of Public Lands" (January 10, 1835), "Speech to the Springfield Scott Club" (August 14, 26, 1852), "Fragment on Government" (July 1, 1854), and "Speech at Edwardsville" (September 11, 1858), in *CW,* 1:7, 27, 28, 32, 2:152, 220–221, and 3:92; Elnathan Winchester, *A Plain Political Catechism Intended for the Use of Schools in the United States of America* (Greenfield, MA: T. Dickmen, 1796), 13; Olivier Fraysse, *Lincoln, Land, and Labor, 1809–1860,* trans. S. Neely (Urbana: University of Illinois Press, 1994), 69, 78.

21. George M. Weston, "Who Are Sectional?," in *Republican Campaign Documents of 1856* (Washington: Lewis Clephane, 1857), 4–5; Lincoln, "Address to the Pennsylvania General Assembly" (February 22, 1861), "To Winfield Scott" (April 25, 1861), and "Message to Congress in Special Session" (July 4, 1861), in *CW,* 4:245, 344, 428; "Topic of the Day" and "Timely Words," *Boston Evening Transcript* (January 2 and 15, 1861); Henry Waldron, "The Tariff Bill" (April 26, 1860), *Congressional Globe,* 36th Congress, 1st session, 1872; Frederick Law Olmsted, *Journeys and Explorations in the Cotton Kingdom: A Traveller's Observations on Cotton and Slavery in the American Slave States* (New York: Mason Bros., 1861), 350; Howell Cobb, in William W. Freehling, *The Road to Disunion: Secessionists Triumphant* (New York: Oxford University Press, 2007), 419; "The Legislature of South Carolina," *Philadelphia Inquirer* (December 1, 1860); *Southern Notes for National Circulation* (Boston: Thayer & Eldredge, 1860), 7; "Secession—Its Effect on Lynching," *Delaware* (OH) *Gazette* (February 1, 1861).

22. Lincoln, "Speech at Hartford, Connecticut" (March 5, 1860) and "Address to the Legislature at Albany, New York" (February 18, 1861), in *CW,* 4:28, 226.

23. Lincoln, "First Inaugural Address Final Text" (March 4, 1861), "Message to Congress in Special Session" (July 4, 1861), and "Reply to Edward Count Piper" (November 8, 1861), in *CW,* 4:270, 426, 5:18; "Democracy on Its Trial," *London Quarterly Review* 110 (July 1861) 139–40; Phillip S. Paludan, "The American Civil War Considered as a

Crisis in Law and Order," *American Historical Review* 77 (October 1972): 1017.

24. Lincoln, "Reply to Committee from Maryland Legislature" (May 4, 1861), "Message to Congress in Special Session" (July 4, 1861), "Annual Message to Congress" (December 8, 1861), "To Cuthbert Bullitt" (July 28, 1862), and "To William S. Rosecrans" (May 20, 1863), in *CW,* 4:356, 426, 432, 5:48–49, 346, 6:224; John Hay and Gideon Welles, in *Recollected Words of Abraham Lincoln,* ed. Don E. and Virginia Fehrenbacher (Stanford, CA: Stanford University Press, 1996), 212, 485.

Chapter Three: An American System

1. "Lincoln Legal Database," parts 1 and 2, *Lincoln Legal Briefs* (October–December 1997), 3, and (April–June 1998), 2–3; George R. Dekle, *Prairie Defender: The Murder Trials of Abraham Lincoln* (Carbondale: Southern Illinois University Press, 2017), 2, 187; Brian Dirck, *Lincoln the Lawyer* (Urbana: University of Illinois Press, 2007), 56, 62–63; Guy S. Fraker, *Lincoln's Ladder to the Presidency: The Eighth Judicial Circuit* (Carbondale: Southern Illinois University Press, 2012), 57–58.

2. Lincoln, "Speech at Peoria, Illinois" (October 16, 1854), "Speech at Indianapolis, Indiana" (September 19, 1859), "First Annual Message to Congress" (December 3, 1861), "Second Annual Message to Congress" (December 1, 1862), "Reply to New York Workingmen's Democratic Republican Association" (March 21, 1864), and "To Henry W. Hoffman" (October 4, 1864), in *CW,* 2:265, 3:468–69, 5:523, 7:259, 8:41; John Locke, *Two Treatises on Government,* ed. Peter Laslett (New York: Signet Classics, 1965), 338.

3. Lincoln, "Discussion in Illinois Legislature" (February 6, 1841), "Fragment on Free Labor" (September 17, 1859), "Address Before the Wisconsin State Agricultural Society, Milwaukee, Wisconsin" (September 19, 1859), and "Speech at New Haven, Connecticut" (March 5, 1860), in *CW,* 1:484, 3:462, 478–79, 481, 4:24.

4. Robert J. Gordon, *The Rise and Fall of American Growth: The U.S. Standard of Living Since the Civil War* (Princeton, NJ: Princeton University Press, 2016), 4, 44, 57; *Historical Statistics of the United States, Colonial Times to 1970* (Washington, DC: U.S. Bureau of the Census, 1975), 1:12, 134; James Haines, in "History of Shelby County," *Historical Encyclopedia of Illinois,* ed. N. Bateman and P. Selby (Chicago: Munsell Publishing, 1910), 2:779; Henry Clay Whitney, *Lincoln the Citizen,* ed. Michael Burlingame (unpublished manuscript, forthcoming from the Univer-

sity of Illinois Press, 2023; Christopher Clark, *The Roots of Rural Capitalism: Western Massachusetts, 1780–1860* (Ithaca, NY: Cornell University Press, 1990), 29; Kenneth J. Winkle, *The Young Eagle: The Rise of Abraham Lincoln* (Dallas, TX: Taylor, 2001), 19, 27, 46, 49–51.

5. Adam Smith, *An Inquiry into the Nature and Causes of the Wealth of Nations,* ed. R. H. Campbell and A. S. Skinner (1776; Indianapolis: Liberty Fund, 1981), 25.

6. Charles de Secondat de Montesquieu, *The Spirit of the Laws,* ed. A. Cohler, B. C. Miller, and H. S. Stone (New York: Cambridge University Press, 1989), 338–39; William Robertson, "A View of the Progress of Society in Europe" (1760), in *Commerce, Culture and Liberty: Readings on Capitalism Before Adam Smith,* ed. Henry C. Clark (Indianapolis, IN: Liberty Fund, 2003), 506; Ritchie Robertson, *The Enlightenment: The Pursuit of Happiness, 1680–1790* (New York: HarperCollins, 2021), 523; Daniel Defoe, *The Complete English Tradesman: In Familiar Letters* (London: Charles Rivington, 1726), 1:373–74.

7. T. G. Onstot, *Pioneers of Menard and Mason Counties* (Peoria, IL: J. W. Franks, 1902), 51.

8. Lincoln, "Communication to the People of Sangamo County" (March 9, 1832), in *CW,* 1:5; Olivier Fraysse, *Lincoln, Land, and Labor, 1809–1860,* trans. S. Neely (Urbana: University of Illinois Press, 1994), 42–44, 116; William W. Freehling, *Becoming Lincoln* (Charlottesville: University of Virginia Press, 2018), 20; Douglas L. Wilson, *Honor's Voice: The Transformation of Abraham Lincoln* (New York: Knopf, 1998), 87–90.

9. Arthur E. Morgan, "New Light on Lincoln's Boyhood," *Atlantic Monthly* 125 (1920): 213.

10. Robert Dawidoff, *The Education of John Randolph* (New York: W. W. Norton, 1979), 29; Stanley Elkins and Eric McKitrick, *The Age of Federalism: The Early American Republic, 1788–1800* (New York: Oxford University Press, 1993), 267; Jefferson to George Mason (February 4, 1791), in *Jefferson: Writings,* ed. Merrill Peterson (New York: Library of America, 1984), 972; Herbert E. Sloan, *Principle and Interest: Thomas Jefferson and the Problem of Debt* (New York: Oxford University Press, 1995), 173–74.

11. Jefferson, "Manufactures," in *Notes on the State of Virginia* (Philadelphia: Prichard & Hall, 1788), 175; "How to Be Rich," *New England Farmer and Horticultural Journal* 8 (October 23, 1829): 112.

12. "Petition to Macon County Commissioners' Court" (May 26, 1830), "Document Drawn for James Eastep" (November 12, 1831), "Bill of Sale Drawn for John Ferguson" (January 25, 1832), "Mortgage Drawn for William Green, Jr. to Reuben Radford" (January 15, 1833), "Bond

of David Rutledge" (January 31, 1833), and "Will of Joshua Short" (August 22, 1836), in *CW*, 1:2–4, 15–16, 51; *The Law Practice of Abraham Lincoln: A Statistical Portrait*, http://www.lawpracticeofabrahamlincoln .org/reference/reference%20html%20files/statisticalportrait.html.

13. Lincoln, "Communication to the People of Sangamo County" (March 9, 1832), "Resolution Introduced in Illinois Legislature regarding Revenue from the Sale of Public Lands" (January 10, 1835), "Resolution Introduced in Illinois Legislature Concerning the Incorporation of a Canal Company" (December 11, 1835), "To the Editor of the Sangamo Journal" (June 13, 1836), "Speech in the Illinois Legislature Concerning the State Bank" (January 11, 1837), "Committee Reporting the Illinois Legislature on Condition of the State Bank" (January 21, 1840), "Remarks in the Illinois Legislature Concerning the Illinois and Michigan Canal" (January 22–23, 1840), and "Seventh and Last Debate with Stephen A. Douglas at Alton, Illinois" (October 15, 1858), in *CW*, 1:6, 40, 43, 65, 69, 194, 196–97, 3:309; Freehling, *Becoming Lincoln*, 52; Gabor S. Boritt, *Lincoln and the Economics of the American Dream* (Memphis, TN: Memphis State University Press, 1977), 14–24; Speed interview with William Henry Herndon (1865–66) in *Herndon's Informants: Letters, Interviews, and Statements About Abraham Lincoln*, ed. Douglas L. Wilson and Rodney O. Davis (Chicago: University of Illinois Press, 1998), 476.

14. Lincoln, "Report on Alton and Springfield Railroad" (August 5, 1847), "Fragments of a Tariff Discussion" (December 1, 1847), and "Speech in United States House of Representatives on Internal Improvements" (June 20, 1848), in *CW*, 1:398, 407–16, 483, 488; Mentor L. Williams, "The Chicago River and Harbor Convention, 1847," *Mississippi Valley Historical Review* 35 (March 1949): 610; "Recent Find: Lincoln as a Peacemaker in Chicago," *For the People: A Newsletter of the Abraham Lincoln Association* 22 (Spring 2021): 7; Freehling, *Becoming Lincoln*, 104. On the telegraph, see Allen C. Guelzo, *Lincoln and Douglas: The Debates That Defined America* (New York: Simon and Schuster, 2008), 97; Boritt, *Lincoln and the Economics of the American Dream*, 109–14.

15. John Pendleton Kennedy, "Address of the Tariff Convention" (October 26, 1831), in *Hazard's Register of Pennsylvania* 8 (December 3, 1831): 357.

16. Henry Clay, "On the Direct Tax, and The State of the Nation After the War of 1812" (January 1816), in *The Speeches of Henry Clay*, ed. Calvin Colton (New York: A. S. Barnes, 1857), 1:98; Robert V. Remini, *Henry Clay: Statesman for the Union* (New York: W. W. Norton, 1991), 137, 225–33; "Home Industry Convention," *New-York Tribune* (April 7, 1842).

17. Horace Greeley, "The Grounds of Protection" (February 10, 1843), in

Notes

The American Laborer, Devoted to the Cause of Protection of Home Industry 1
(March 1843): 364; Edward Joy Morris, "Speech...in Favor of Home
Industry and Protective Duties" (March 4, 1842), in *The Protector* 1
(April 13, 1842): 55; Michael Hudson, *America's Protectionist Takeoff: The
Neglected American School of Political Economy* (Islet, 2010), 149; Michael
Lind, *What Lincoln Believed: The Values and Convictions of America's
Greatest President* (New York: Doubleday, 2004), 73–84.

18. Remini, *Henry Clay*, 463; "Home Industry Convention," *New-York Tribune* (April 7, 1842). Adam Smith, as a free trader, was skeptical that
tariffs would do anything to "increase the general industry of the society" and might actually increase "the wretched spirit of monopoly,"
but even Smith conceded that "it will generally be advantageous to
lay some burden upon foreign, for the encouragement of domestick,
industry." See Smith, *Wealth of Nations*, 1:453, 461, 463.

19. *The American Almanac and Repository of Useful Knowledge for the Year 1859*
(Boston: Crosby, Nichols, and Co., 1859), 169, 218; Lincoln, "Protest in
Illinois Legislature on Slavery" (March 3, 1837), "Speech at Peoria,
Illinois" (October 16, 1854), "To Joshua Speed" (August 24, 1855), and
"Speech at Greeneville, Illinois" (September 13, 1858), in *CW*, 1:75, 2:255,
320, 3:96.

20. George Fitzhugh, *Cannibals All!: Or, Slaves Without Masters* (Richmond,
VA: A. Morris, 1857), ix, 163; and *Sociology for the South, or the Failure of
Free Society* (Richmond, VA: A. Morris, 1854), 245, 302.

21. Lincoln, "Fragment on Slavery" (July 1, 1854), "Fragment on Free
Labor" (September 1859), "Speech at Cincinnati" (September 17, 1859),
and "Speech at Indianapolis, Indiana" (September 19, 1859), in *CW*,
2:222, 3:459, 462, 468; Eric Foner, "Free Labor and Nineteenth-Century
Political Ideology," in *The Market Revolution in America: Social, Political, and Religious Expressions, 1800–1880*, ed. Melvyn Stokes and Stephen
Conway (Charlottesville: University Press of Virginia, 1998), 106–7.

22. Rufus Choate, "The Importance of Illustrating New-England His-
tory by a Series of Romances like the Waverly Novels" (1833), in *The
Works of Rufus Choate: With a Memoir of His Life*, ed. S. G. Brown (Bos-
ton: Little, Brown, 1862), 1:331, 333; Greeley, "Fourier and His Ideas" and
"The Relations of Learning to Labor" (1844), in *Hints Toward Reforms:
In Lectures, Addresses, and Other Writings* (New York: Harper & Bros.,
1850), 133, 291; Daniel Walker Howe, *The Political Culture of the American
Whigs* (Chicago: University of Chicago Press, 1979), 191.

23. John Romine to Herndon, in *Recollected Words of Abraham Lincoln*, ed.
Don and Virginia Fehrenbacher (Stanford, CA: Stanford University

Press, 1996), 385; John Hanks to Herndon (June 13, 1865), in *Herndon's Informants*, 118; Michael Burlingame, *The Inner World of Abraham Lincoln* (Urbana: University of Illinois Press, 1994), 39; "To John D. Johnston" (December 24, 1848, and November 4, 1851), and "To John M. Brockman" (September 25, 1860), in *CW*, 2:16, 211, 4:121; Robert Todd Lincoln to Isaac Markens (February 13, 1918), in *A Portrait of Abraham Lincoln in Letters by His Oldest Son*, ed. Paul Angle (Chicago: Chicago Historical Society, 1968), 56; Edward D. Neill, *Four Reminiscences of the Last Year of President Lincoln's Life* (St. Paul, MN: Pioneer Press Co., 1885), 4–5.

Chapter Four: Political Economy and the Nation

1. William Herndon to Jesse Weik (January 1, 1886), in *Herndon on Lincoln: Letters*, ed. D. L. Wilson and R. O. Davis (Urbana: University of Illinois Press, 2016), 181; Shelby Cullom, in Walter B. Stevens, *A Reporter's Lincoln*, ed. Michael Burlingame (Lincoln: University of Nebraska Press, 1998), 154. There has been a persistent attempt to link Lincoln with Marx, based on a perceived commonalty in Lincoln's espousal of a "labor theory of value" and the priority of labor to capital. A particularly foolish example of this is Gillian Brockell's op-ed, "You Know Who Was into Karl Marx?," *Washington Post* (July 27, 2019). Brockell asserts that Lincoln was "regularly reading Karl Marx" through Marx's journalism pieces in the *New-York Tribune*, after Marx was hired in 1852 by Horace Greeley as a stringer to report on European politics. But in the years Marx wrote for the *Tribune*, he contributed exactly seven signed pieces, all of them energetic but straightforward political reporting from London. Whether Lincoln read any of these articles is pure conjecture; whether he would have recognized Marx's name as an off-the-shelf brand is even more conjectural. The only letter of Marx's Lincoln is likely to have read was a petition Marx helped draft for the International Workingmen's Association in support of the Emancipation Proclamation. Nevertheless, the foolishness keeps getting repeated, as in the concluding paragraphs of John Nichols's "Liz Cheney Is No Abraham Lincoln," *The Nation* (August 17, 2022). On the other hand, if it tortures credulity to identify Lincoln and Marx, Herndon may be guilty of exaggerating the influence of Wayland, especially on the subject of tariffs.

2. David Demaree, "A Stumping Sucker: Reception of Abraham Lincoln in Massachusetts, September 11–23, 1848," *Civil War History* 68 (March 2022): 95 (henceforth *CWH*); Richard Gamble, *A Fiery Gospel: The Battle*

Hymn of the Republic and the Road to Righteous War (Ithaca, NY: Cornell University Press, 2019), 39; *The Life and Letters of James Abram Garfield, 1831–1877,* ed. Theodore Clark Smith (New Haven, CT: Yale University Press, 1925), 1:266; "Intelligence by the Mails," *New York Herald* (September 3, 1848); Samuel P. Hadley, "Recollections of Lincoln in Lowell in 1848 and Reading of Concluding Portion of the Emancipation Proclamation," *Contributions of the Lowell Historical Society* (Lowell, MA: Butterfield Printing, 1913), 371; Frederick Law Olmsted to Mary Cleveland Bryant Olmsted (October 1861), in *The Papers of Frederick Law Olmsted—Defending the Union: The Civil War and the U.S. Sanitary Commission, 1861–1863,* ed. Jane Turner Censer (Baltimore: Johns Hopkins University Press, 1986), 4:213; John Hay, diary entry for July 25, 1863, in *Inside Lincoln's White House: The Complete Civil War Diary of John Hay,* ed. Michael Burlingame and J. R. T. Ettlinger (Carbondale: Southern Illinois University Press, 1997), 67–68; John Todd Stuart, in *The Lincoln Papers,* ed. David C. Mearns (Garden City, NY: Doubleday, 1948), 159; George Tuthill Borrett, *Letters from Canada and the United States* (London: J. E. Adlard, 1865), 253–54.

3. "To James H. Hackett" (August 17, 1863), in *CW,* 6:392; Joshua Speed and Leonard Swett, in *Herndon's Informants: Letters, Interviews, and Statements About Abraham Lincoln,* ed. Douglas L. Wilson and Rodney O. Davis (Chicago: University of Illinois Press, 1998), 499, 636; Noah Brooks, "Personal Recollections of Abraham Lincoln," in *Lincoln Observed: Civil War Dispatches of Noah Brooks,* ed. Michael Burlingame (Baltimore: Johns Hopkins University Press, 1998), 218–19; William Herndon to "The Editor of *The Liberal Age*" (December 4, 1882), in *Herndon on Lincoln: Letters,* 139; Thomas F. Pendel, *Thirty-Six Years in the White House: Lincoln-Roosevelt* (Washington, DC: Neale, 1902), 25–26; David Homer Bates, *Lincoln in the Telegraph Office* (New York: Century, 1907), 194–95.

4. Robert Todd Lincoln to Isaac Markens (November 4, 1917), in *A Portrait of Abraham Lincoln,* 48; Robert Bray, *Reading with Lincoln* (Carbondale: Southern Illinois University Press, 2010), 121–29, 158–62; John Hay, "The Heroic Age in Washington," in *At Lincoln's Side: John Hay's Civil War Correspondence and Selected Writings,* ed. Michael Burlingame (Carbondale: Southern Illinois University Press, 2000), 138; Douglas L. Wilson, "The Frigate and the Frugal Chariot," in *Lincoln Before Washington: New Perspectives on the Illinois Years* (Urbana: University of Illinois Press, 1997), 10–11; "A Romance of Reality," *Menard Axis* (February 15, 1862), in *Herndon's Informants,* 25–26; Herndon to Cyrus O. Poole (January 5, 1886), *Herndon on Lincoln: Letters,* 183. On Lincoln's read-

ing of Euclid—which in the English-speaking nineteenth century was not nearly so abstract as it sounds—see Glenn W. LaFantasie, "Lincoln, Euclid, and the Satisfaction of Success," *JALA* 41 (Winter 2020): 24–46.

5. Lincoln, "Fragments of a Tariff Discussion" (December 1, 1847), "Address Before the Wisconsin State Agricultural Society, Milwaukee, Wisconsin" (September 30, 1859) and "Annual Message to Congress" (December 3, 1861), in *CW*, 1:412, 3:477, 5:51; Adam Smith, *An Inquiry into the Nature and Causes of the Wealth of Nations*, ed. R. H. Campbell and A. S. Skinner (1776; Indianapolis: Liberty Fund, 1981), 1:10, 224, 292, 296, 2:687; Paul J. McNulty, "Adam Smith's Concept of Labor," *Journal of the History of Ideas* 34 (July 1973): 346; Jesse Norman, *Adam Smith: What He Thought, and Why It Matters* (London: Allen Lane, 2018), 96; Ritchie Robertson, *The Enlightenment: The Pursuit of Happiness, 1680–1790* (New York: HarperCollins, 2021), 537–42; Michael P. Zuckert, *A Nation So Conceived: Abraham Lincoln and the Paradox of Democratic Sovereignty* (Lawrence: University of Kansas Press, 2023), 165. Lincoln made a similar argument in defense of tariffs fourteen years later, after his election to the presidency:

> *I have long thought that if there be any article of necessity which can be produced at home with as little or nearly the same labor as abroad, it would be better to protect that article. Labor is the true standard of value. If a bar of iron, got out of the mines of England, and a bar of iron taken from the mines of Pennsylvania, be produced at the same cost, it follows that if the English bar be shipped from Manchester to Pittsburgh, and the American bar from Pittsburgh to Manchester, the cost of carriage is appreciably lost. If we had no iron here, then we should encourage its shipment from foreign countries; but not when we can make it as cheaply in our own country. This brings us back to our first proposition, that if any article can be produced at home with nearly the same cost as abroad, the carriage is lost labor.* "Speech at Pittsburgh Pennsylvania" (February 15, 1861), in *CW*, 4:212.

Herndon identifies John Ramsay McCulloch, rather than Smith, as one of Lincoln's models, which is odd, since McCulloch followed the lead of David Ricardo and particularly questioned any labor theory of value; but McCulloch also produced the four-volume 1828 edition of Smith's *Wealth of Nations*, which "first gained a wide readership in the 1840s and 1850s," at just the moment when many of the other volumes

Herndon itemizes were circulating. See Hiroshi Mizuta, *A Critical Bibliography of Adam Smith* (London: Routledge, 2016), 38.

6. Lincoln, "Fragment on Free Labor," in *CW,* 3:462; John Stuart Mill, *Principles of Political Economy, with Some of the Their Applications to Social Philosophy* (Boston: Little & Brown, 1848), 2:327–28.

7. Mill, *Principles of Political Economy,* 1:86, 171, 279–80; 2:343, 524. During the Civil War, Mill was quick to defend Lincoln's administration as "the most hopeful sign of the moral state of the American mind which has appeared for many years." See Mill's *The Contest in America—Reprinted from Fraser's Magazine* (Boston: Little, Brown, 1862), 10. Alongside Mill, the twin masters of the "Manchester School"—Richard Cobden and John Bright—offer another uncanny transatlantic resemblance to Lincoln. Cobden and Bright both lauded middle-class commerce as the embodiment of public virtue, and moaned over a British society still locked in the grip of a landed aristocracy. "What a country we live in," exclaimed Bright, "where accident of birth is supreme over almost every description and degree of merit." Cobden frankly described the Anti–Corn Law League crusade, not as "merely a battle about a customs duty," but as the "first serious attempt of a new class to assert its claim to take a foremost place" in British life. "Nothing can be…better calculated for…obstructing the growth of democratic government, than this insane advocacy of national interference," Cobden complained. See Herman Ausubel, *John Bright: Victorian Reformer* (New York: John Wiley, 1966), 56; Cobden to Francis Place (May 11, 1838) and to William Ewart Gladstone (January 22, 1841), in *The Letters of Richard Cobden,* vol. 1, *1815–1847,* ed. Anthony Howe (New York: Oxford University Press, 2007), 135, 213; John Morley, *The Life of Richard Cobden* (Boston, 1881), 126.

It is strange, given the larger similarities of Lincoln and English liberalism, that Cobden, Bright, and Lincoln should be most readily characterized in opposition, and by the one issue upon which they did *not* agree, which was tariffs. Significantly, this seemed never to have provoked from Cobden or Bright the kind of criticism which the Manchester School leveled at the Corn Laws; and with good reason, since the economic positions of the United States and Great Britain were almost exactly inverted. American industry was still struggling to find its legs and required protection; British industry was struggling to escape from restriction, and wanted deliverance from protection. In both cases, the strategy was aimed at a hostile and reactionary agrarianism. Bright denounced the Confederacy's effort to paint itself as a champion of free trade, and Mill insisted that "Slavery alone" and not tariffs "was thought of, alone talked of" by the South. See Marc-William Palen, "The Civil War's Forgotten Transatlantic Tariff Debate and the Confederacy's Free Trade Diplomacy," *Journal of the Civil War Era* 3 (March 2013): 50–51; Heather Cox Richardson, *The Greatest Nation of the Earth: Republican Economic Policies During the Civil War* (Cambridge, MA: Harvard University Press, 1997), 133; Richard Franklin Bensel, *Yankee Leviathan: The Origins of Central State Authority in America, 1859–1877* (New York: Cambridge University Press, 1990), 80.

8. Henry Carey, *Principles of Political Economy* (Philadelphia: Carey, Lea & Blanchard, 1837), 1:x, xiv, 14, 19, *The Slave Trade, Domestic and Foreign: Why It Exists, and How It May Be Extinguished* (Philadelphia: A. Hart, 1853), 294, 299–300, and *Money: A Lecture Delivered Before the New York Geographical and Statistical Society* (Philadelphia: H. C. Baird, 1860), 27; Anthony F. C. Wallace, *Rockdale: The Growth of an American Village in the Early Industrial Revolution* (New York: Knopf, 1978), 394–97; Daniel Walker Howe, *Transforming the American Self: Jonathan Edwards to Abraham Lincoln* (Cambridge, MA: Harvard University Press, 1997), 139.

9. "Second Republican National Platform," in Eugene Virgil Smalley, *A History of the Republican Party from Its Organization to the Present Time* (St. Paul, MN: E. V. Smalley, 1896), 106; Carey to Lincoln (June 20, 1861), in Abraham Lincoln Papers (Series 1, General Correspondence, 1833–1916), Library of Congress; William Belmont Parker, *The Life and Public Services of Justin Smith Morrill* (Boston: Houghton Mifflin, 1924), 108; Richard Rogers Bowker, *A Primer for Political Education* (New York: Society for Political Education, 1886), 17; John T. Nixon, "Revision of the Tariff" (May 4, 1860), in *Congressional Globe*, 36th Congress, 1st session, 295; "Annual Report of the Secretary of the Treasury on the State of the Finances" (July 4, 1861), Senate Executive Document no. 2, 37th Congress, 1st session, 13; Roger Lowenstein, *Ways and Means: Lincoln and His Cabinet and the Financing of the Civil War* (New York: Penguin, 2022), 28–29, 286; Richardson, *Greatest Nation of the Earth*, 133–35; Lincoln to Edward Wallace (May 12, 1860), in *CW*, 4:49; Bensel, *Yankee Leviathan*, 73–74; Gabor S. Boritt, *Lincoln and the Economics of the American Dream* (Memphis, TN: Memphis State University Press, 1977), 209; Edward K. Spann, *Gotham at War: New York City, 1860–1865* (Wilmington, DE: Scholarly Resources, 2002), 8; "The News," *New York Herald* (March 16, 1861); "Journey of the President Elect. Important Speeches of Mr. Lincoln on the Crisis and the Tariff Questions," *New York Herald* (February 16, 1861).

10. *Report of the Secretary of the Treasury on the State of the Finances for the Year Ending June 30, 1861* (Washington, DC: Government Printing Office, 1861), 17–19; John Sherman, "National Bank Currency" (February 10, 1863), in *Selected Speeches and Reports on Finance and Taxation, from 1859 to 1878* (New York: D. Appleton, 1879), 69–70; J. W. Schuckers, *The Life and Public Services of Salmon Portland Chase* (New York: D. Appleton, 1874), 408–9; Fergus Bordewich, *Congress at War: How Republican Reformers Fought the Civil War, Defied Lincoln, Ended Slavery, and Remade America* (New York: Knopf, 2020), 211–13; Lincoln, "To the Senate and House of Representatives" (January 17, 1863), in *CW*, 6:60–61; William O. Stoddard, *Inside the White House in War Times: Memoirs and Reports of Lincoln's Secretary*, ed. Michael Burlingame (Lincoln: University of Nebraska Press, 2000), 103–4.

11. "An Act to Secure Homesteads to Actual Settlers on the Public Domain," in *The Statutes at Large, Treaties and Proclamations of the United States of America*, ed. George P. Sanger (Boston: Little, Brown, 1863), 12:392–93; Lincoln, "Annual Message to Congress" (December 1, 1862), in *CW*, 5:532; Richardson, *Greatest Nation of the Earth*, 144–49; Wigfall, "Homestead Bill" (March 22, 1860), *Congressional Globe*, 36th Congress, 1st session, 1299; William C. Harris, *Lincoln and Congress* (Carbondale: Southern Illinois University Press, 2017), 44–45; Sen. Carl T. Curtis (July 26, 1961), in *Homestead Act Centennial: Hearing Before the Subcommittee on Federal Charters, Holidays and Celebrations* (Washington, DC: Government Printing Office, 1961), 2.

12. Michael Lind, "The Politics of Tollbooth Capitalism," *American Affairs* 5 (Spring 2021): 84–85; Henry Carey, *The North and the South* (New York: Tribune, 1854), 8, 15; Bensel, *Yankee Leviathan*, 136–37; John Elwood Clark, *Railroads in the Civil War: The Impact of Management on Victory and Defeat* (Baton Rouge: Louisiana State University Press, 2001), 35–36; Thomas Weber, *The Northern Railroads in the Civil War* (1952; Bloomington: Indiana University Press, 1999), 102–3; Lincoln, "Annual Message to Congress" (December 3, 1861), in *CW*, 5:37; Boritt, *Lincoln and the Economics of the American Dream*, 210. Michael Lind (*What Lincoln Believed*, 229) suggests that "if Lincoln had lived and promoted the industrialization of the highland South, American economic and political history might have been very different. The poor mining areas of the Appalachians and Ozarks might have become the sites of industrial cities like Pittsburgh, Detroit, and Chicago, providing employment for Southern blacks as well as poor Southern whites and white immigrants from Europe and other parts of the United States,"

instead of declining into the economic and racial morass of the Jim Crow South.

13. Curtis, "Pacific Railroad" (May 24, 1860), in *Congressional Globe*, 36th Congress, 1st session, 2332; Richardson, *Greatest Nation of the Earth*, 173; Bordewich, *Congress at War*, 133; William D. Kelley, "Pacific Railroad Bill" (April 17, 1862), in *Congressional Globe*, 37th Congress, 2nd session, 1707; Lincoln, "Order Extending the Pacific Railroad" (July 11, 1862), "Order Establishing Gauge of Union Pacific Railroad" (January 21, 1863), "To the Officers of the Union Pacific Railroad" (October 16, 1863), "Order Concerning Union Pacific Railroad" (November 17, 1863), "Order Fixing Western Base of the Union Pacific Railroad" (January 12, 1864), in *CW*, 5:314, 6:68, 519, 7:16, 122; Olivier Fraysse, *Lincoln, Land, and Labor, 1809–1860*, trans. S. Neely (Urbana: University of Illinois Press, 1994), 106; Harris, *Lincoln and Congress*, 45–48.

14. William Pitt Kellogg, in *Recollected Words of Abraham Lincoln*, ed. Don E. and Virginia Fehrenbacher (Stanford, CA: Stanford University Press, 1996), 277; Jeremy Atack and Peter Passel, *A New Economic View of American History*, 2nd ed. (New York: W. W. Norton, 1995), 192; William W. Freehling, *Becoming Lincoln* (Charlottesville: University of Virginia Press, 2018), 312; James L. Huston, *The British Gentry, The Southern Farmer, and the Northern Family Farmer: Agriculture and Sectional Antagonism in North America* (Baton Rouge: Louisiana State University Press, 2015), 228; Lincoln, "Address Before the Wisconsin State Agricultural Society, Milwaukee, Wisconsin" (September 30, 1859), "Annual Message to Congress" (December 1, 1862), and "To the Senate and House of Representatives" (January 17, 1863), in *CW*, 3:481, 5:552, 6:61; Lowenstein, *Ways and Means*, 170; Jon D. Schaff, *Abraham Lincoln's Statesmanship and the Limits of Liberal Democracy* (Carbondale: Southern Illinois University Press, 2019), 122; Francis B. Carpenter, *Six Months at the White House with Abraham Lincoln* (New York: Hurd and Houghton, 1867), 84; Schuckers, *Salmon Portland Chase*, 409; *A History of the County of Berkshire, Massachusetts; in Two Parts* (Pittsfield, MA: Samuel W. Bush, 1829), 269.

15. Thomas J. DiLorenzo, *Lincoln Unmasked: What You're Not Supposed to Know About Dishonest Abe* (New York: Three Rivers Press, 2006), 13; Murray Rothbard, "America's Two Just Wars—1775 and 1861," in *The Costs of War: America's Pyrrhic Victories*, ed. John V. Denson (New Brunswick, NJ: Transaction Publishers, 1999), 128–29; David Gordon, "Harry V. Jaffa and the Indefensible Abe," *Mises Review* 7 (Summer 2001), at https://mises.org/library/new-birth-freedom-abraham-lincoln-and

-coming-civil-war-harry-v-jaffa. The most important statement of the comparison of Lincoln and Bismarck is Carl Degler in "The American Civil War and the German Wars of Unification: The Problem of Comparison," in Stig Förster and Jörg Nagler, eds., *On the Road to Total War: The American Civil War and the German Wars of Unification, 1861–1871* (New York: Cambridge University Press, 1997), 53–72. For an extended rebuttal of the libertarian and Degler comparisons, see Michael Knox Beran, *Forge of Empires, 1861–1871: Three Revolutionary Statesmen and the World They Made* (New York: Free Press, 2007); and Thomas L. Krannawitter, *Vindicating Lincoln: Defending the Politics of Our Greatest President* (Lanham, MD: Rowman and Littlefield, 2008), 298–302.

16. *Historical Statistics of the United States, Colonial Times to 1970* (Washington, DC: U.S. Government Printing Office, 1975), 2:1103–4; Paul P. Van Riper and Keith A. Sutherland, "The Northern Civil Service, 1861–1865," *CWH,* 11 (December 1965): 347; *Register of Officers and Agents, Civil, Military and Naval, in the Service of the United States on the Thirtieth September, 1863* (Washington, DC: Government Printing Office, 1864), 1–2, 40–41, 57–96, 97, 122, 125, 265; Mark E. Neely Jr., *Lincoln and the Triumph of the Nation: Constitutional Conflict in the American Civil War* (Chapel Hill: University of North Carolina Press, 2011), 109.

17. Ralph Waldo Emerson, "Abraham Lincoln. Remarks at the Funeral Services of the President, in Concord, April 27, 1865," *The Liberator* (May 5, 1865); Lincoln, "Application for Patent on an Improved Method of Lifting Vessels over Shoals" (March 10, 1849), "Second Lecture on Discoveries and Inventions" (February 11, 1859), "Speech at Hartford, Connecticut" (March 5, 1860), and "Emancipation Proclamation" (January 1, 1863), in *CW,* 2:31, 3:363, 4:7, 6:30.

18. Herbert Croly, *The Promise of American Life* (New York: Macmillan, 1914), 275; Helen Nicolay, *Personal Traits of Abraham Lincoln* (New York: Century, 1912), 381–82; Albert J. Beveridge, *Abraham Lincoln, 1809–1858* (Boston: Houghton Mifflin, 1928), 1:236; Arnold S. Cohen letter, *New York Times* (January 16, 2023); Richard Hofstadter, "Abraham Lincoln and the Self-Made Myth," in *The American Political Tradition and the Men Who Made It* (1948; New York: Knopf, 1973), 102, 105; David S. Brown, *Richard Hofstadter: An Intellectual Biography* (Chicago: University of Chicago Press, 2006), 59.

19. James L. Huston, *The British Gentry, the Southern Planter, and the Northern Family Farmer,* 75, and *Calculating the Value of the Union: Slavery, Property Rights, and the Economic Origins of the Civil War* (Chapel Hill: University of North Carolina Press, 2003), 75–76; David Montgom-

ery, *Beyond Equality: Labor and the Radical Republicans, 1862–1872* (New York: Knopf, 1967), 4–5, 8; Robert J. Gordon, *The Rise and Fall of American Growth: The U.S. Standard of Living Since the Civil War* (Princeton, NJ: Princeton University Press, 2016), 97, 102–5; Amel Toukabri and Lauren Medina, "Latest City and Town Population Estimates of the Decade Show Three-Fourths of the Nation's Incorporated Places Have Fewer Than 5,000 People" (May 21, 2020), at https://www.census.gov/library/stories/2020/05/america-a-nation-of-small-towns.html; Jared Hecht, "Are Small Businesses Really the Backbone of the Economy?" *Inc.* (December 17, 2014), at https://www.inc.com/jared-hecht/are-small-businesses-really-the-backbone-of-the-economy.html; Maryam Mohsin, "10 Small Business Statistics Every Future Entrepreneur Should Know in 2020," *Oberlo* (January 23, 2020), at https://www.oberlo.com/blog/small-business-statistics; Melissa Angell, "Small Business Applications Smash Another New Record in 2022," *Inc.* (January 18, 2023); Lincoln, "Speech at Indianapolis, Indiana" (September 19, 1859) and "Speech at New Haven, Connecticut" (March 6, 1860), in *CW*, 3:469, 4:24–25.

Chapter Five: Democratic Culture

1. Plato, *Republic,* trans. G. M. A. Greve (Indianapolis, IN: Hackett Publishing, 1992), 215; Alexis de Tocqueville, *Democracy in America,* ed. H C. Mansfield and D. Winthrop (Chicago: University of Chicago Press, 2000), 352; John Burt, "Lincoln's Dred Scott: Contesting the Declaration of Independence," *American Literary History* 21 (Winter 2009): 743. This is what Michael Polanyi described in the 1960s when he said that every law or constitution depends on what "we have assumed from the start," on what "exceeds the powers of articulation," and what Robert Bellah would call "habits of the heart." See Polanyi, *Personal Knowledge: Towards a Post-Critical Philosophy* (1962; Chicago: University of Chicago Press, 2015), 34, 92; and Bellah, *Habits of the Heart: Individualism and Commitment in American Life* (Berkeley: University of California Press, 1985), 22–26.

2. Drew R. McCoy, *The Last of the Fathers: James Madison and the Republican Legacy* (New York: Cambridge University Press, 1989), 234; Forrest A. Nabors, *From Oligarchy to Republicanism: The Great Task of Reconstruction* (Columbia: University of Missouri Press, 2017), 266; Albion W. Tourgée, *A Fool's Errand, by One of the Fools: The Famous Romance of American History* (New York: Fords, Howard & Hulbert, 1880), 156; James G.

Blaine, *Twenty Years of Congress: from Lincoln to Garfield, with a Review of the Events which led to the Political Revolution of 1860* (Norwich, CT: Henry Bill, 1884), 1:256, 257; Frederick Douglass, "Reconstruction," *Atlantic Monthly* 18 (December 1866): 762; Alex Gourevitch, *From Slavery to the Cooperative Commonwealth: Labor and Republican Liberty in the Nineteenth Century* (New York: Cambridge University Press, 2015), 22–47.

3. John Pettit, "The Nebraska and Kansas Bill" (February 20, 1854), *Congressional Globe,* 33rd Congress, 1st session, appendix, 214; Sidney Blumenthal, *The Political Life of Abraham Lincoln: Wrestling with His Angel, 1849–1856* (New York: Simon & Schuster, 2017), 304; Lincoln, "Speech at Springfield, Illinois" (June 26, 1857) and "Speech at Edwardsville, Illinois" (September 11, 1858), in *CW,* 2:404, 3:95. Not surprisingly, the Jacobins justified tyranny on the grounds that they represented the "general will" of the people, whereas the Convention merely represented the particular wills of its members; see Alan Charles Kors, "The Ethics of Democracy," *Georgetown Journal of Law and Public Policy* 18 (Summer 2020): 694–95.

4. Allan Kulikoff, "The American Revolution, Capitalism, and the Formation of the Yeoman Classes," in *Beyond the American Revolution: Explorations in the History of American Radicalism,* ed. Alfred J. Young (DeKalb: Northern Illinois University Press, 1993), 87; Hector St. John de Crèvecoeur, *Letters from an American Farmer and Sketches of Eighteenth-Century America,* ed. Albert Stone (New York: Penguin, 1981), 69–70; Georges Fisch, *Nine Months in the United States During the Crisis* (London: James Nisbet, 1863), 99; "Nathaniel Hawthorne," *North American Review* 76 (January 1853): 247.

5. John Randolph, in Henry F. May, *The Enlightenment in America* (New York: Oxford University Press, 1978), 330; *Oakes v. Hill* (October 1830), in *Reports of Cases Argued and Determined in the Supreme Judicial Court of Massachusetts,* ed. O. Pickering (Boston: Hilliard, Gray, 1833), 10:240; Fisch, *Nine Months in the United States,* 37; Tocqueville, *Democracy in America,* 275, 278–79.

6. Crèvecoeur, "Sketches of Eighteenth-Century America," in *Letters from an American Farmer,* 324.

7. Hawthorne, *The Blithedale Romance* (Boston: Ticknor, Reed & Fields, 1852), 76; John Henry Hopkins, *The American Citizen: His Rights and Duties, According to the Spirit of the Constitution of the United States* (New York: Pudney & Russell, 1857), 77; David Hackett Fischer, *African Founders: How Enslaved People Expanded American Ideals* (New York: Simon & Schuster, 2022), 95–96, 720.

8. "Testimony Taken by the Committee on Privileges and Elections, in Relation to the Alleged Frauds Committed upon the Ballot-Boxes in Schenectady County, at the Election in November, 1839," in *Documents of the Assembly of the State of New York, Sixty-Third Session, 1840* (Albany: Thurlow Weed, 1840), 7:21, 26; *Memoirs of Gustave Koerner*, ed. T. J. McCormick (Cedar Rapids, IA: Torch Press, 1909), 2:613; Joel H. Silbey, *The American Political Nation, 1838–1893* (Stanford, CA: Stanford University Press, 1991), 47; Ernest Duvergier de Haranne, *Huit Mois en Amerique: Lettres et Notes de Voyage, 1864–1865* (Paris, 1866), 3, 7, 9. See his comment on an election meeting:

> *I followed them to the Court-house where I found mobs being harangued by speakers while two men posted at the windows flooded them with a rain of small paper booklets. We were rushing to pick them up, and I had some difficulty in grasping one. It was one of those strange election pamphlets, part sermon, part poster, in slogans about this or that, with a lot of capital letters, enlarged and underlined words, and exclamations which Americans are so good at creating for the general public. . . . These meetings are all alike, like those clubs whose torchlight processions fill the streets of the city all night. Last night, when everyone was asleep, a din of band instruments sounded in the street; a long line of torches and lanterns stopped under our windows for some time, pulsing to the cadence of Hip! Hip! Hoorah!*

Charles Fried, "Foreword," *Harvard Journal of Law and Public Policy* 39 (March 2016), 333; Walt Whitman, "Election Day, November 1884," in *Leaves of Grass* (New York: D. Appleton, 1912), 391; Lincoln, "Fragment of Speech Intended for Kentuckians" (February 12, 1861), in *CW,* 4:200.

9. Lincoln, "Whig Protest in Illinois Legislature Against the Reorganization of the Judiciary" (February 26, 1841), "Fragment on Formation of the Republican Party" (February 26, 1857), and "To Erastus Corning and Others" (June 12, 1863), in *CW,* 1:247, 2:391, and 6:267; Burt, "Lincoln's Dred Scott," 738; Herman Belz, "Lincoln's View of Direct Democracy and Public Opinion," in *Democracy: How Direct? Views from the Founding Era and the Polling Era*, ed. Elliott Abrams (Lanham, MD: Rowman & Littlefield, 2002), 34.

10. Lincoln, "To Millard Fillmore" (March 11, 1851), "Speech at Paris, Illinois" (September 7, 1858), and "To Lyman Trumbull" (December 10, 1860), in *CW,* 2:102, 3:90, and 4:149.

11. Lincoln, "Speech at a Republican Banquet, Chicago, Illinois" (Decem-

ber 10, 1856), "First Debate with Stephen A. Douglas at Ottawa, Illinois" (August 21, 1858), "Speech at Cincinnati, Ohio" (September 17, 1859), and "Speech at Hartford, Connecticut" (March 5, 1860), in *CW,* 2:385, 3:27, 442, and 4:9.

12. Lincoln, "Remarks in Illinois Legislature Concerning Appropriation for Building the State House" (January 7, 1839), "First Inaugural Address Final Text" (March 4, 1861), "Message to Congress in Special Session" (July 4, 1861), and "Opinion on the Admission of West Virginia into the Union" (December 31, 1862), in *CW,* 1:126, 4:202–3, 4:428, and 6:28. Even as he journeyed eastward by train for his inauguration as president, Lincoln was still promising deference and accommodation toward public opinion. "I deem it due to myself and the whole country," he said in Cincinnati, "in the present extraordinary condition of the country and of public opinion, that I should wait and see the last development of public opinion before I give my views or express myself at the time of the inauguration." See "Speech to Germans at Cincinnati, Ohio" (February 12, 1861), in *CW,* 4:270; and Belz, "Lincoln's View of Direct Democracy and Public Opinion," 51–52.

13. Lincoln, "Speech at Springfield, Illinois" (June 26, 1857), "First Lecture on Discoveries and Inventions" (April 6, 1858), "Speech at Springfield, Illinois" (July 17, 1858), "Second Lecture on Discoveries and Inventions" (February 11, 1859), "Speech at Indianapolis, Indiana" (September 19, 1859), and "Speech at Hartford Connecticut" (March 5, 1860), *CW,* 2:409, 437, 440, 520, 3:363, 469, and 4:2, 9. Curiously, as president, Lincoln signed two congressional property confiscation acts into law. But his administration was unenthusiastic about enforcing them in any sweeping way. He waited six months after the passage of the second Confiscation Act in July 1862 to authorize Attorney General Edward Bates to begin enforcement of the *first* Confiscation Act (from August 1861). Even then, he assured the widow of Stephen Douglas, whose stepsons had inherited property in Louisiana, that she need "not expect the property of absent minor children will be confiscated." In the case of property used by the Confederacy for military purposes, he would grant that such "property may be destroyed for proper military objects," but the emphasis was on *proper,* "none shall be destroyed in wantonness or malice," if he could help it. Even then, "accounts shall be kept, sufficiently accurate, and in detail to show quantities and amounts and from whom, both property, and such persons shall have come, as a basis upon which compensation can be made in proper cases." When an Arkansan, Mary Morton, appealed the confiscation

of her property by a Union general in 1865, Lincoln ordered the property returned, warning that "the true rule for the Military is to seize such property as is needed for Military uses and reasons, and let the rest alone." Taken together, the entire value of property seized during the Civil War amounted to only $300,000 and just over 15,000 acres of land. See Lincoln, "Advice to Mrs. Stephen A. Douglas" (November 17, 1861), "To Edwin M. Stanton" (July 22, 1862), and "To Joseph J. Reynolds"(January 20, 1865), in *CW*, 5:32, 8:229, Supplement 1:141; Burrus M. Carnahan, *Lincoln on Trial: Southern Civilians and the Law of War* (Lexington: University Press of Kentucky, 2010), 43–46, Daniel W. Hamilton, *The Limits of Sovereignty: Property Confiscation in the Union and the Confederacy During the Civil War* (Chicago: University of Chicago Press, 2007), 146; John Syrett, "The Confiscation Acts: Efforts at Reconstruction During the Civil War" (PhD dissertation, University of Wisconsin, 1971), 93; James G. Randall, *The Confiscation of Property During the Civil War* (Indianapolis, IN: Mutual Printing, 1913), 48, and *Constitutional Problems Under Lincoln* (New York: D. Appleton, 1926), 289–92.

14. "To Martin S. Morris" (March 26, 1843) and "Handbill Replying to Charges of Infidelity" (July 31, 1846), in *CW*, 1:319, 382; Henry C. Deming, in *Recollected Words of Abraham Lincoln*, ed. Don E. and Virginia Fehrenbacher (Stanford, CA: Stanford University Press, 1996), 137.

15. Lincoln, "Meditation on the Divine Will" (September 2, 1862) and "Second Inaugural Address" (March 4, 1865), in *CW*, 5:403, 8:332.

16. Lincoln, "Speech at Chicago, Illinois" (July 10, 1858), in *CW*, 2:499–500.

17. Lincoln, "Eulogy on Henry Clay" (July 6, 1852) and "To Joshua Speed" (August 24, 1855), in *CW*, 2:126, 322; "Federal Whigs, Alias Native Americans," *Springfield State Register* (June 21, 1844).

18. Lincoln, "To William H. Herndon" (June 22, 1848), "To Thomas Cory" (July 29, 1859), "To Jesse W. Fell, Enclosing Autobiography" (December 20, 1859), "First Inaugural Address—First Edition and Revision" (March 4, 1861), and "Memorandum Concerning His Probable Failure of Re-election" (August 23, 1864), in *CW*, 1:490, 3:395, 511, 4:259, 7:514; John Hay and John Nicolay, "Abraham Lincoln: A History—Cabinet Changes—Lincoln Reelected—Chase as Chief-Justice," *Century Magazine* 38 (September 1889), 699; Lucius E. Chittenden, in Fehrenbacher, *Recollected Words of Abraham Lincoln*, 104.

19. Adam Smith, *The Theory of Moral Sentiments* (1759; London: Henry G. Bohn, 1853), 342; Lincoln, "Address Before the Young Men's Lyceum of Springfield, Illinois" (January 27, 1838), in *CW*, 1:114.

20. Carl Schurz, in Francis F. Browne, *The Every-day Life of Abraham Lincoln* (New York: N. D. Thompson, 1887), 423; Jesse Weik, *The Real Lincoln: A Portrait* (Boston: Houghton Mifflin, 1922), 215–16; Hay, diary entry for September 24, 1862, in *Inside Lincoln's White House: The Complete Civil War Diary of John Hay*, ed. Michael Burlingame and J. R. T. Ettlinger (Carbondale: Southern Illinois University Press, 1997), 41; "Conversation with Hon. J. P. Usher" (October 8, 1878), in *An Oral History of Abraham Lincoln: John G. Nicolay's Interviews and Essays*, ed. Michael Burlingame (Carbondale: Southern Illinois University Press, 1996), 67; William O. Stoddard, *Inside the White House in War Times: Memoirs and Reports of Lincoln's Secretary*, ed. Michael Burlingame (Lincoln: University of Nebraska Press, 2000), 148.

21. Lincoln, "Fragment on Sectionalism" (July 23, 1856), "Speech at Edwardsville, Illinois" (September 11, 1858), and "Speech at Columbus, Ohio" (September 16, 1859), in *CW*, 2:352–53, 3:92, 410; Weik, *The Real Lincoln*, 231.

22. Lincoln, "Speech at Springfield, Illinois" (June 26, 1857), "First Debate with Stephen A. Douglas at Ottawa, Illinois" (August 21, 1858), "Speech at Carlinville, Illinois" (August 31, 1858), "Fourth Debate with Stephen A. Douglas at Charleston, Illinois" (September 18, 1858), "Sixth Debate with Stephen A. Douglas, at Quincy, Illinois" (October 13, 1858), "Seventh and Last Debate with Stephen A. Douglas at Alton, Illinois" (October 15, 1858), and "Speech at New Haven, Connecticut" (March 6, 1860), in *CW*, 2:409, 3:14, 78, 181, 255, 304, 4:16, 17.

23. "Fragment on Pro-Slavery Theology" (October 1, 1858), "To Simon Cameron" (October 25, 1861), and "Response to Methodists" (May 18, 1864), in *CW*, 3:204, 5:3, 7:351; Carnahan, *Lincoln on Trial*, 43–46; Martin Borden, "The Christian Amendment," *CWH* 25 (June 1979): 160, 163.

24. John Hay, in Fehrenbacher, *Recollected Words*, 216.

Chapter Six: Democracy and Civil Liberties

1. Lincoln, "Address to the Pennsylvania General Assembly at Harrisburg" (February 22, 1861), "Message to Congress in Special Session" (July 4, 1861), "Proclamation Revoking General Hunter's Order of Military Emancipation of May 9, 1862" (May 19, 1862), and "To Alexander Ramsay" (August 27, 1862), in *CW*, 4:245, 426, 429, 438, 5:222, 396; James G. Randall, *Constitutional Problems Under Lincoln* (New York: D. Appleton, 1926), 513.

2. James Buchanan, "Annual Message of December 3, 1860," in George

Ticknor Curtis, *Life of James Buchanan, Fifteenth President of the United States* (New York: Harper & Bros., 1883), 2:347.

3. Lincoln, "First Inaugural Address" (March 4, 1861), in *CW*, 4:264.

4. Hamilton, Nos. 28 and 69, *The Federalist Papers*, 136, 357. That role would have been even more marginal in Hamilton's original scheme for a Constitution in 1787: "He shall be the Commander in Chief of the army and navy of the United States, and of the militia within the several States, and shall have the direction of war when commenced; but he shall not take the actual command in the field of an army, without the consent of the Senate and Assembly." See "Draft of a Constitution," in *The Papers of Alexander Hamilton,* ed. H. C. Syrett (New York: Columbia University Press, 1962), 4:263.

5. "To Erastus Corning and Others" (June 12, 1863) and "Message to Congress in Special Session" (July 4, 1861), in *CW*, 6:267, 4:426; Harry V. Jaffa, *A New Birth of Freedom: Abraham Lincoln and the Coming of the Civil War* (Lanham, MD: Rowman & Littlefield, 2000), 361; Daniel A. Farber, *Lincoln's Constitution* (Chicago: University of Chicago Press, 2003), 8.

6. Michael P. Zuckert, *A Nation So Conceived: Abraham Lincoln and the Paradox of Democratic Sovereignty* (Lawrence: University of Kansas Press, 2023), 278–88; James A. Dueholm, "Lincoln's Suspension of the Writ of Habeas Corpus: An Historical and Constitutional Analysis," *JALA* 29 (Summer 2008): 49–51, 61–62; Robert O. Faith, "Public Necessity or Military Convenience? Reevaluating Lincoln's Suspensions of the Writ of Habeas Corpus During the Civil War," *CWH* 62 (September 2016): 285–86; Jonathan W. White, *Abraham Lincoln and Treason in the Civil War: The Trials of John Merryman* (Baton Rouge: Louisiana State University Press, 2011), 14–15; Louis Fisher, "Abraham Lincoln: Preserving the Union and the Constitution," *Albany Government Law Review* 3 (2010): 24. For subsequent suspensions of the writ in 1861, see "To Winfield Scott" (June 20, July 2, and October 14, 1861), in *CW*, 4:414, 419, 554.

7. "To Salmon P. Chase" (September 2, 1863), in *CW*, 6:428–29.

8. Lincoln, "Message to Congress in Special Session" (July 4, 1861), in *CW*, 4:426; Herman Belz, "Lincoln, Secession, and Revolution: The Civil War Challenge to the Founding," in *Constitutionalism in the Approach and Aftermath of the Civil War,* ed. Paul Moreno and Johnathan O'Neill (New York: Fordham University Press, 2013), 98.

9. Lincoln, "Address Before the Young Men's Lyceum of Springfield, Illinois" (January 27, 1838), "Message to Congress in Special Session" (July 4, 1861), "Revision of William H. Seward to Charles Francis

Adams" (May 21, 1861), and "To James C. Conkling" (August 26, 1863), in *CW,* 1:109, 112, 115, 4:379, 428, 436, 6:407.

10. "Arrest and Detention of Certain Members of the Maryland Legislature," *The War of the Rebellion: A Compilation of the Official Records of the Union and Confederate Armies* (Washington, DC: Government Printing Office, 1894), series 2, 1:667–75; Jennifer L. Weber, *Copperheads: The Rise and Fall of Lincoln's Opponents in the North* (New York: Oxford University Press, 2006), 36; Bruce Tap, "Race, Rhetoric, and Emancipation: The Election of 1862 in Illinois," *CWH* 39 (June 1993): 119; "Terrorism in Indiana," *Bedford Gazette* (November 11, 1864); Stephen E. Towne, "Worse Than Vallandigham: Governor Oliver P. Morton, Lambdin P. Milligan, and the Military Arrest and Trial of Indiana State Senator Alexander J. Douglas During the Civil War," *Indiana Magazine of History* 106 (March 2010): 7.

11. Diary entry for August 25, 1862, in *A Philadelphia Perspective: The Civil War Diary of Sidney George Fisher,* ed. Jonathan W. White (New York: Fordham University Press, 2007), 160; Frank Key Howard, *Fourteen Months in American Bastiles* (Baltimore: Kelly, Hedian & Piet, 1863), 7–8; John A. Marshall, *American Bastille: A History of the Illegal Arrests and Imprisonment of American Citizens During the Late Civil War* (Philadelphia: Thomas W. Hartley, 1869), 586–605.

12. William C. Harris, *Two Against Lincoln, Reverdy Johnson and Horatio Seymour: Champions of the Loyal Opposition* (Lawrence: University Press of Kansas, 2017), 171–72; Frank L. Clement, *Lincoln's Critics: The Copperheads of the North* (Shippensburg, PA: White Mane Books, 1999), 28; Norma Ann Paul, "Suppression of the *Chicago Times:* June 1863" (MA thesis, Loyola University of Chicago, 1932), 101; Craig D. Tenney, "To Suppress or Not to Suppress: Abraham Lincoln and the *Chicago Times,*" *CWH* 27 (September 1981): 253; Stephen E. Towne, "Killing the Serpent Speedily: Governor Morton, General Hascall, and the Suppression of the Democratic Press in Indiana, 1863," *CWH* 52 (March 2006): 51–53; John W. Robinson, "A California Copperhead: Henry Hamilton and the Los Angeles Star," *Arizona and the West* 23 (Autumn 1981): 220–21; Dennis A. Mahony, *The Prisoner of State* (New York: Carleton, 1863), 119. Other arrests included James McMaster of the *New York Freeman's Journal,* Albert Boileau of the *Philadelphia Evening Journal,* Dennis A. Mahony of the *Dubuque Herald,* and Samuel Medary (a former territorial governor under President James Buchanan) of the *Columbus Crisis.*

13. "The Widow-Maker of the Nineteenth Century," in *LaCrosse Democrat*

(August 25, 1864); "Released," *Huntington Democrat* (November 20, 1862); Edward Holcomb Stiles, *Recollections and Sketches of Notable Lawyers and Public Men of Early Iowa* (Des Moines, IA: Homestead Publishing, 1916), 862–63; Peter J. Barry, "'I'll Keep Them in Prison Awhile...'" Abraham Lincoln and David Davis on Civil Liberties in Wartime," *JALA* 28 (Winter 2007): 24; David W. Bulla, "'Palpable Injury': Abraham Lincoln and Press Suppression in the Civil War North," in *An Indispensable Liberty: The Fight for Free Speech in Nineteenth-Century America* (Carbondale: Southern Illinois University Press, 2016), 45–46; Lincoln, "Memorandum: Military Arrests" (May 17, 1861), "To John W. Davis" (September 15, 1861), and "To William H. Seward" (October 4, 1861), in *CW*, 4:522, 549.

14. "The Election at Home," *New-York Tribune* (November 9, 1864); Monroe Porter to Horace Congar (November 11, 1864), in Daniel W. Crofts, "Re-electing Lincoln: The Struggle in Newark," *CWH* 30 (March 1984): 76; Mark E. Neely Jr., *The Fate of Liberty: Abraham Lincoln and Civil Liberties* (New York: Oxford University Press, 1991), 147, 194–95; Samuel Negus, "A Notorious Nest of Offense: Neutrals, Belligerents, and Union Jails in Civil War Blockade Running," *CWH* 56 (December 2010): 385; "City Intelligence," *Philadelphia Evening Telegraph* (November 9, 1864); John Syrett, "The Confiscation Acts: Efforts at Reconstruction During the Civil War" (PhD dissertation, University of Wisconsin, 1971), 153.

15. Lincoln, "To Orville Hickman Browning" (September 22, 1861), in *CW*, 4:532.

16. Julie Roy Jeffrey, "'They Cannot Expect...That a Loyal People Will Tolerate the Utterance of Such Sentiments': The Campaign Against Treasonous Speech During the Civil War," *CWH* 65 (March 2019): 9; Mark E. Neely Jr., "The Lincoln Administration and Arbitrary Arrests: A Reconsideration," *JALA* 5 (Winter 1983): 8, 12–16, and *Lincoln and the Democrats: The Politics of Opposition in the Civil War* (New York: Cambridge University Press, 2017), 127; Paul Finkelman, "Civil Liberties and Civil War: The Great Emancipator as Civil Libertarian," *Michigan Law Review* 91 (May 1993): 1361.

17. Lincoln, "To John Brough and Samuel P. Heintzelman" (June 20, 1864), in *CW*, 7:402.

18. William H. Egle, *An Illustrated History of the Commonwealth of Pennsylvania, Civil, Political, and Military* (Philadelphia: E. M. Gardner, 1880), 272; William Schouler, *A History of Massachusetts in the Civil War* (Boston: John Wilson & Son, 1871), 2:12; Richard F. Miller, ed., *States at War*, vol. 3,

Notes

A Reference Guide for Pennsylvania in the Civil War (Hanover, NH: University Press of New England, 2014), 3.

19. Lincoln, "To Edwin M. Stanton" (March 18, 1864), in *CW,* 7:255; Michael Les Benedict, "'The Perpetuation of Our Political Institutions': Lincoln, the Powers of the Commander in Chief, and the Constitution," *Cardozo Law Review* 29 (2008): 930; William Blair, *With Malice Toward Some: Treason and Loyalty in the Civil War Era* (Chapel Hill: University of North Carolina Press, 2014), 307.

20. W. H. Smith, in *Reminiscences About Abraham Lincoln: Newspaper Clippings, Accounts, and Memories of Those Whose Lives Included an Encounter with the 16th President of the United States,* ed. W. R. Wilson (Elmira, NY: Cayuga Press, 1945), 269–70.

Chapter Seven: Democracy and Race

1. Michael Mann, *The Dark Side of Democracy: Explaining Ethnic Cleansing* (New York: Cambridge University Press, 2005), 55.

2. This is what Susan Lane describes as "autochthonous ancestry," in *Race and Citizen Identity in the Classical Athenian Democracy* (New York: Cambridge University Press, 2010), 16–18. See also Michael G. Hanchard, *The Spectre of Race: How Discrimination Haunts Western Democracy* (Princeton, NJ: Princeton University Press, 2018), 74.

3. Alexis de Tocqueville, *Democracy in America,* ed. H. C. Mansfield and D. Winthrop (Chicago: University of Chicago Press, 2000), 303–5, 326, 329, 335, 341, 348. Yet, years later, Tocqueville helped draft the legislation in the French Chamber of Deputies which abolished slavery in the French colonies. See Joel Lieske, "Race and Democracy," *PS: Political Science and Politics* 32 (June 1999): 218–23. Nor is the American democracy the only modern democratic regime with a race problem. Brazilians have often touted their democracy for blending several races into a single *ethnos,* but this has been challenged by Thomas E. Skidmore in *Black into White: Race and Nationality in Brazilian Thought* (New York: Oxford University Press, 1974); and by Michael G. Hanchard in *Orpheus and Power: The Movimento Negro of Rio de Janeiro and São Paulo, Brazil, 1945–1988* (Princeton, NJ: Princeton University Press, 1994).

4. George H. Moore, *Notes on the History of Slavery in Massachusetts* (New York: D. Appleton, 1866), 145; David Hackett Fisher, *African Founders: How Enslaved People Expanded American Ideals* (New York: Simon & Schuster, 2022), 80; "Debates in the Federal Convention of 1787 as

Reported by James Madison" (August 8, 1787), in *Documents Illustra-tive of the Formation of the Union of the American States,* ed. Charles C. Tansill (Washington, DC: Government Printing Office, 1927), 616; Sean Wilentz, *No Property in Man: Slavery and Antislavery at the Nation's Founding* (Cambridge, MA: Harvard University Press, 2018), 154, 165, 167–69, 176; Paul Finkelman, "The First Civil Rights Movement: Black Rights in the Age of the Revolution and Chief Taney's Originalism in *Dred Scott," University of Pennsylvania Journal of Constitutional Law* 24 (June 2022): 707; Mark E. Neely Jr., *Lincoln and the Triumph of the Nation: Constitutional Conflict in the American Civil War* (Chapel Hill: University of North Carolina Press, 2011), 113.

5. Moore, *Notes on the History of Slavery in Massachusetts,* 186; James Oliver Horton, "Urban Alliances: The Emergence of Race-Based Populism in the Age of Jackson," in *The African American Urban Experience: Per-spectives from the Colonial Period to the Present,* ed. Joe W. Trotter (New York: Macmillan 2004), 30; Marc W. Kruman, *Between Authority and Liberty: State Constitution-Making in Revolutionary America* (Chapel Hill: University of North Carolina Press, 1997), 103–8.

6. "An Act Regulating Black Suffrage, 1811," in *Jim Crow New York: A Doc-umentary History of Race and Citizenship, 1777–1877,* ed. D. N. Gellman and D. Quigley (New York: New York University Press, 2003), 64–65; David A. Bateman, *Disenfranchising Democracy: Constructing the Elector-ate in the United States, the United Kingdom, and France* (New York: Cam-bridge University Press, 2018), 87; Eugene H. Berwanger, *The Frontier Against Slavery: Western Anti-Negro Prejudice and the Slavery Extension Controversy* (Urbana: University of Illinois Press, 1967), 23; Daniel W. Wilder, "The Story of Kansas," in *Transactions of the Kansas State His-torical Society, 1897–1900,* ed. G. W. Martin (Topeka, KS: W. Y. Morgan, 1900), 6:337.

7. Richard Wightman Fox, *Lincoln's Body: A Cultural History* (New York: W. W. Norton, 2015), 226, 234–36; "Delegates to Pay Visit to Lincoln Memorial," *Washington Evening Star,* August 5, 1926; William E. Lilly, "Abraham Lincoln: Never Was a Man More Worthy of the Love of a People," *Chicago Defender,* February 15, 1930. Lilly collected the series in book form under the title *Set My People Free: A Negro's Life of Lincoln* in 1932.

8. Lerone Bennett Jr., *Forced into Glory: Abraham Lincoln's White Dream* (Chicago: Johnson Publishing, 2000), 624; Lincoln, "Fifth Debate with Stephen A. Douglas, at Galesburg, Illinois" (October 7, 1858) and "Sec-ond Lecture on Discoveries and Inventions" (February 11, 1859), in *CW,*

3:235, 358; Daryl Michael Scott, "The Scandal of Thirteentherism," *Liberties: A New Journal of Culture and Politics* 2 (Winter 2021), http://web .archive.org/web/20210308113949/https://libertiesjournal.com/now -showing/the-scandal-of-thirteentherism/.

9. Jared Sexton, "Racial Profiling and the Societies of Control," in *Warfare in the American Homeland: Policing and Prison in a Penal Democracy*, ed. Joy James (Durham, NC: Duke University Press, 2007), 202; Frank B. Wilderson, *Afro-Pessimism* (New York: Liveright, 2020), 14–15; Michael Kazin, "Criticize and Thrive: The American Left in the Obama Years," in Julian Zelizer, *The Presidency of Barack Obama* (Princeton, NJ: Princeton University Press, 2018), 246, 250–53; Joshua S. Sellers, "Race, Reckoning, Reform, and the Limits of the Law of Democracy," *University of Pennsylvania Law Review* 169 (July 2021): 1997; Eddie Glaude, *Democracy in Black: How Race Still Enslaves the American Soul* (New York: Broadway Books, 2017), 7, 34, 146.

10. Lawrence Blum, *I'm Not a Racist, But . . .: The Moral Quandary of Race* (Ithaca, NY: Cornell University Press, 2002), 9, 32; George M. Fredrickson, *Racism: A Short History* (Princeton, NJ: Princeton University Press, 2002), 151; Glenn C. Loury, *The Anatomy of Racial Inequality* (Cambridge, MA: Harvard University Press, 2002), 9–11; J. L. A. Garcia, "The Heart of Racism," *Journal of Social Philosophy* 27 (Fall 1996): 5–45; Dante Puzzo, "Racism and the Western Tradition," *Journal of the History of Ideas* 25 (October/December 1964): 579–86; Sterling Stuckey, "Racism," in *The Oxford Companion to United States History*, ed. Paul S. Boyer (New York: Oxford University Press, 2001), 644–45; Winthrop Jordan, *White over Black: American Attitudes Toward the Negro, 1550–1812* (Chapel Hill: University of North Carolina Press, 1968), 64; Scott L. Malcolmson, *One Drop of Blood: The American Misadventure of Race* (New York: Farrar, Straus & Giroux, 2000), 133–84; Werner Sollors, "Ethnicity: Early Theories," *Encyclopedia of American Cultural and Intellectual History*, ed. M. K. Cayton and P. W. Williams (New York: Charles Scribner's Sons, 2001), 3:101–6; Thomas L. Carson, *Lincoln's Ethics* (New York: Cambridge University Press, 2015), 337–43.

11. Lincoln, "To Albert G. Hodges" (April 4, 1864), "Protest in Illinois Legislature on Slavery" (March 3, 1837), "Remarks in Illinois Legislature Concerning Resolutions in Relation to Fugitive Slaves" (January 5, 1839), "Remarks and Resolution Introduced in United States House of Representatives Concerning Abolition of Slavery in the District of Columbia" (January 10, 1849), and "To Joshua F. Speed" (August 24, 1855), in *CW*, 1:75, 126, 2:20–22, 320, 7:281; Michael Burlingame, "The First

Servant/Slave Liberated by Lincoln," *For the People: A Newsletter of the Abraham Lincoln Association* 24 (Summer 2022): 6; Douglas L. Wilson, *Honor's Voice: The Transformation of Abraham Lincoln* (New York: Knopf, 1998), 162–66; Kenneth J. Winkle, *The Young Eagle: The Rise of Abraham Lincoln* (Dallas, TX: Taylor, 2001), 257; Elmer Gertz, "The Black Laws of Illinois," *Journal of the Illinois State Historical Society* 56 (Autumn 1963): 461, 463–66; Robert E. May, *Slavery, Race, and Conquest in the Tropics: Lincoln, Douglas, and the Future of Latin America* (New York: Cambridge University Press, 2013), 86–87; Blumenthal, *The Political Life of Abraham Lincoln: A Self-Made Man, 1809–1849* (New York: Simon & Schuster, 2016), 40–42, 424–29, 436; Michael Burlingame, *Abraham Lincoln: A Life* (Baltimore, MD: Johns Hopkins University Press, 2008), 1:122; "Lincoln Completely Fused—His Abolitionism Avowed," *Springfield State Register* (October 19, 1854); Kenneth J. Winkle, *Lincoln's Citadel: The Civil War in Washington, DC* (New York: W.W. Norton, 2013), 35, 53; Lincoln to James Quay Howard, in *Recollected Words of Abraham Lincoln,* ed. Don and Virginia Fehrenbacher (Stanford, CA: Stanford University Press, 1996), 260.

12. Wendell Phillips, "Lincoln's Election" (November 7, 1860), in *Speeches, Lectures, and Letters* (Boston: James Redpath, 1863), 302; Frederick Douglass, "Address at Framingham, Massachusetts, July 4, 1860," in *Knowing Him by Heart: African Americans on Abraham Lincoln,* ed. F. L. Hord and M. D. Norman (Urbana: University of Illinois Press, 2023), 22; Roy P. Basler, *The Lincoln Legend: A Study in Changing Conceptions* (Boston: Houghton Mifflin, 1935), 69–74, 78–81; Carl Adams, "Lincoln's First Freed Slave: A Review of *Bailey v. Cromwell,* 1841," *Journal of the Illinois State Historical Society* 101 (Winter 2008): 243, 255; Gossie H. Hudson, "William Florville: Lincoln's Barber and Friend," *Negro History Bulletin* 37 (August–September 1974): 279–81; David S. Reynolds, *Abe: Abraham Lincoln in His Times* (New York: Penguin Press, 2020), 407–9, 417–22; Lincoln, "To Charles R. Welles" (September 27, 1852); Blumenthal, *A Self-Made Man,* 329–30, 338–41; "To Salmon Chase" (June 9, 1859) and "To Major W. Packard" (February 10, 1860), in *CW,* 2:159, 3:384, 518; "Rev. Billious Pond," at https://www.geni.com/people/Rev-Billious-Pond/6000000003147185518; Noah Brooks, *Abraham Lincoln and the Downfall of Slavery* (New York: G. P. Putnam's, 1888), 127; Jonathan W. White, *A House Built by Slaves: African American Visitors to the Lincoln White House* (Lanham, MD: Rowman & Littlefield, 2022), 6–8. On the John Shelby case, see Josiah G. Holland, *The Life of Abraham Lincoln* (Springfield, MA: Gurdon Bill, 1866), 127-28; Roger D. Bridges, "1857: Lincoln, Gov-

ernor Bissell, and a Black Man's Freedom," *For the People: A Newsletter of the Abraham Lincoln Association* 24 (Spring 2022); Catharine H. Dall, "Pioneering," *Atlantic Monthly* 19 (April 1867): 414–15; Brooks, *Lincoln and the Downfall of Slavery,* 125–26; Charles Segal, "Lincoln, Benjamin Jonas and the Black Code," *Journal of the Illinois State Historical Society* 46 (Autumn 1953): 278–79. On the Matson slave case, see Charles R. McKirdy, *Lincoln Apostate: The Matson Slave Trial* (Jackson: University Press of Mississippi, 2011), 20.

13. Lincoln, "Speech at Worcester, Massachusetts" (September 12, 1848), "Speech at Boston, Massachusetts" (September 15, 1848), "Debate at Jacksonville, Illinois" (October 21, 1848), "Speech at Lacon, Illinois" (November 1, 1848), "Speech at Peoria, Illinois" (October 16, 1854), and "To George Robertson" (August 15, 1855), in *CW,* 2:2, 3–4, 5, 12, 14, 255–56, 317.

14. Lincoln, "Speech at Dayton, Ohio" (September 17, 1859), "Speech at Indianapolis, Indiana" (September 19, 1859), in *CW,* 3:437, 470; Sidney Blumenthal, *The Political Life of Abraham Lincoln: Wrestling with His Angel, 1849–1856* (New York: Simon & Schuster, 2017), 104; Michael Lind, *What Lincoln Believed: The Values and Convictions of America's Greatest President* (New York: Doubleday, 2004), 126–32.

15. Lincoln, "To Henry J. Raymond" (December 18, 1860) in *CW,* 4:156.

16. Lincoln, "Speech at Tremont, Illinois" (May 2, 1840), "Speech at Bloomington, Illinois" (September 12, 1854), "First Debate with Stephen A. Douglas" (August 21, 1858), "Speech at Columbus, Ohio" (September 16, 1859), and "To William H. Seward" (February 1, 1861), in *CW,* 1:210, 2:232, 260, 3:16, 407, 4:183; Fehrenbacher, *Recollected Words of Abraham Lincoln,* 61; May, *Slavery, Race, and Conquest,* 24; Mark E. Neely Jr., *The Boundaries of American Political Culture in the Civil War Era* (Chapel Hill: University of North Carolina Press, 2005), 112; Herndon to Mr. Swanson (February 8, 1888), in *Herndon on Lincoln: Letters,* ed. Douglas L. Wilson and Rodney O. Davis (Urbana: University of Illinois Press, 2016), 273; Grover, in Fehrenbacher, *Recollected Words of Abraham Lincoln,* 188; Herndon and Jesse K. Weik, in *Herndon's Lincoln,* ed. D. L. Wilson and R. O. Davis (Urbana: University of Illinois Press, 2006), 196, 218; Henry Clay Whitney, *Life on the Circuit with Lincoln,* ed. Paul M. Angle (Caldwell, ID: Caxton Printers, 1940), 103; Jesse Weik, *The Real Lincoln: A Portrait* (Boston: Houghton Mifflin, 1922), 75, 86–88. William W. Newcomb, "one of the best known performers of minstrelsy," began his stage career in 1851, and in 1857 struck up a partnership with H. S. Rumsey which lasted until 1862 and brought Newcomb & Rumsey's

Minstrels to Canada, Cuba, and England; see E. L. Rice, *Monarchs of Minstrelsy, from "Daddy" Rice to Date* (New York: Kenny Publishing, 1911), 40.

17. Elizabeth Brown Pryor, *Six Encounters with Lincoln: A President Confronts Democracy and Its Demons* (New York: Penguin Books, 2017), 163, 169–70, 207; John Hay, diary entry for April 30, 1861, in *Inside Lincoln's White House: The Complete Civil War Diary of John Hay*, ed. Michael Burlingame and J. R. T. Ettlinger (Carbondale: Southern Illinois University Press, 1997), 14; Benjamin Brown French, diary entry for March 28, 1863, in *Witness to the Young Republic: A Yankee's Journal, 1828–1870*, ed. D. B. Cole and J. J. McDonough (Hanover, NH: University Press of New England, 1989), 419; "The President and the Wild Indians," *Washington Evening Star* (March 27, 1863); "Grand Council of Indians," *Washington National Republican* (March 27, 1863); Charles H. Coleman, "Lincoln's Lincoln Grandmother," *Journal of the Illinois State Historical Society* 52 (Spring 1959): 79; *Herndon's Lincoln*, ed. D. L. Wilson and R. O. Davis, 20; Burrus Carnahan, "Lincoln and the 1862 Minnesota Sioux Trials," *Lincoln Lore* 1934 (Summer 2022): 8–9. The military tribunal which tried 397 Sioux defendants for crimes committed during the uprising condemned 307 of them to death. Lincoln, who seems to have reviewed the cases in conjunction with two officers from the State and Interior departments, commuted the sentences of all but 38 of the Sioux, reserving the death penalty only for those found guilty of rape and/or murder. (Two more, who had fled to Canada and were later extradited, were executed in 1865.) How thorough the review could have been is a matter of dispute, and there is no evidence that Lincoln gave any later attention to the plight of those imprisoned. Lincoln was later told by Minnesota governor Alexander Ramsey that the commutations had cost Lincoln votes in the 1864 election, but Lincoln merely replied, "I could not afford to hang men for votes." Lincoln promised Episcopal bishop Henry Whipple that "if we get through this war, and I live, this Indian system shall be reformed." But he did not, and the 1862 Sioux uprising became the pretext for wholesale removal of the Dakota from Minnesota. See Duane Schultz, *Over the Earth I Come: The Great Sioux Uprising of 1862* (New York: St. Martin's Press, 1992), 253, 259, 275; Andrew F. Lang, *A Contest of Civilizations: Exposing the Crisis of American Exceptionalism in the Civil War Era* (Chapel Hill: University of North Carolina Press, 2021), 227; and Burlingame, *Abraham Lincoln: A Life*, 2:483.

18. Basler, *The Lincoln Legend*, 101.

Notes

Chapter Eight: Democracy and Emancipation

1. John Gardner, *On Writers and Writing,* ed. Stewart O'Nan (Reading, MA: Addison-Wesley Publishing, 1994), 111.

2. Lincoln, "Speech at Springfield, Illinois" (July 17, 1858), in *CW,* 2:520; George H. Fredrickson, *Big Enough to Be Inconsistent: Abraham Lincoln Confronts Slavery and Race* (Cambridge, MA: Harvard University Press, 2008), 77.

3. Nicholas Buccola, "What If Honest Abe Was Telling the Truth? Natural Rights, Race, and Legalism in the Political Thought of Lincoln," in *Abraham Lincoln and Liberal Democracy,* ed. N. Buccola (Lawrence: University Press of Kansas, 2016), 125.

4. Lincoln, "Speech at Carlinville, Illinois" (August 31, 1858), "Speech at Springfield, Illinois" (July 17, 1858), and "Seventh and Last Debate with Stephen A. Douglas at Alton, Illinois" (October 15, 1858), in *CW,* 2:520, 3:79, 80, 301; Jonathan W. White, *A House Built by Slaves: African American Visitors to the Lincoln White House* (Lanham, MD: Rowman & Littlefield, 2022), 87. In this comment, Lincoln is very close to restating Locke's distinction in the *Two Treatises on Government:* "Though I have said … *That all Men by Nature are equal,* I cannot be supposed to understand all sorts of *Equality: Age or Virtue* may give Men a just Precedency: *Excellency of Parts and Merit* may place others above the Common Level: *Birth* may subject some, and *Alliance* or *Benefits* others, to pay an Observance to those whom Nature, Gratitude, or other Respects, may have made it due: and yet all this consists with the *Equality* … that every Man hath, *to his Natural Freedom,* without being subjected to the Will or Authority of any other Man." [Italics in the original.] See *Two Treatises on Government,* ed. Peter Laslett (New York: Signet Classics, 1965), 346.

5. Lincoln, "Fragment on Slavery" (July 1, 1854), "Speech at Springfield, Illinois" (October 4, 1854), "Fragment of a Speech" (May 18, 1858), and "To James N. Brown" (October 18, 1858), in *CW,* 2:222, 245, 449, 3:328.

6. Lincoln, "Speech at Beardstown, Illinois" (August 12, 1858) and "Speech at Hartford, Connecticut" (March 5, 1860), in *CW,* 2:538, 4:9; *The Lincoln-Douglas Debates,* ed. D. L. Wilson and R. O. Davis (Urbana: University of Illinois Press, 2008), 14, 162; Robert W. Johannsen, "Lincoln, Liberty and Equality," in *The Frontier, the Union, and Stephen A. Douglas* (Urbana: University of Illinois Press, 1989), 262.

7. Lincoln, "To the Editor of the Sangamo Journal" (June 13, 1836), "Speech at Indianapolis, Indiana" (September 19, 1859), "Speech at Hartford, Connecticut" (March 5, 1860), and "Speech at New Haven,

Connecticut" (March 6, 1860), in *CW,* 1:48, 3:469, 4:9, 24–25; *Julian M. Sturtevant: An Autobiography,* ed. J. M. Sturtevant Jr. (New York: Fleming H. Revell, 1896), 287; Lucius E. Chittenden, *Recollections of President Lincoln and His Administration* (New York: Harper, 1891), 76; Robert Bray, *Reading with Lincoln* (Carbondale: Southern Illinois University Press, 2010), 174.

8. Lincoln, "Speech at Chicago, Illinois" (July 10, 1858), "Speech at Janesville, Wisconsin" (October 1, 1859), and "Speech at New Haven, Connecticut" (March 6, 1860), in *CW,* 2:501, 3:486, 4:20; James Oakes, *The Radical and the Republican: Frederick Douglass, Abraham Lincoln, and the Triumph of Antislavery Politics* (New York: W. W. Norton, 2007), 84–85; Julian Kune, *Reminiscences of an Octogenarian Hungarian Exile* (Chicago, 1911), 87–88, 93.

9. Lincoln, "To John L. Scripps" (June 23, 1858) and "To John M. Schofield" (June 22, 1863), in *CW,* 2:471, 6:291.

10. Gilbert J. Greene, *Lincoln the Comforter,* ed. C. T. White (Hancock, NY: Herald Press, 1916), 35–36; Lincoln, "To Williamson Durley" (October 3, 1845) and "To John L. Scripps" (June 23, 1858), in *CW,* 1:347, 2:471; Jean H. Baker, "A Loyal Opposition: Northern Democrats in the Thirty-Seventh Congress," *CWH* 25 (June 1979): 150. Nor was Lincoln unusual in thinking this way. Not even many abolitionists looked for national overthrow of the slave system. "Free Soil men disclaim all right on the part of Congress to touch the institution of slavery where it exists," conceded the abolitionist Indiana Republican George Washington Julian. "We all agree that…Congress has no more right to abolish slavery in South Carolina, than it has to abolish free schools in Massachusetts…no more concern than with slavery in Russia or Austria." Even the towering Thaddeus Stevens grudgingly conceded that though he might "greatly dislike" tolerating slavery, "Congress has no power over slavery in the States." But like Lincoln, he took consolation in the belief that if Congress can "confine this malady within its present limits," it would asphyxiate for want of new lands. "Surround it by a cordon of freemen that it cannot spread, and in less than twenty-five years every slave-holding state in this Union will have on its statute books a law for the gradual and final extinction of slavery." See William Miller, *Lincoln's Virtues: An Ethical Biography* (New York: Knopf, 2002), 367; George Washington Julian, "The Slavery Question" (May 14, 1850), in *Speeches on Political Questions* (New York: Hurd & Houghton, 1872), 8; Thaddeus Stevens, "The Slave Question: Speech of Mr. T. Stevens of Pennsylvania" (February 20, 1850), *Congressio-*

nal Globe, 31st Congress, 1st session, Appendix, 142. Stevens, like Lincoln in the Matson slave case, had represented a slaveowner trying to reclaim a fugitive early in his legal career, in *Butler v. Delaplaine;* see Hans L. Trefousse, *Thaddeus Stevens: Nineteenth-Century Egalitarian* (1997; Mechanicsburg, PA: Stackpole, 2001), 14. On the ease with which even prominent abolitionists denigrated blacks as a race, see David S. Reynolds, *Abe: Abraham Lincoln in His Times* (New York: Penguin Press, 2020), 350. Radical Republican abolitionist senator Benjamin F. Wade was a bitter critic of Lincoln's slowness on emancipation, yet Wade freely used racial epithets and racial denigration, even as he maintained that "equality before the law, without respect to race, color or nationality" was the "polar star" of his politics. See Hans L. Trefousse, *Benjamin Franklin Wade: Radical Republican from Ohio* (New York: Twayne, 1965), 311.

11. Lincoln, "To George Robertson" (August 15, 1855), "Speech at Springfield, Illinois" (June 17, 1857), "Fragment of a Speech" (May 18, 1858), "'A House Divided': Speech at Springfield, Illinois" (June 16, 1858), "Speech at Chicago, Illinois" (July 10, 1858), "Speech at Springfield, Illinois" (July 17, 1858), in *CW,* 2:318, 404, 453, 461, 491, 492, 514; Michael F. Holt, *The Election of 1860: "A Campaign Fraught with Consequences"* (Lawrence: University Press of Kansas, 2017), 90, 92–96.

12. John G. Nicolay, "Memorandum, Springfield, 5 November 1860," in *With Lincoln in the White House: Letters, Memoranda, and Other Writings of John G. Nicolay, 1860–1865,* ed. Michael Burlingame (Carbondale: Southern Illinois University Press, 2000), 7; "Important Statement by the Ex-Governor of Kentucky," *Liverpool Mercury* (October 13, 1862); Lincoln, "First Inaugural Address—Final Text" (March 4, 1861), "To the Regent Captains of the Republic of San Marino" (May 7, 1861), "To Horace Greeley" (August 22, 1862), in *CW,* 4:263, 360, 5:388; Orville Hickman Browning, diary entry for December 1, 1861, in *The Diary of Orville Hickman Browning,* ed. T. C. Pease and J. G. Randall (Springfield: Illinois State Historical Library, 1925), 1:512.

13. Lincoln, "To Horace Greeley" (March 24, 1862), "To Nathaniel Banks" (August 5, 1863), and "To John A. J. Creswell" (March 7, 1864), in *CW,* 5:169, 6:365, 7:226.

14. Lincoln, "Outline for Speech to the Colonization Society" (January 4, 1855), "Speech at Springfield, Illinois" (June 26, 1857), "Speech at Springfield, Illinois" (July 17, 1858), "Fifth Debate with Stephen A. Douglas, at Galesburg, Illinois" (October 7, 1858), and "Annual Message to Congress" (December 3, 1861), in *CW* 2:299, 409, 521, 3:233, 5:48; Mark

Steiner, "Recent Discovery: Lincoln on Colonization," *For the People: A Newsletter of the Abraham Lincoln Association* 23 (Summer 2021): 2. The literature on Lincoln and colonization is surprisingly deep, considering how narrow a question this is. See John G. Nicolay and John Hay, *Abraham Lincoln: A History* (New York: Century, 1890), 6:354–67; Paul J. Schieps, "Lincoln and the Chiriqui Colonization Project," *Journal of Negro History* 37 (October 1952): 418–53; Robert Zoellner, "Negro Colonization: The Climate of Opinion Surrounding Lincoln," *Mid-America* 42 (July 1960): 131–50; James M. McPherson, *The Negro's Civil War: How American Blacks Felt and Acted During the War for the Union* (New York: Pantheon, 1965), 79–99; Warren A. Beck, "Lincoln and Negro Colonization in Central America," *Abraham Lincoln Quarterly* 6 (September 1950): 171; Michael Vorenberg, "Abraham Lincoln and the Politics of Black Colonization," *JALA* (Summer 1993): 22–45; Gabor S. Boritt, "Did He Dream of a Lily-White America? The Voyage to Linconia," in *The Lincoln Enigma: The Changing Faces of an American Icon* (New York: Oxford University Press, 2001), 1–19; Sebastian N. Page, "Lincoln and Chiriquí Colonization Revisited," *American Nineteenth Century History* 12 (December 2011): 289–325; Kate Masur, *An Example for All the Land: Emancipation and the Struggle over Equality in Washington* (Chapel Hill: University of North Carolina Press, 2010), 13–40; Phillip W. Magness and Sebastian N. Page, *Colonization After Emancipation: Lincoln and the Movement for Black Resettlement* (Columbus: University of Missouri Press, 2011), 1–12.

15. The "committee" had been formed on August 14, 1862, at the request of Lincoln, "who had sent them word that he had something to say to them of interest to themselves and to the country," thus making Lincoln the first president ever formally to request an official meeting with an African American delegation in the White House. It is difficult now to grasp what a thrill of horror Lincoln stimulated in the minds of whites when they read he had met them, "shaking hands very cordially with each one." See "The President's Colonization Scheme," *Washington National Republican* (August 15, 1862), and "Interview Between President Lincoln and a Committee of Colored Men," *Washington Evening Star* (August 15, 1862).

16. Lincoln, "Address on Colonization" (August 14, 1862), in *CW,* 5:373; Dennis A. Mahony, *The Prisoner of State* (New York: Carleton, 1863), 200–201.

17. "Thirty-Seventh Congress," *New York Daily Herald* (March 5, 1862), "Political," *New York Daily Herald* (March 14, 1862), "Proceedings of

Congress," *New York Times* (March 28, 1862); Frederick Milnes Edge, *Major-General McClellan and the Campaign on the Yorktown Peninsula* (London: Trubner & Co., 1865), 61; Michael Burlingame, "President Lincoln's Meetings with African Americans," *JALA* 42 (Winter 2021): 44–45; Hay, diary entry for July 1, 1864, in *Inside Lincoln's White House: The Complete Civil War Diary of John Hay,* ed. Michael Burlingame and J. R. T. Ettlinger (Carbondale: Southern Illinois University Press, 1997), 217; Willis D. Boyd, "The Île a Vache Colonization Venture, 1862–1864," *Americas* 16 (July 1959): 49, 51, 55–56; and Lincoln, "To Edwin M. Stanton" (February 1, 1864), in *CW,* 7:164. One constituency which preferred Lincoln's colonization plans were the freed slaves themselves at Fortress Monroe, especially since there was no guarantee, even as late as 1864, that the Emancipation Proclamation would survive a postwar court challenge. "Their sufferings at the South, and fears of reenslavement, together with their dread of the cold climate of the North, led them to look with approval on the project of emigration to some free tropical country." See "News from Washington," *New York Times* (October 19, 1862). My thanks to the generous Michael Burlingame for bringing this detail to my attention.

18. Josiah Grinnell, in *Recollected Words of Abraham Lincoln,* ed. Don E. and Virginia Fehrenbacher (Stanford, CA: Stanford University Press, 1996), 187; Isaac J. Hill, in *Knowing Him by Heart: African Americans on Abraham Lincoln,* ed. F. L. Hord and M. D. Norman (Urbana: University of Illinois Press, 2023), 154; William O. Stoddard, *Inside the White House in War Times: Memoirs and Reports of Lincoln's Secretary,* ed. Michael Burlingame (Lincoln: University of Nebraska Press, 2000), 139; White, *A House Built by Slaves,* 59–60. Only four days before his death, Lincoln publicly advocated the extension of voting rights and free education in the South for "those who have served our cause as soldiers." He limited this to the veterans and "the very intelligent." But this was exactly the portion of the black community that racists, North and South, most dreaded, and strove the most to insist should not even exist. See Lincoln, "Last Public Address" (April 11, 1865), in *CW,* 8:403.

19. Harold M. Hyman, "Lincoln and Equal Rights for Negroes: The Irrelevancy of the 'Wadsworth Letter,'" *CWH* 12 (September 1966): 262; "Speech of Frederick Douglass," *The Liberator* (January 29, 1864); Frederick Douglass, in *Reminiscences of Abraham Lincoln by Distinguished Men of His Time,* ed. A. T. Rice (New York: North American Publishing, 1886), 193; John Eaton, *Grant, Lincoln and the Freedmen: Reminiscences of the Civil War* (New York: Longmans, Green, and Co., 1907), 175; Carle-

ton Mabee, "Sojourner Truth and President Lincoln," *New England Quarterly* 61 (December 1988): 521; Charles-Adolphe Pineton, marquis de Chambrun, "Personal Recollections of Mr. Lincoln," *Scribner's Magazine* 13 (January 1893): 28; Horace White, "Recollections of Abraham Lincoln," *The Magazine of History* 3 (February 1906): 72; "Richard J. Hinton Interview with Abraham Lincoln," *For the People: A Newsletter of the Abraham Lincoln Association* 22 (Spring 2020): 9.

20. One serious objection to this judgment appeals to the use by Lincoln of racial epithets, and in particular what can simply be called *the* epithet. Lincoln's modern critics point out that this epithet occurs twenty-eight times in the standard Basler edition of the *Collected Works of Abraham Lincoln*, which is more than enough to indict him for racial insensitivity, if not outright contempt. But if we examine the appearances of the epithet attributed to Lincoln, we find that all but three appear in secondhand reports of Lincoln's comments, frequently from hostile newspapers who routinely employed the epithet whenever *anyone* referred to blacks, whether or not the epithet was even actually used. One account of this nature, reporting on a speech Lincoln gave in Council Bluffs, Iowa, in 1859, derisively contrasts its own free use of the epithet with Lincoln's wording—"the 'eternal Negro,' to use his own language." For his first debate with Stephen Douglas in 1858, the standard edition uses a transcription prepared by reporters from the *Chicago Tribune* which has Lincoln freely using the epithet; but a transcript prepared by two reporters from the *Chicago Times* (an anti-Lincoln newspaper) gives an entirely different version, *sans* any such usage. (See Lincoln, "First Debate with Stephen A. Douglas" [August 21, 1858], in *CW*, 3:20, 27; but compare with "The First Joint Debate at Ottawa" [August 21, 1858], in *The Lincoln-Douglas Debates: The First Complete, Unexpurgated Text*, ed. Harold Holzer [New York: HarperCollins, 1993], 67, 74.) In all, twenty-two of the examples of the epithet attributed to Lincoln come, not from Lincoln, but from newspaper accounts summarizing Lincoln's speeches in their own words. On the three occasions when we actually find Lincoln using the term in writing, two of those instances are quotes of comments by others, and in the other, he sets off the term in quotation marks, so that it will not be mistaken for his own voice. Even Lincoln's ethnic humor was comparatively mild stuff. Paul M. Zall's catalog of Lincoln's humor, *Abe Lincoln Laughing* (University of California Press, 1982), cites seventeen jokes about blacks out of 325 stories attributed to Lincoln. All but one poke fun at ignorance rather than race (he made the same jokes

about Irish and Germans); and all of them, again, come down to us at second or third hand.

21. Lincoln, "Address on Colonization to a Deputation of Negroes" (August 14, 1862), in *CW*, 5:371-72; John E. Roll, in Fehrenbacher, *Recollected Words*, 383; "Oration of Fred. Douglass," *New York Daily Herald* (June 2, 1865); Fredrickson, *Big Enough to Be Inconsistent*, 84; Carson, *Lincoln's Ethics*, 13, 352–58, 372, 395–96.

22. Lincoln, "Message to Congress in Special Session" (July 4, 1861), in *CW*, 4:438; Danyelle Solomon, et al., "Systematic Inequality and American Democracy," Center for American Progress (August 7, 2019), https://www.americanprogress.org/article/systematic-inequality-american-democracy/; James Oakes, *The Crooked Path to Abolition: Abraham Lincoln and the Antislavery Constitution* (New York: W. W. Norton, 2021), 107.

Chapter Nine: Democracy's Deficits

1. Rawls believed that "deeply opposed though reasonable comprehensive doctrines may live together and all affirm the political conception of a constitutional regime" because no questions of that nature were really of any compelling significance. This is not the same as Lincoln's understanding of toleration, which was always a gradualism in motion toward resolution rather than indifference. Lincoln could respect those who stood against him on slavery, and even conceded that "I have no prejudice against the Southern people. They are just what we would be in their situation. If slavery did not now exist amongst them, they would not introduce it. If it did now exist amongst us, we should not instantly give it up." But he could not accommodate indifference to slavery itself, and he believed that the United States must logically become "all one thing or all the other." See Rawls, *Political Liberalism* (New York: Columbia University Press, 1993), xviii, 95; and Lincoln, "Speech at Peoria, Illinois" (October 16, 1854), in *CW*, 2:255; Kyle Scott, *Federalism: A Normative Theory and Its Practical Relevance* (London: Continuum, 2011), 35; and Hans Kelsen, "Foundations of Democracy" (1955), in *Verteidigung der Demokratie: Abhandlungen zur Demokratietheorie* (Tubingen: Moor Siebeck, 2006), 2, 4, 44. See also Michael Sandel's judgment that "liberal political theory does not see political life as concerned with the highest human ends or with the moral excellence of its citizens," in *Democracy's Discontent: America in Search of a Public Philosophy* (Cambridge, MA: Harvard University Press, 1996), 7. This seems to me an exceedingly narrow view of liberal political theory,

one which has little regard for liberalism's history before the twentieth century and one which puts weapons in the hands of liberal democracy's hostile critics.

2. Amy Gutmann and Dennis F. Thompson, *Democracy and Disagreement* (Cambridge, MA: Harvard University Press, 1996), 75; David B. Wong, *Moral Relativity* (Berkeley: University of California Press, 1984), 146; Lincoln, "Speech at Peoria, Illinois" (October 16, 1854), "'A House Divided': Speech at Springfield, Illinois" (June 16, 1858), and "Third Debate with Stephen A. Douglas at Jonesboro, Illinois" (September 15, 1858), in *CW* 2:271, 461, 3:121.

3. Lincoln, "To John L. Scripps" (June 23, 1858), in *CW*, 2:471; John Finnis, "'Public Reason' and Moral Debate," in *Reason in Action: Collected Essays* (New York: Oxford University Press, 2011), 1:265.

4. Lincoln, "Speech at Peoria, Illinois" (October 16, 1854), "To Norman B. Judd" (October 30, 1858), "Address at Sanitary Fair, Baltimore Maryland" (April 18, 1864), and "To Joseph Holt" (February 27, 1865), in *CW*, 2:265, 3:330, 7:301–2, 8:321.

5. David Pantier to William Herndon, in *Herndon's Informants: Letters, Interviews, and Statements About Abraham Lincoln*, ed. Douglas L. Wilson and Rodney O. Davis (Chicago: University of Illinois Press, 1998), 78. Herndon heard Lincoln claim that "I hate the stuff" because "it is unpleasant to me and always makes me feel flabby and undone" (*Herndon's Lincoln*, ed. D. L. Wilson and R. O. Davis [Urbana: University of Illinois Press, 2006], 53–54). There are entries in Kentucky store ledgers for whiskey sold by the pint to Thomas Lincoln, Lincoln's father; his great-aunt Elizabeth was "in the habit of frequent intoxication" and his uncle Mordecai "was a heavy drinker." See William H. Townsend, "Lincoln and Liquor," *Atlantic Monthly* 153 (February 1934): 129–43.

6. David Davis, David Turnham, and Henry McHenry to Herndon (May 29, 1865, February 21 and September 20, 1866), in *Herndon's Informants*, 14, 217, 350; Herndon to Jesse Weik (February 5, 1887), in *Herndon on Lincoln: Letters*, ed. Douglas L. Wilson and Rodney O. Davis (Urbana: University of Illinois Press, 2016), 229; Lucas Morel, "Lincoln Among the Reformers: Tempering the Temperance Movement," *JALA* 20 (Winter 1999): 13–15.

7. Lincoln, "Temperance Address" (February 22, 1842), in *CW*, 1:271–79; John Channing Briggs, *Lincoln's Speeches Reconsidered* (Baltimore: Johns Hopkins University Press, 2005), 72–73; Daniel Walker Howe, "Why Lincoln Was a Whig," *JALA* 16 (Winter 1995): 34–35.

8. The response was not entirely favorable. The Democratic *Illinois State Register* sniffed afterwards that the Washingtonians' "parades and assemblies" were nothing but a "Federal-whig" political tactic, and a month later accused Lincoln of joining the Washingtonians in order to foist a "Federal-bank-whig mayor upon us." The absolutists were even more put out. Herndon "was at the door of the church" as the audience left and heard complaints from "the professing Christians" that asked why "he should be permitted to abuse us so in the house of the Lord." They had not forgotten, either, that Lincoln had consistently voted against prohibition legislation when it surfaced in the state legislature. "The New Reign of Temperance" and "The Washington Society," *Illinois State Register* (February 25 and March 11, 1842); *Herndon's Lincoln*, ed. Wilson and Davis, 166; Townsend, "Lincoln and Liquor," 136; Harry V. Jaffa, *Crisis of the House Divided: An Interpretation in the Lincoln-Douglas Debates* (New York: Doubleday, 1959), 244–45, Briggs, *Lincoln's Speeches Reconsidered*, 76.

9. Mark E. Neely Jr., "The Kansas-Nebraska Act in American Political Culture: The Road to Bladensburg and the Appeal of the Independent Democrats," in *The Nebraska-Kansas Act of 1854*, ed. J. R. Wunder and J. M. Ross (Lincoln: University of Nebraska Press, 2008), 33–34, 38, 44–45; Lincoln, "Speech at Peoria, Illinois" (October 16, 1854), *CW*, 2:282.

10. Afterwards, Yates told Edward G. Miner that "I have heard this winter all the big men in Congress talk on this question, but Lincoln's is the strongest speech I ever heard on the subject." James Miner, in Rufus Rockwell Wilson, *Intimate Memories of Lincoln* (Elmira, NY: Primavera Press, 1945), 166. Lincoln, "To George W. Shaw" (July 27, 1854), "To Richard Yates" (August 18, 1854), "Speech at Winchester, Illinois" (August 26, 1854), "Speech at Springfield, Illinois" (September 9, 1854), "Editorial on the Kansas-Nebraska Act" (September 11, 1854), "Speech at Springfield, Illinois" (July 17, 1858), and "Speeches at Clinton, Illinois" (September 2, 1858), in *CW*, 2:226–27, 229–30, 514, 3:82, and Supplement 2:8–9; Douglas, "Kansas-Lecompton Constitution" (March 22, 1858), *Congressional Globe*, 35th Congress, 1st session (Appendix), 195, 200.

11. Louis E. Lehrman, *Lincoln at Peoria: The Turning Point* (Mechanicsburg, PA: Stackpole, 2008), 56–57; Lincoln, "Speech at Peoria, Illinois" (October 16, 1854), in *CW*, 2:255.

12. Lincoln, "Speech at Peoria, Illinois" (October 16, 1854), in *CW*, 2.255. 264–65, 266, 267, 270, 273, 276.

13. Lincoln, "Drafts of Resolutions Recommending Amendment of the Kansas Nebraska Act" (January 4, 1855) and "To George Robertson" (August 15, 1855), in *CW*, 2:300, 318.

14. Lincoln, "To James C. Conkling" (August 26, 1863), in *CW*, 6:408; William O. Stoddard, *Inside the White House in War Times: Memoirs and Reports of Lincoln's Secretary*, ed. Michael Burlingame (Lincoln: University of Nebraska Press, 2000), 97.

15. Grant, *The Personal Memoirs of Ulysses S. Grant: The Complete Annotated Edition*, ed. John F. Marszalek (Cambridge, MA: Harvard University Press, 2017), 279. In *Campaigning with Grant* (New York: Century, 1897), Horace Porter has Grant put the question directly to Lincoln: " 'Never for a moment,' was the prompt and emphatic reply, as Mr. Lincoln leaned forward in his camp-chair and enforced his words by a vigorous gesture of his right hand."

16. Orville Hickman Browning, Montgomery Meigs, and Samuel Wilkeson, in *Recollected Words of Abraham Lincoln*, ed. Don E. and Virginia Fehrenbacher (Stanford, CA: Stanford University Press, 1996), 87, 328, 497; Noah Brooks, *Washington in Lincoln's Time* (New York: Century, 1895), 57–58; Michael Burlingame, *The Inner World of Abraham Lincoln* (Urbana: University of Illinois Press, 1994), 105, and *Lincoln and the Civil War* (Carbondale: Southern Illinois University Press, 2011), 74, 78.

17. Lincoln, "Response to a Serenade" (July 7, 1863), in *CW*, 6:319–320.

18. Douglas Wilson, *Lincoln's Sword: The Presidency and the Power of Words* (New York: Knopf, 2006), 232–33; Briggs, *Lincoln's Speeches Reconsidered*, 314–15; Henry John Chetwynd-Talbot, 18th Earl of Shrewsbury, in "Lord Malmesbury, General Peel, The Earl of Shrewsbury, and Sir J. Pakington, on Public Affairs," *Nottingham Daily Guardian* (November 2, 1861). The principal speaker at the Gettysburg cemetery dedication was not Lincoln, but the Harvard scholar and onetime Whig politico Edward Everett, who was much more interested in casting stones at the Confederate leadership, those "bold bad men," who, like Clarendon's Cromwell, deluded themselves and others with "wretched sophistries."

19. Heine, "Jetzt wohin?" [Where To Now?] in *Heinrich Heine's Sämmtliche Werke: Dichtungen* (Hamburg: Hoffman & Sampe, 1853), 152; Sydney Smith, "America," *Edinburgh Review* 33 (January 1820): 79; Charles Dickens, *The Life and Adventures of Martin Chuzzlewit* (London: Chapman & Hall, 1854), 279. I have translated the stanza from Heine somewhat freely:

…Manchmal kommt mir in den Sinn
Nach Amerika zu segeln,
Nach dem großen Freiheitstall,
Der bewohnt von Gleichheits-Flegeln

Doch es ängstet mich ein Land,
Wo die Menschen Tabak käuen
Wo sie ohne König kegeln,
Wo sie ohne Spuknapf speien.

> …*Sometimes it comes to my mind*
> *To sail to America*
> *To that big outhouse of freedom*
> *Where dolts lounge in disarray.*
> *But a country frightens me*
> *Whose citizens chomp tobacco,*
> *Live without law,*
> *And spit into everything.*

20. Samuel Toombs [13th New Jersey], *New Jersey Troops in the Gettysburg Campaign from June 5 to July 31, 1863* (Orange, NJ: Evening Mail Publishing, 1888), 330–31.
21. Lincoln, "Speech at Chicago, Illinois" (July 10, 1858), "To Agenor-Etienne de Gasparin" (August 4, 1862), "Serenade in Honor of Emancipation Proclamation" (September 24, 1862), and "To Alexander Reed" (February 22, 1863), in *CW,* 2:501, 5:355, 438, 6:114; Phillip S. Paludan, "Lincoln's PreWar Constitutional Vision," *JALA* 15 (Summer 1994): 9; Richard Brookhiser, *Give Me Liberty: A History of America's Exceptional Idea* (New York: Basic Books, 2019), xx.
22. Lincoln, "To William S. Rosecrans" (November 19, 1864), in *CW,* 8:116.
23. Ron Soodalter, *Hanging Captain Gordon: The Life and Trial of an American Slave Trader* (New York, 2006), 6, 58, 146, 242; John B. Alley and Henry P. H. Bromwell, in Fehrenbacher, *Recollected Words of Abraham Lincoln,* 2, 40; Lincoln, "Stay of Execution for Nathaniel Gordon" (February 4, 1862), in *CW,* 5:128; John Hay, diary entry for October 28, 1863, in *Inside Lincoln's White House,* ed. Burlingame, 101; John Hay and John Nicolay, *Abraham Lincoln: A History* (New York: Century, 1909), 10:85.
24. Burlingame, *Abraham Lincoln: A Life,* 2:758; William C. Harris, *Lincoln's Last Months* (Cambridge, MA: Harvard University Press, 2004), 115–21.

25. Lincoln, "To Edwin M. Stanton" (May 17, 1864), in *CW*, 7:344; *Memoirs of General William T. Sherman by Himself* (New York: D. Appleton, 1875), 326–27; Lloyd Lewis, *Sherman—Fighting Prophet* (New York: Harcourt, Brace, 1932), 524; Joan Waugh, *Lincoln and the War's End* (Carbondale: Southern Illinois University Press, 2014), 79; John Avlon, *Lincoln and the Fight for Peace* (New York: Simon & Schuster, 2022), 121; Noah Andre Trudeau, *Lincoln's Greatest Journey: Sixteen Days That Changed a Presidency, March 24–April 8, 1865* (El Dorado, CA: Savas Beatie, 2016), 186–93; Charles A. Dana, in *Reminiscences of Abraham Lincoln by Distinguished Men of His Time*, ed. Allen T. Rice (New York, 1886), 376; Gideon Welles, "Lincoln and Johnson," in *Selected Essays by Gideon Welles: Civil War and Reconstruction*, ed. Albert Mordell (New York: Twayne, 1959), 191. He told John Sanford Barnes, while "lamenting the great loss of life and the sufferings of the wounded," that "he hoped that...there would be no more bloodshed or ruin of homes," and "many times did he reiterate the same hope with grave earnestness." See Barnes, "With Lincoln from Washington to Richmond in 1865," *Appleton's Magazine* 9 (May 1907): 522. In the end, only one war-crimes trial was actually conducted—that of Henry Wirz, the commandant at Andersonville—and that was after Lincoln's death.

26. "Additional Details of the Inauguration Ceremonies" and "President Lincoln's Second Inaugural—The Negro Question," *New York Daily Herald* (March 5, 1865); Wilson, *Lincoln's Sword*, 253.

27. Lincoln, "Second Inaugural Address" (March 4, 1865), in *CW*, 8:332; Briggs, *Lincoln's Speeches Reconsidered*, 324.

28. Lincoln, "Second Inaugural Address" (March 4, 1865), in *CW*, 8:333; Sean A. Scott, *A Visitation of God: Northern Civilians Interpret the Civil War* (New York: Oxford University Press, 2011), 240–41; Mark A. Noll, *The Civil War as a Theological Crisis* (Chapel Hill: University of North Carolina Press, 2006), 89–90.

29. "The Inaugural," *Detroit Free Press* (March 5, 1865); Colleen Shogan, *The Moral Rhetoric of American Presidents* (College Station: Texas A&M University Press, 2006), 111–12; A .G. Riddle, *The Life of Benjamin F. Wade* (Cleveland, OH: William W. Williams, 1886), 268–69; Lincoln, "To Thurlow Weed" (March 15, 1865), in *CW*, 8:356.

Epilogue: What If Lincoln Had Lived?

1. Stephen V. Ash, *Middle Tennessee Society Transformed, 1860–1870: War and Peace in the Upper South* (Baton Rouge: Louisiana State University

Press, 1988), 107; Hans L. Trefousse, *Andrew Johnson: A Biography* (New York: W. W. Norton, 1989), 280; *Speeches, Correspondence and Political Papers of Carl Schurz,* ed. F. Bancroft (New York: G. P. Putnam's Sons, 1913), 1:283, 2:256.

2. Lincoln, "To Michael Hahn" (March 13, 1864) and "Last Public Address" (April 11, 1865), in *CW,* 7:243, 8:400–401.

3. Lincoln, "To James S. Wadsworth" (January 1864), in *CW,* 7:101.

4. "Interview with Delegation of Blacks" (February 7, 1866), in *The Papers of Andrew Johnson,* vol. 10, *February–July 1866,* ed. P. H. Bergeron (Knoxville: University of Tennessee Press, 1992), 48; Frederick Douglass, "An Appeal to Congress for Impartial Suffrage," *Atlantic Monthly* 19 (January 1867): 116.

5. Lincoln, "Address Before the Wisconsin State Agricultural Society, Milwaukee, Wisconsin" (September 30, 1859) and "Last Public Address" (April 11, 1865), in *CW,* 3:480, 8:403; Roger Lowenstein, *Ways and Means: Lincoln and His Cabinet and the Financing of the Civil War* (New York: Penguin, 2022), 212.

6. Lincoln, "Opinion on Land Titles in Beloit, Wisconsin" (March 24, 1856) and "Order Concerning Lessees and Owners of Plantations Worked by Freedmen" (September 30, 1864), in *CW,* 6:337, 8:30.

7. "By the President of the United States: A Proclamation" (May 20, 1865), in *The War of the Rebellion: A Compilation of the Official Records of the Union and Confederate Armies* (Washington, DC: Government Printing Office, 1894), series 2, 8:579.

8. Don E. and Virginia Fehrenbacher, eds., *Recollected Words of Abraham Lincoln* (Stanford, CA: Stanford University Press, 1996), 131, 132, 486; Edward D. Neill, *Reminiscences of the Last Year of President Lincoln's Life* (St. Paul, MN: Pioneer Press Co., 1885), 14; Joshua Speed, *Reminiscences of Abraham Lincoln and Notes of a Visit to California: Two Lectures* (Louisville, KY: John P. Morton, 1884), 33; Sumner to the Duchess of Argyll (April 24, 1865), in *The Selected Letters of Charles Sumner,* ed. B. W. Palmer (Boston: Northeastern University Press, 1990), 2:295; Charles A. Dana to Edwin M. Stanton (April 7, 1865), in *The War of the Rebellion: A Compilation of the Official Records of the Union and Confederate Armies* (Washington, DC: Government Printing Office, 1894), series 1, 46(pt 3): 619; Lincoln, "To Godfrey Weitzel" (April 12, 1865), in *CW,* 8:407.

9. Robert K. Scott, in *Piedmont Farmer: The Journals of David Golightly Harris, 1855–1870,* ed. P. N. Racine (Knoxville: University of Tennessee Press, 1990), 556.

10. LaWanda and John H. Cox, "Negro Suffrage and Republican Politics:

The Problem of Motivation in Reconstruction Historiography," in *Reconstruction: An Anthology of Revisionist Writings*, ed. K. M. Stampp and L. F. Litwack (Baton Rouge: Louisiana State University Press, 1969), 159–65.

11. Sidney Andrews, "Three Months Among the Reconstructionists," *Atlantic Monthly* 17 (February 1866): 238.

12. See Frederick Douglass's comment that, because Lincoln was "a humane man, an honorable man, and at heart an anti-slavery man" who "looked to the principles of liberty and justice, for the peace, security, happiness and prosperity of his country," the results of Reconstruction must point in a different direction than Johnson's. Twenty-three years later, Douglass had not changed his mind: Lincoln was "a man so broad in his sympathy…so free from narrow prejudice…that all classes and conditions of men could claim him as a…friend, a brother, and a benefactor." Joseph R. Fornieri, "Lincoln on Black Citizenship," in *Constitutionalism in the Approach and Aftermath of the Civil War*, ed. P. D. Moreno and J. G. O'Neill (New York: Fordham University Press, 2013), 80; Frederick Douglass, "In Honor of Lincoln," *Washington National Republican* (February 13, 1888).

13. Lincoln, "Seventh and Last Debate with Stephen A. Douglas at Alton, Illinois" (October 15, 1858), "Speech at Pittsburgh, Pennsylvania" (February 4, 1861), and "Speech in Independence Hall, Philadelphia, Pennsylvania" (February 12, 1861), in *CW*, 3:316, 4:211, 241; David Runciman, *The Confidence Trap: A History of Democracy in Crisis from World War I to the Present* (Princeton, NJ: Princeton University Press, 2013), 29, and "Democracy's Dual Dangers," *Chronicle of Higher Education* (November 18, 2018); George F. Kennan, "The Sources of Soviet Conduct," *Foreign Affairs* (July 1947), https://www.foreignaffairs.com/articles/russian-federation/1947-07-01/sources-soviet-conduct.

14. Suzanne Mettler and Robert C. Lieberman, *Four Threats: The Recurring Crises of American Democracy* (New York: St. Martin's Press, 2020), 137, 151–58; Jan-Werner Müller, *Democracy Rules* (New York: Farrar, Straus & Giroux, 2021), 126; Runciman, *How Democracy Ends* (New York: Basic Books, 2018), 152–53; Adrian Pabst, "Democratic Corporatism," *American Affairs* 6 (Spring 2022): 112.

15. J. C. B. Davis, *The Case of the United States, to Be Laid Before the Tribunal of Arbitration to Be Convened at Geneva* (Washington, DC: Government Printing Office, 1872), 23; Welles, diary entry for September 14, 1864, in *Diary of Gideon Welles*, ed. J. T. Morse (Boston: Houghton Mifflin, 1911), 2:144; William O. Stoddard, *Inside the White House in War Times: Mem-*

oirs and Reports of Lincoln's Secretary, ed. Michael Burlingame (Lincoln: University of Nebraska Press, 2000), 160; Mark E. Neely Jr., "Lincoln's Political Education," *Lincoln Lore* #1704 (February 1980).

16. Emanuel Hertz, *The Wizardry of Lincoln's Political Appointments and Party Management* (New York: n.p., 1930), 21.

17. Max Weber, "Politics as a Vocation," in *The Vocation Lectures,* ed. D. Owen and T. B. Strong (Indianapolis, IN: Hackett, 2004), 71–72; Paul A. Rahe, *Soft Despotism, Democracy's Drift: Montesquieu, Rousseau, Tocqueville, and the Modern Prospect* (New Haven, CT: Yale University Press, 2009), 244; Alexis de Tocqueville, *Democracy in America,* ed. H. C. Mansfield and D. Winthrop (Chicago: University of Chicago Press, 2000), 229.

18. Adams, *Speech of John Quincy Adams of Massachusetts, upon the Right of the Peple, men and Women, to Petition on the Freedom of Speech and of Debate* (Washington, DC: Gales & Seaton, 1838), 65; Lincoln, "Fragment on the Dred Scott Case" (January 1857), "Speech at Springfield, Illinois" (June 26, 1857), "Speech at Chicago" (July 10, 1858), "Speech at Springfield, Illinois" (July 17, 1858), and "First Inaugural Address" (March 4, 1861), in *CW* 2:387, 400–402, 495–96, 516–17, 520, 4:268; Michael P. Zuckert, *A Nation So Conceived: Abraham Lincoln and the Paradox of Democratic Sovereignty* (Lawrence: University of Kansas Press, 2023), 136.

19. Lincoln, "To Stephen A. Hurlbut" (July 31, 1863), in *CW,* 6:358; John Hay and John Nicolay, "Abraham Lincoln: A History—The Edict of Freedom," *Century Magazine* 37 (March 1889): 703; Jonathan W. White, "The Strangely Insignificant Role of the U.S. Supreme Court in the Civil War," *Journal of the Civil War Era* 3 (June 2013): 21–238; Robert A. Nisbet, *The Present Age: Progress and Anarchy in Modern America* (New York: Harper & Row, 1988), 68–69.

20. Daniel J. Mahoney, *De Gaulle: Statesmanship, Grandeur, and Modern Democracy* (New Brunswick, NJ: Transaction Pubs., 2000), 16, 60; Noah Brooks, "Personal Recollections of Abraham Lincoln," *Harper's New Monthly Magazine* 31 (July 1865): 224; Charles B. Johnson, "The Presidential Campaign of 1860," *Transactions of the Illinois State Historical Society for the Year 1927* (Danville: Illinois Printing, 1927), 121; Lincoln, "To James H. Hackett" (November 2, 1863), in *CW,* 6:559; "The Cordelia Harvey Manuscript," Part 1, ed. Robert C. Bray, *JALA* 43 (Spring 2022): 86. See also "Statement by Dr. Parker," in *An Oral History of Abraham Lincoln: John G. Nicolay's Interviews and Essays,* ed. Michael Burlingame (Carbondale: Southern Illinois University Press, 1996), 87: "I may not

be a great man—(straightening up to his full height)—I *know* I am not a great man—and perhaps it is better that it is so—for it makes me rely upon One who is great and who has the wisdom and power to lead us safely through this great trial."

21. Lincoln, "Second Lecture on Discoveries and Inventions" (February 11, 1859), in *CW*, 3:358; Steven B. Smith, "Abraham Lincoln's Kantian Republic," in *Abraham Lincoln and Liberal Democracy*, ed. Nicholas Buccola (Lawrence: University Press of Kansas, 2016), 233.

22. Lincoln, "Speech at Hartford, Connecticut" (March 5, 1860) and "Speech at New Haven, Connecticut" (March 6, 1860), in *CW*, 4:7, 24; Robert J. Gordon, *Rise and Fall of American Growth: The U.S. Standard of Living Since the Civil War* (Princeton, NJ: Princeton University Press, 2016), 554–55.

23. Aristotle, *Politics*, trans. Joe Sachs (Indianapolis, IN: Hackett, 2012), 174–75. I am paraphrasing Ernest Renan: *Avoir des gloires communes dans le passé, une volonté commune dans le présent, avoir fait de grandes choses ensemble, vouloir en faire encore.* See Richard M. Chadbourne, *Ernest Renan* (New York: Twayne Publishers, 1969), 101.

24. Lincoln, "Remarks at Springfield, Illinois" (November 20, 1860) and "First Inaugural Address" (March 4, 1861), in *CW*, 4:142–43, 264; Stephen A. Douglas, in *The Lincoln-Douglas Debates*, ed. Douglas L. Wilson and Rodney O. Davis (Urbana: University of Illinois Press, 2008), 162; James Oakes, *Freedom National: The Destruction of Slavery in the United States, 1861–1865* (New York: W. W. Norton, 2013), 356–57; Roy P. Basler, "Did President Lincoln Give the Smallpox to William H. Johnson?" *Huntington Library Quarterly* 35 (May 1972): 279–84; "William Johnson," in John E. Washington, *They Knew Lincoln*, ed. K. Masur (New York: Oxford University Press, 2018), 127–34; Phillip W. Magness and Sebastian Page, "Mr. Lincoln and Mr. Johnson," *New York Times* (February 1, 2012); Michael Burlingame, "Reflections on the Gravestone of William H. Johnson," in *Final Resting Places: Reflections on the Meaning of Civil War Graves*, ed. J. W. White and B. M. Jordan (Athens: University of Georgia Press, 2023), 243.

25. Boker, "Lincoln," in Sculley Bradley, *George Henry Boker: Poet and Patriot* (Philadelphia: University of Pennsylvania Press, 1927), 224; Runciman, *How Democracy Ends*, 169–70; Müller, *Democracy Rules*, xvi; Lincoln, "Seventh and Last Debate with Stephen A. Douglas at Alton, Illinois" (October 15, 1858) and "Notes for Speeches at Columbus and Cincinnati" (September 16, 17, 1859), in *CW*, 3:301, 436.

Index

A NOTE ABOUT THE AUTHOR

Allen C. Guelzo is the Thomas W. Smith Distinguished Research Scholar and Director of the Initiative on Politics and Statesmanship in the James Madison Program in American Ideals and Institutions at Princeton University. He is the author of *Abraham Lincoln: Redeemer President, Lincoln's Emancipation Proclamation: The End of Slavery in America,* and *Gettysburg: The Last Invasion,* all winners of the Lincoln Prize. His essays, reviews, and articles have appeared in publications ranging from the *American Historical Review* and the *Journal of American History* to *National Review* and *The Wilson Quarterly,* and in newspapers such as *The New York Times, The Washington Post, The Philadelphia Inquirer,* and *The Wall Street Journal.*

A NOTE ON THE TYPE

This book was set in Janson, a typeface named for the Dutchman Anton Janson, but is actually the work of Nicholas Kis (1650–1702). The type is an excellent example of the influential and sturdy Dutch types that prevailed in England up to the time William Caslon (1692–1766) developed his own incomparable designs from them.

Composed by North Market Street Graphics,
Lancaster, Pennsylvania

Printed and bound by Berryville Graphics,
Berryville, Virginia

Designed by Michael Collica